Dean Fearing's
Southwest Cuisine

DEAN FEARING'S

Southwest Cuisine

BLENDING ASIA AND THE AMERICAS

DEAN FEARING

EDITED BY JUDITH CHOATE

 Grove Weidenfeld · NEW YORK

Published by Grove Weidenfeld
A division of Grove Press, Inc.
841 Broadway
New York, NY 10003-4793

Published in Canada by General Publishing Company, Ltd.

Library of Congress Cataloging-in-Publication Data

Fearing, Dean.
  Southwest cuisine / Dean Fearing.
    p.   cm.
  ISBN 0-8021-1321-4
    1. Cookery, American—Southwestern style.   I. Title.
TX715.2.S69F43   1990
  641.5979—dc20   90-41972
                                    CIP

Manufactured in the United States of America

This book is printed on acid-free paper

Designed by Irving Perkins Associates

First Edition

10 9 8 7 6 5 4 3 2 1

All photography by Greg Booth + Associates / Dallas

Color separations, printing and binding
by R. R. Donnelley & Sons Company

To an Innkeeper . . .

Acknowledgments

I WOULD ESPECIALLY LIKE to acknowledge The Mansion on Turtle Creek, which has always been more than just a hotel or restaurant to me. The Mansion on Turtle Creek is more than a home to Southwest cuisine, it is also my home. Never have I come across an environment so committed to quality, innovation, and excellence, filled with warm, enthusiastic people who love their workplace and their work.

As the best things always are, this book was made possible—and made a great deal more fun to work on—by the support of some very special colleagues:

The management team of both The Mansion on Turtle Creek and Rosewood Hotel Group, whose support, understanding, humor, and constant vigilance were invaluable.

All of my associates in the kitchen, in particular my sous chefs, who held the reins during my absences and kept our quality at its constant creative best, who stimulated many of the recipes and kept our spirit and imagination firing on full burners.

The administrative support staff, who selflessly carried out the least glamorous, but no less important task of detail, detail, detail.

Judith Choate—Our second time around together, and I can't think of anyone else I would rather have standing beside me providing me with guidance on this cookbook. Thank you for giving the book a special touch.

Greg Booth & Associates—The talents of Barth Tillotson and Mark Bumgarner gave us beautiful food photography that literally leaps off the pages. Thank you.

Kyra Effren and Richard Effren—Their devotion, determination, and an amazing amount of culinary talent meant the recipes were expertly and lovingly tested.

Special thanks also to my literary agent, Jan Miller, and to Sandra Burrowes for coordinating the many details involved in this book.

To my editor, Walt Bode, who picked up the ball and ran with it. Thanks for your enthusiasm.

To the people at Gumps, who provided beautiful dishes and props for our photo shoots; and to Stanley Korshak and Neiman Marcus.

And to Caroline Rose Hunt and her family. They are the reason for The Mansion's very existence, but even more than that, their faith has allowed us the creative freedom to establish our unique culinary style. Thank you.

The single biggest vote of thanks goes to our patrons. Above all else, their support is truly the difference at The Mansion.

Contents

The New Alliance in Southwest Cuisine

With the passing of the 1980s we witnessed the birth of a new cuisine, American Cookery. As a young chef working in Dallas, Texas, I helped pioneer one integral part of it, Southwest Cuisine. From my first attempts to refine Tex-Mex fare, a definitive American style of cooking arose. Using the spirit of the Southwest to involve indigenous foods which are characterized by intense flavors, vibrant colors, and earthy aromas, I could reflect my passion for what tastes good. At The Mansion on Turtle Creek, we have cultivated our own special cuisine and raised it into its prime, joining all of the wonderful American regional characteristics to create an innovative, legitimate culinary form.

The cuisine at The Mansion on Turtle Creek has now gone beyond the set boundaries of the American Southwest. My Southern heritage and love for Asian foods represent the "allies" that, when merged with the Southwest style of cooking, create a synergistic union that can best be described as the New Alliance in Southwest Cuisine. This alliance blends three uniquely different cultures, refining their elements into a sophisticated provincial menu. The techniques and foods of Mexico and the Plains Indians, the customs and specialties of the American South, and the philosophy and delicacies of Asia are united with locally produced foodstuffs and time-honored traditions to create a cuisine in tune with the 1990s.

Each ally brings to the table diverse flavors and cooking techniques:

Old Mexico presents earthy flavors such as beans, dried chilies, masa, tortillas, corn, peppers, epazote, pozole, cilantro, cumin, coriander, and jicama. The traditions of the American South offer tomatoes, scallions, filé gumbo, rice, mustard, cornmeal, melons, okra, sweet potatoes, green beans, pecans, black-eyed peas, and molasses. The flavors of Asia include ginger, Thai chilies, fish sauce, soy sauce, mangoes, tamarind, curries, rice vinegar, daikon, and wasabi.

Food preparation techniques from all three cultures are intertwined on the stoves of our kitchen. Tamales, moles, stews, smoking, and barbecuing have their roots in the Southwest. Deep-frying, pan-frying, curing, baking, and breading are traditional Southern cooking methods. Stir-frying, grilling, marinating, pickling, tea smoking, steaming, and tempura all come from Asia. All of these influence our cuisine and are a reflection of America's assimilation of divergent cultures and traditions.

As we experimented with this New Alliance, we also noticed a change in our eating habits. As our relatively young kitchen staff became increasingly aware of the dangers of the excessive use of salt, butter, cream, and animal fats to their continued good health, food preparation began to evolve to another level. As our eating habits changed so did our cooking practices. And we found that our restaurant diners were demanding the same changes. With this joint concern for healthy diets, reduced fats, and low sodium and cholesterol, our kitchen has pioneered and is using "hybrid" sauces as the base for the New Alliance. Containing no butter or cream, these sauces are fat-free stocks infused with herbs, spices, and vegetable flavors, finished at the final moment of service. Intensely flavorful, honest, truly natural and fresh, hybrid sauces are, I feel, the healthy foundation to a cuisine which is not only delicious, but wholesome.

Great sauces are the herald of advanced cooking, influencing the style and spirit of a particular cuisine. The New Alliance in Southwest Cuisine is complemented by the innovative hybrid sauces which are designed to bring out the intense flavors that especially characterize our cuisine. The direction of the New Alliance moved us away from "classical" sauce preparations which traditionally incorporate large amounts of demi-glace, butter, cream, and liquor. We wanted to create sauces which were complex, but not cloying, and which would enhance the flavors in each recipe.

In addition, we sought to develop a series of base sauces which would reflect today's dietary health consciousness. To do this we had to discover whether we could make a sauce which would stand on its own, in texture and flavors, without using substantial amounts of fat or alcohol. As we began to experiment with Asian cooking techniques, which include the use of flavor-infused stocks, slightly thickened and finished to order, we knew we had the foundation of a repertoire of healthy sauces.

The creation of a hybrid sauce involves a two-step process. The first step is to infuse a neutral base stock, be it veal, chicken, or vegetable, with vegetables, herbs, fruits, and occasionally roasted bones. A small amount of binding agent, either corn starch or fruit or vegetable purée, is added for body and consistency. The blend is simmered for 20 to 40 minutes and then strained. The first stage yields a base sauce which will

be finished by the addition of specific vegetables, herbs, or fruit, and accented with some acidity (most often fresh lemon or lime juice).

The most wonderful aspect of hybrid sauces is their adaptability to the different influences in this alliance cookery. To make a hybrid base sauce with an Old Mexico flair, we might infuse the base with fresh dried chilies, corn, or cilantro. Southern flavors might call for black pepper, onions, or sage. To get the taste of Asia, ginger, rice vinegars, curry spices, or soy sauce might be used. From these bases, the sauces are then finished by incorporating the vegetables, fruits, and herbs highlighted elsewhere in an individual recipe.

The hybrid sauce approach is now found throughout the Mansion on Turtle Creek kitchen and is pervasive in all of our meals. Our hybrids are a superb marriage of sauces, intense and rich with flavor, with very little of those ingredients known to be unhealthy. I believe hybrid sauces allow diners to enjoy the fullness that a complex cuisine can offer while remaining true to health-responsive eating.

Although we have incorporated our prized hybrid sauces into many recipes, we still use classical sauces in some of our dishes. And let's face it, a good Cabernet-reduced demi-glace sauce is worth cheating for! In addition, we are aware that most people do not eat traditionally rich foods on a daily basis so that an occasional lapse is acceptable even to the most health-conscious dieter.

All of the recipes in this book come from The Mansion on Turtle Creek Restaurant, which has a special staff that researches, and has at its disposal, the freshest and highest quality specialty foods the world can offer. I am aware that many ingredients listed in these recipes may not be available throughout the United States (although grocery stores, ethnic markets, and local purveyors have recently expanded their inventories to include many unusual products), but this should not dissuade you from creating any of my dishes. Recipes are not written in stone, each is capable of change. It is commonly thought that if you do not have a specific ingredient then a recipe should not be attempted. I do not believe this when developing my recipes. They are designed to be followed step by step, but are also flexible enough to accommodate substitutions whenever necessary. When substituting ingredients, always make changes based on the same food type. For example, if you cannot find a fresh mango, use fresh papaya or pineapple. If wild game is unavailable, use domestic lamb or beef. Be creative. That is the fun of cooking. By understanding the reasoning behind the creation of hybrid sauces and the development of the New Alliance, you can have at your disposal a whole new foundation for creating great meals on your own.

This collection of recipes is not just another cookbook. It is another step in my continuing endeavor to share the best of American cookery. My kitchen philosophy is, fundamentally, to use select local ingredients to create menus that remain honest to their origins; to present a plate that is beautiful to look at, and of nutritional value; and to share all that I have learned with other food enthusiasts. *Dean Fearing's Southwest Cuisine* brings my philosophy and the Mansion on Turtle Creek kitchen directly to you. I hope you join me and renew our alliance to the best that America has to offer.

PART ONE

The Roots of the New Alliance

CHAPTER ONE

Old Mexico

THE CUISINE of Old Mexico is the backbone of the Mansion on Turtle Creek kitchen. Chilies and herbs are used in many guises to enhance our Southwestern menu. Frequently thought of as only spicy, the dishes of Old Mexico are more often subtle in flavor than simply hot, with a complex melding of textures and tastes—not the fast food of taco stands, but a highly developed and sophisticated cuisine. Although traditionally most Old Mexico meals were handmade—from the grinding of the corn to the tedious mortar-and-pestle-pounded salsas—modern equipment has eased the task of preparing these once special-occasion-only dishes.

Pozole-Poblano Soup with Corn Sticks

SERVES 4

The mystery word here is *pozole*, large white dried cacahuazin corn kernels, used in traditional Mexican soups and stews. Canned hominy may be used as a substitute.

1 tablespoon corn oil (or olive oil)
³/4 pound boneless pork shoulder, cut into 1-inch cubes*
Salt to taste
1 onion, peeled and diced
1 large clove garlic, peeled and minced
1 serrano chili, minced
¹/2 tablespoon chopped fresh Mexican oregano (or regular fresh oregano)
5 cups chicken stock (see page 236)
4 ancho chilies
1 cup cooked pozole (or 1 cup canned yellow hominy, well rinsed and drained)

1 poblano chili, roasted, peeled, and cut into ¹/2-inch dice
Fresh lime juice to taste
¹/2 cup husked, washed, and diced tomatillos
¹/2 cup ¹/2-inch-dice jicama
¹/3 cup julienned radish
1 tablespoon chopped fresh cilantro
1 cup grated jalapeño jack cheese
4 thin slices lime
8 Corn Sticks

Heat oil in a large saucepan over medium-high heat. When hot, add pork cubes and salt and sauté for about 5 minutes or until lightly browned. Stir in onion and sauté for 4 minutes or until transparent. Add garlic, serrano, and oregano and sauté for 1 minute. Add 4 cups chicken stock and bring to a boil. Skim off scum and reduce heat. Simmer for 20 minutes, stirring occasionally.

Remove and discard seeds from anchos. Combine with remaining 1 cup chicken stock in a small saucepan and bring to a boil over high heat. Reduce heat and simmer for 15 minutes or until anchos are very soft. Pour mixture into a blender and purée until very smooth. Immediately add to soup mixture and continue to simmer for 20 minutes, skimming and stirring occasionally.

Add pozole and poblano to soup. Raise heat and bring to a boil. When boiling, reduce heat and simmer for 10 minutes. Season with salt and lime juice. Stir in tomatillos, jicama, radish, and cilantro. When well blended, remove from heat.

Pour equal portions into four warm soup bowls, making certain that each contains a mixture of vegetables. Sprinkle cheese over top of soup and float a lime slice on top. Serve immediately with warm Corn Sticks on the side.

* To further enhance the pork flavor, cold smoke the cubes for 15 minutes (see page 230).

Pozole-Poblano Soup with Corn Sticks

CORN STICKS

1 cup yellow cornmeal
1 cup all-purpose flour
4 teaspoons baking powder
¹/₂ teaspoon salt
1 cup milk
*2 extra-large eggs, lightly
   beaten*

¹/₄ cup molasses
*¹/₄ cup unsalted butter (or
   bacon fat), melted*
*1 tablespoon unrefined
   corn oil*

Preheat oven to 375°.

Place an iron corn-stick pan in preheated oven for 20 minutes.

While pan is heating, combine cornmeal, flour, baking powder, and salt. Stir in milk, eggs, molasses, and melted butter with a few rapid strokes until dry ingredients are just moistened. Remove corn-stick pan from oven and brush with unrefined corn oil. Spoon in batter to the top of each slot. Return to oven and bake for 12 minutes or until golden brown. Remove from oven and serve hot.

Creamy Masa Vegetable Soup

SERVES 4

You may ask, what is masa harina? It is corn flour, which in this recipe
we use as a thickener and for great flavor.

1 teaspoon peanut oil
*1 medium onion, peeled
  and chopped*
*1 medium carrot, peeled
  and chopped*
*1 stalk celery, trimmed and
  chopped*
*1 clove garlic, peeled and
  chopped*
*1 serrano chili, seeded and
  chopped*
*1 small yellow squash,
  thinly sliced*
*1 green bell pepper, seeded
  and membranes
  removed, chopped*
*1/2 tablespoon chopped fresh
  cilantro*
*1/2 tablespoon chopped fresh
  thyme*
*1/4 tablespoon cracked black
  pepper*
*1/4 cup masa harina**
1/4 cup water
*2 1/2 cups vegetable stock
  (see page 238) or
  chicken stock (see page
  236)*

1 cup heavy cream
Salt to taste
*1 teaspoon fresh lime juice
  or to taste*
*1 medium yellow squash
  (only part with yellow
  skin attached), cut into
  1/4-inch dice*
*1/2 small carrot, peeled and
  cut into 1/4-inch dice*
*1/2 small stalk celery, peeled
  and cut into 1/4-inch
  dice*
*1/2 yellow bell pepper, seeded
  and membranes
  removed, cut into fine
  julienne*
*1/2 red bell pepper, seeded
  and membranes
  removed, cut into fine
  julienne*
*1 ear corn, roasted, kernels
  cut from cob*
*1 cup cooked, drained black
  beans*

Heat oil in a heavy saucepan over medium
heat. When hot, stir in chopped onion, carrot,
and celery. Sauté for 5 minutes or until onions
are soft and juices have begun to evaporate. Do
not brown. Then stir in garlic, serrano, squash,
chopped green pepper, cilantro, thyme, and
pepper. Sauté for 3 minutes. Mix masa and 1/4
cup water and add to soup along with vegetable stock. Bring to a boil, stirring frequently.
Reduce heat and simmer for 20 minutes. Stir
in cream and return soup to heat. Bring to a
simmer and cook for five minutes or until
slightly reduced.

Remove from heat and pour into a blender.
Process until very smooth. Strain and season
with salt and lime juice. Set aside and keep
warm.

Fill a large pot three-quarters full with water. Bring to a boil. Season lightly with salt.
Add finely diced squash, carrot, and celery, and
julienned bell peppers. Cook for 2 minutes.
Quickly drain vegetables well, and immediately fold into warm soup. Add corn kernels
and beans.

Pour equal portions into four warm soup
bowls and serve immediately.

* Available at Mexican or ethnic food markets.

Ancho Navy Bean Soup

SERVES 4

2 cups dried white navy
    beans, picked over and
    rinsed clean
4 thick slices smoked bacon
1 large onion, peeled and
    chopped
1 stalk celery, trimmed and
    chopped
2 large shallots, peeled and
    chopped
2 cloves garlic, peeled and
    chopped

2 serrano chilies, chopped
4 cups Ham Stock
4 cups chicken stock (see
    page 236)
Ancho Chili Paste
Salt to taste
Fresh lime juice to taste
1 red onion, peeled and cut
    into 1/4-inch dice
8 leaves fresh cilantro

Cover navy beans with at least 8 cups of cold water. Allow to soak at least 8 hours. Drain well.

Render fat from bacon in a large stockpot over medium heat. Add chopped onion, celery, shallots, garlic, and serranos and sauté for 3 minutes. Add beans, Ham Stock, and chicken stock. Bring to a boil, then lower heat and simmer for 40 minutes.

When done, combine soup and Ancho Chili Paste in a blender and purée until smooth. Stir in salt and lime juice and strain. Recheck seasoning.

Pour soup into four warm soup bowls and garnish with red onion and cilantro leaves just before serving.

HAM STOCK

MAKES ABOUT 4 CUPS

2 tablespoons bacon fat
1 large onion, peeled and
    chopped
2 stalks celery, trimmed
    and chopped
1 carrot, chopped
1 bunch fresh cilantro,
    chopped
2 jalapeño chilies, seeded
    and chopped

1 pound ham bones
1 pig's foot
1 bay leaf
1 tablespoon chopped fresh
    thyme
1 teaspoon black
    peppercorns
1 gallon cold water

Heat bacon fat in a large saucepan over medium-high heat. Add onion, celery, carrot, cilantro, and jalapeños and sauté for 4 minutes or until transparent. Do not brown the vegetables. Add ham bones, pig's foot, bay leaf, thyme, and peppercorns. Cover with cold water and bring to a boil. Lower heat and simmer for 4 hours, then strain stock through a fine sieve.

ANCHO CHILI PASTE

MAKES ABOUT 1 CUP

4 ancho chilies, seeded
1 small onion, peeled and
    chopped
1 clove garlic, peeled and
    chopped

1 small bunch fresh
    cilantro
1 cup chicken stock (see
    page 236)

Place anchos, onion, garlic, cilantro, and chicken stock in a small saucepan over medium heat. Simmer for 10 minutes, then pour into a blender and purée until smooth. Set aside until ready to use.

APPETIZERS

Spicy Veal Tacos with Cabbage, Peanut, and Mango Salad
SERVES 4

Using veal gives this dish a twist on the traditional meat taco. Any meat may be used, but I came up with this version for Jamie Nichols, who owns and runs a "naturally raised" veal farm in Virginia. I felt that they needed some "spice of life" up there.

2 tablespoons olive oil
1 cup finely diced onion
2 tablespoons minced garlic
3 serrano chilies, seeded and finely chopped
2 pounds ground veal, cooked and drained
1 tablespoon minced fresh oregano
1 tablespoon minced fresh cilantro
1 small bay leaf
1 tablespoon ground cumin
1 tablespoon chili powder
1 teaspoon ground coriander

1 teaspoon ground cinnamon
1 cup tomato sauce
1 tablespoon ground roasted pumpkin seeds (optional)
Salt to taste
Fresh lime juice to taste
8 taco shells, warmed
2 cups finely grated jalapeño jack cheese
Cabbage, Peanut, and Mango Salad

Heat oil in a large saucepan over medium-high heat. When hot, add onions. Lower heat and sauté for 4 minutes. Stir in garlic and serranos and sauté for 1 minute. Add veal and stir to blend. Add herbs, spices, and tomato sauce. Bring to a simmer and cook for 15 minutes, stirring frequently. Add pumpkin seeds, if desired, and season with salt and lime juice. Remove bay leaf.

Place 2 taco shells on each of four serving plates. Spoon equal portions of meat mixture into each shell and top with a layer of cheese. Place Cabbage, Peanut, and Mango Salad on top of cheese and serve immediately.

CABBAGE, PEANUT, AND MANGO SALAD

2 cups julienned red cabbage, leafy part only
1 cup julienned white cabbage, leafy part only
1/2 cup roasted skinless peanut halves
1/2 mango (or papaya), cut into 1/4-inch dice

1 tablespoon finely chopped fresh cilantro
2 tablespoons virgin olive oil
Salt to taste
Juice of 2 medium limes or to taste

Combine all ingredients in a large bowl and toss to blend. Adjust seasonings and serve immediately.

8

Barbecued Quail Nachos with Jalapeño Jack Cheese and Refried Black Beans, Served with Yellow Tomato Pico de Gallo

SERVES 4

4 whole 6-ounce quail,
　wings and wishbone
　removed
1/3 cup Mansion Barbecue
　Spice Mix (see page
　234)
1/2 cup corn oil
Salt to taste
3 whole fresh yellow corn
　tortillas (or a
　combination of yellow,
　blue, and ancho corn
　tortillas)

Refried Black Beans
1 cup grated jalapeño jack
　cheese
12 leaves fresh cilantro
Yellow Tomato Pico de
　Gallo

Prepare smoker for cold smoke (see page 230).

Coat quail with Mansion Barbecue Spice Mix and place on a smoker rack. Place in smoker for 12 minutes, making sure quail do not cook. Remove from smoker.

Preheat oven to 350°.

Heat a medium ovenproof sauté pan over medium heat. When hot, add 2 tablespoons oil. Season each quail with salt. Place in pan and cook for about 3 minutes, turning to brown both sides of breast. When brown, remove pan from top of stove and place in preheated oven. Cook for 6 to 8 minutes or until done. Do not overcook. When done, remove quail from pan and set aside to cool.

Lower oven temperature to 300°.

Remove breast meat from quail using a sharp boning knife. Cut into a fine julienne, reserving rest of quail meat for another use.

Cut tortillas into quarters. Heat remaining 6 tablespoons oil in a heavy sauté pan over medium-high heat. When hot, add tortilla triangles, a few at a time, and fry for about 2 minutes or until crisp. Remove from oil and drain on paper towel.

Using a small spatula, spread Refried Black Beans on each tortilla triangle, making sure not to break them. Sprinkle a portion of julienned quail on top. Then mound a small amount of cheese on top of quail meat.

Carefully place the nachos on a baking sheet. Bake at 300° for 3 minutes or until cheese has completely melted.

Place 3 nachos on each of four serving plates and garnish each nacho with a cilantro leaf. Spoon a portion of Yellow Tomato Pico de Gallo on each or on the side. Serve immediately.

REFRIED BLACK BEANS

1 cup cooked, drained black beans
1/3 cup chicken stock (see page 236) or liquid from beans

3 tablespoons bacon fat (or peanut oil)
Salt to taste

Place beans and chicken stock in a blender and purée until smooth.

Heat a large sauté pan over medium-high heat. Add bacon fat. When hot, spoon black bean purée into the pan. Fry carefully, rolling the mixture back and forth by jerking the pan with short thrusts. Cook, rolling constantly, for 5 minutes or until very thick. Season with salt and set aside until ready to use.

YELLOW TOMATO PICO DE GALLO

2 large ripe yellow tomatoes, peeled, cored, seeded, and diced
1/2 small onion, peeled and cut into 1/4-inch dice
2 cloves garlic, peeled and minced
2 serrano chilies, 1 of them seeded, both finely chopped

1 tablespoon chopped fresh cilantro
1/2 tablespoon fresh lime juice or to taste
Salt to taste

Place all ingredients in a medium bowl and toss to combine. Let sit for about 5 minutes, then recheck seasonings.

Thin-Cut Scallop Ceviche with Mango

Thin-Cut Scallop Ceviche with Mango

SERVES 4

This is a modern version of the traditional-style ceviche. For a more traditional dish, add all the ingredients and marinate for 2 hours or more.

12 large, very fresh scallops (if small, additional scallops may be needed)

1 ripe mango, peeled and cut into 1/4-inch dice

1 cold-smoked red bell pepper (see page 230), seeded and membranes removed, cut into 1/4-inch dice

1 cold-smoked yellow bell pepper, seeded and membranes removed, cut into 1/4-inch dice

5 tomatillos, husked, cored, and cut into 1/4-inch dice

1 shallot, peeled and cut into 1/4-inch dice

1 clove garlic, peeled and minced

2 serrano chilies, seeded and minced

2 teaspoons chopped fresh cilantro

1/4 cup fresh lime juice

1/4 cup fresh orange juice

Salt to taste

Virgin olive oil to taste

Fresh cracked black pepper (optional)

Using a very sharp, thin knife, cut the scallops into very thin rounds. You will need 2 cups scallop slices.

Cover the entire bottom of each of four cold serving plates with a single layer of scallop circles. Cover with clear plastic wrap and refrigerate.

In a medium bowl, combine mango, bell peppers, tomatillos, shallot, garlic, serranos, cilantro, and fruit juices. Stir to blend. Season with salt and let stand for 10 minutes.

When ready to serve, remove scallop plates from refrigerator. Uncover, and spoon a thin coating of mango sauce over scallops on each plate. Sprinkle with olive oil and serve immediately. Fresh cracked black pepper may be passed.

Barbecued Duck Wrapped in Flour Tortillas with Mango Pico de Gallo
SERVES 4

When Kyra Effren and I were testing the recipes, this particular one stood out in my mind as a perfect combination of flavors—but then I love barbecue!

4 whole boneless, skinless duck breasts, soaked in brine (see page 231)

1/2 cup Mansion Barbecue Spice Mix (see page 234)

1 tablespoon corn oil

1/4 cup diced shallots

3/4 cup cooked, drained black beans

1/2 cup Mansion Barbecue Sauce

Salt to taste

4 Flour Tortillas, cooked and warm (see page 28)

1/2 cup grated jalapeño jack cheese

1 tablespoon chopped fresh cilantro

Mango Pico de Gallo

4 fresh serrano chilies

4 sprigs fresh cilantro

Prepare smoker for hot smoke (see page 229).

Dredge duck breasts with Mansion Barbecue Spice Mix, coating evenly and well. Place breasts on a smoker rack and put in smoker for 12 minutes. Remove from smoker and cool.

Using a sharp, thin knife, julienne duck breasts.

Place oil in a large sauté pan over medium heat. When hot, add julienned duck and sauté for 1 minute. Add shallots and sauté for an additional minute. Stir in black beans and Mansion Barbecue Sauce and bring to a boil. When boiling, remove from heat immediately. Season with salt.

Place a warm tortilla on each of four warm serving plates. Spoon equal portions of duck mixture into the middle of each tortilla and sprinkle with cheese and cilantro. Then roll tortilla around filling and center in the middle of the plate. Spoon Mango Pico de Gallo beside each rolled tortilla and garnish with a chili (to be eaten like a pickle for the adventurous) and cilantro sprig.

MANSION BARBECUE SAUCE

MAKES ABOUT 1½ CUPS

1 tablespoon bacon fat (or vegetable oil)
1 large yellow onion, peeled and cut into ¼-inch dice
1 cup ketchup
4 tablespoons Worcestershire sauce
1 tablespoon malt vinegar

2 tablespoons molasses
2 teaspoons Creole mustard
1 teaspoon Tabasco sauce
Salt to taste
Fresh lemon juice to taste
Meat drippings from smoker to taste (optional)

Preheat oven to 375°.

Heat bacon fat in a small sauté pan over medium-high heat. When hot, add onion and cook for 4 minutes or until soft.

Place onion in a small ovenproof pan. Combine remaining ingredients in a small bowl and pour over onion. Cover and bake in preheated oven for 30 minutes. Remove pan from oven and keep warm until ready to serve.

MANGO PICO DE GALLO

2 ripe mangoes, peeled and cut into ¼-inch dice
1 tomato, peeled, cored, seeded, and cut into ¼-inch dice
½ small red onion, peeled and cut into ¼-inch dice
1 clove garlic, peeled and minced

2 small serrano chilies, seeded and minced
1 tablespoon finely chopped fresh cilantro
½ teaspoon ground ancho chili powder
¼ cup fresh lime juice
Salt to taste

Place all ingredients in a medium bowl and toss to combine. Let stand for at least 10 minutes before serving.

Crab Tostadas with Cabbage Salad, Avocado Relish, and Tomato Salsa

SERVES 4

Chef Robert Del Grande of Cafe Annie and I have a musical group called the Barbed Wires. When I am in Houston to see what Robert is doing new with food and to strum some C & W songs, I always ask him to make crab tostadas. Robert always asks, "Again?", implying, "Don't you remember what they taste like from the hundreds you had before?" I still love them.

6 whole fresh corn tortillas
1/2 cup peanut oil
2 tablespoons heavy cream
1 teaspoon mayonnaise
12 ounces fresh lump crabmeat, picked clean of shell and cartilage

Cabbage Salad
Avocado Relish
Tomato Salsa
12 leaves fresh cilantro

Cut twelve 3-inch tortilla rounds from tortillas. Heat oil in a small skillet over medium-high heat. When hot, fry tortillas for about 2 minutes or until golden brown and crisp. Set aside on a paper towel to drain.

In a mixing bowl, combine cream and mayonnaise and blend until smooth. Add crabmeat and mix to coat. Do not overwork.

Place 3 tortillas on each of four serving plates. Spread Cabbage Salad on each crisp tortilla. Layer Avocado Relish over the cabbage and place crabmeat on top. Serve with Tomato Salsa. Garnish tostadas with cilantro leaves.

CABBAGE SALAD

1/4 small head white cabbage
1/4 cup sour cream
1 tablespoon fresh lime juice

2 small serrano chilies, seeded and minced
Salt to taste
Ground black pepper to taste

Slice cabbage into a very fine chiffonade. Blend sour cream, lime juice, and serranos in a bowl until smooth. Add the cabbage and mix until well coated. Season with salt and pepper and refrigerate until ready to serve.

AVOCADO RELISH

2 ripe 8-ounce avocados
1/2 cup finely chopped red
   bell pepper
1 cup finely chopped red
   onion
1 tablespoon minced
   serrano chili
3/4 cup chopped fresh
   cilantro

2 tablespoons hazelnut oil
   (or peanut oil)
2 tablespoons fresh lime
   juice
Salt to taste
Ground black pepper to
   taste

Split, seed, and peel avocados. Cut into very small cubes. Combine avocado, red pepper, onion, serrano, cilantro, hazelnut oil, and lime juice and mix to form a coarse relish. Season with salt and pepper and set aside until ready to use.

TOMATO SALSA

2 cups cored and chopped
   fresh plum tomatoes
1/2 cup minced red onion
3/4 cup chopped fresh
   cilantro
2 teaspoons minced
   jalapeño chili

2 tablespoons fresh lime
   juice
Salt to taste
Ground black pepper to
   taste

Combine tomatoes, onion, cilantro, and jalapeño. Add lime juice and mix thoroughly. Season with salt and pepper. Set aside until ready to use.

SALADS

Southwest Caesar Salad with Pan-Fried Crab Cakes

SERVES 4

The original Caesar Salad was made in Tijuana, Mexico, in 1924 by an Italian restaurateur named Caesar Cardini. The crab cakes add a new twist to a great old classic.

16 small center leaves
   romaine lettuce
2 large egg yolks
3 cloves garlic, peeled and
   minced
2 shallots, peeled and
   minced
4 anchovy fillets (more if
   desired)
2 tablespoons hot mustard
1 tablespoon Worcestershire
   sauce
2 teaspoons Tabasco sauce
2 teaspoons balsamic
   vinegar
1 cup peanut oil
1/2 cup olive oil
1 tablespoon cold-smoked
   1/4-inch-dice red bell
   pepper (see page 230)

1 tablespoon cold-smoked
   1/4-inch-dice yellow bell
   pepper
1 tablespoon cold-smoked
   1/4-inch-dice green bell
   pepper
2 tablespoons diced jicama
2 tablespoons fresh corn
   kernels
2 jalapeño chilies, seeded
   and finely diced
Juice of 2 limes
1 tablespoon minced fresh
   cilantro
Salt to taste
2 ounces Montosio cheese
   (or any other aged
   goat cheese), shaved
20 leaves fresh cilantro
12 Pan-Fried Crab Cakes

Wash and dry romaine lettuce. Refrigerate.

In a blender, combine egg yolks, garlic, shallots, anchovies, mustard, Worcestershire, Tabasco, and balsamic vinegar. When smooth, combine oils and add in a thin stream until dressing is emulsified and creamy.

Pour dressing into a small bowl. Fold in smoked bell peppers, jicama, corn, jalapeños, lime juice, and minced cilantro until well combined. Season with salt. The dressing should be chunky and slightly thick. If too thick, thin with a little water and adjust seasoning.

Place chilled romaine leaves in a large bowl. Add dressing in small amounts and toss lightly. The leaves should be coated lightly with dressing and speckled with garnish. Place leaves in a semicircle around each salad plate. Drizzle extra dressing over top of leaves if necessary, obtaining as much garnish as possible. Add shaved Montosio cheese over top and sprinkle with cilantro leaves. Place 3 hot Pan-Fried Crab Cakes in front of salad on each plate. Serve immediately.

PAN-FRIED CRAB CAKES

1 extra-large egg, beaten
1 tablespoon mayonnaise
½ teaspoon paprika
¼ teaspoon ground black pepper
¼ teaspoon curry powder
¼ teaspoon dry mustard
¼ teaspoon celery salt
⅓ teaspoon cayenne pepper
⅛ teaspoon ground cloves
1 tablespoon Worcestershire sauce

1 tablespoon fresh lemon juice
3 or 4 drops Tabasco sauce
½ pound fresh jumbo lump crabmeat, picked clean of shell and cartilage
1½–2 tablespoons dry bread crumbs
½ cup corn oil, approximately

In a mixing bowl, combine egg, mayonnaise, and seasonings. Add crabmeat and enough bread crumbs to absorb excess moisture. Toss to blend well, but do not overmix. Mixture should be just firm enough to hold together. Adjust seasonings as desired. Form into 12 patties and place on wax paper in a cold place for 20 minutes to dry slightly.

Pour oil into a skillet to a depth of ½ inch. Place over high heat and heat to 350° on a food thermometer. When temperature is right, gently add crab cakes and fry for about 3 minutes per side or until golden brown on both sides. Do not crowd pan; fry in several batches if necessary. Drain on paper towel and serve immediately.

Orange, Jicama, and Cilantro Salad with Cayenne-Lime Dressing

SERVES 4

Patricia Quintana, chef and cookbook author from Mexico, invited a group of Southwest chefs to her family *ranchero* in Veracruz. For days, we dined—morning, noon, and night—on the most incredible meals prepared and served by Patricia and her cooks. I got a first-hand education on the real foods of Mexico. This is my version of one of her salads.

4 seedless oranges
1 large red onion
1½ cups julienned jicama
¼ cup chopped fresh cilantro

Cayenne-Lime Dressing
4 sprigs fresh cilantro

Peel oranges and cut, crosswise, into 4 slices each, keeping oranges intact.

Peel and slice onion, crosswise, into 12 very thin slices.

Place the bottom slice of each orange in the middle of each of four salad plates. Place 1 slice of red onion on top of each orange. Sprinkle a small amount of jicama on top of red onion, then a small amount of chopped cilantro on jicama. Spoon about 1½ teaspoons Cayenne-Lime Dressing over top of cilantro. Put the next slice of orange on top, and repeat procedure for every slice of orange except the top one. Spoon extra dressing over top piece of orange to run down the sides and onto the plate. Garnish each with a cilantro sprig and serve.

CAYENNE-LIME DRESSING

¼ cup peanut oil
¼ cup olive oil
¼ cup fresh lime juice
½ teaspoon cayenne pepper

½ teaspoon ground cumin
½ teaspoon ground coriander
Salt to taste

Whisk all ingredients together in a small bowl to combine. Set aside until ready to use.

Wood-Grilled Redfish with Toasted Chili, Garlic, and Lime Sauce and Mango–Black Bean Relish

SERVES 4

On my first trip to Mexico City a couple of years ago, I brought back an idea for this delicious dish. Simple in execution, but complex in flavor, the thought of this traditional dish made great sense to me.

4 7-ounce redfish fillets,
*   trimmed of skin and*
*   bones*
2 tablespoons olive oil
Salt to taste

Toasted Chili, Garlic, and
*   Lime Sauce*
Mango–Black Bean Relish
4 sprigs fresh cilantro

Prepare wood fire for grilling. Make sure grates are clean and lightly rubbed or brushed with oil just before placing fish on grill.

Dip fillets in oil and season with salt. Place on preheated grill, skin side up. Grill for about 3 minutes. Turn fillets and grill for another 2 minutes or just until firm. Do not overcook as fish should be very moist.

Remove from grill and place 1 fillet on each of four hot serving plates. Ladle Toasted Chili, Garlic, and Lime Sauce over fillets, making sure the chilies and garlic stay on top of the fish and the sauce runs onto the plate. Place a mound of Mango–Black Bean Relish beside each fillet and garnish with a sprig of cilantro. Serve immediately.

TOASTED CHILI, GARLIC, AND LIME SAUCE

1 cup olive oil
1 bulb garlic, cloves peeled
*   and thinly sliced*
2 ancho chilies, seeded and
*   cut into thin strips*
3 pasilla chilies, seeded and
*   cut into thin strips*
3 cascabel chilies, seeded
*   and cut into thin strips*

2 chipotle chilies, seeded
*   and cut into thin strips*
1/2 cup fresh lime juice
2 tablespoons chopped fresh
*   cilantro*
Salt to taste

Place oil and garlic in a medium saucepan over medium heat. Stirring constantly, lightly brown garlic as oil heats up. Do not over-brown. Add chilies and fry, stirring constantly, for 3 minutes or until just beginning to crisp. Add lime juice, cilantro, and salt. Mix and serve immediately.

Wood-Grilled Redfish with Toasted Chili, Garlic, and Lime Sauce and Mango–Black Bean Relish

MANGO–BLACK BEAN RELISH

1 cup cooked, drained black beans
1 cup diced ripe mango or papaya
2 teaspoons white wine vinegar

2 teaspoons maple syrup
2 teaspoons finely chopped fresh cilantro
Salt to taste
Fresh lime juice to taste

Combine all ingredients in a mixing bowl and toss to blend. Serve at room temperature.

Epazote-Glazed Red Snapper with Plantain Mole and Pico de Gallo Rice

SERVES 4

Epazote is a very pungent herb used in various types of Mexican cooking, such as stews, beans—and even in the Mansion on Turtle Creek's Tortilla Soup. In this recipe, I used it as a marinade. If you can't find fresh epazote, you may try dried, which can be found in any true Mexican market.

1 small bunch fresh epazote, leaves only
1 small bunch fresh cilantro
1 small bunch fresh Italian parsley
1 small onion, peeled and finely chopped
3 cloves garlic, peeled and finely chopped
2 teaspoons fresh thyme leaves
1/2 cup olive oil

Salt to taste
Ground black pepper to taste
Fresh lime juice to taste
4 7-ounce red snapper fillets, trimmed of skin, bones, and dark membrane
1 tablespoon peanut oil
Pico de Gallo Rice
Plantain Mole
Triangle Tortilla Chips
4 sprigs fresh cilantro

Combine epazote, cilantro, parsley, onion, garlic, thyme, and olive oil in a blender and mix until smooth. Pour mixture into a medium bowl and season with salt, black pepper, and lime juice.

Place fish fillets in epazote marinade. Cover and marinate for at least 30 minutes at room temperature.

Preheat oven to 350°.

Heat oil in a large ovenproof sauté pan over medium heat. Remove fillets from marinade and let any excess marinade drip off. Place in hot pan, skin side up. Sauté for 3 minutes, then turn. Place pan in preheated oven and cook for 5 to 8 minutes (depending on thickness of fish) or until just cooked through. Remove pan from oven and place fish on a warm serving platter. Keep warm.

Spoon a small mound of Pico de Gallo Rice in the center of each of four warm serving plates. Wedge a snapper fillet against each rice mound. Place small pools of Plantain Mole around the rim of each plate. Place Triangle Tortilla Chips between each sauce pool. Garnish with a cilantro sprig on each fillet and serve immediately.

PLANTAIN MOLE

2 ancho chilies, seeded
2 cascabel chilies, seeded
2 chipotle chilies, seeded
1/3 cup sesame oil
1/4 cup almonds
1/4 cup pistachio nuts
2 tablespoons sesame seeds
2 tablespoons pumpkin
    seeds
1 large yellow onion, peeled
    and chopped
3 shallots, peeled and
    chopped
5 cloves garlic, peeled and
    chopped
2–3 ripe plantains
1 cup chopped fresh
    pineapple
1/2 mango, peeled, seeded,
    and chopped
1/2 papaya, peeled, seeded,
    and chopped

1 large tomato, peeled,
    cored, and chopped
4 large tomatillos, husked
    and chopped
1 teaspoon mustard seeds
1 teaspoon whole coriander
    seeds
1 teaspoon whole cumin
    seeds
1 clove
1 cinnamon stick
4 cups chicken stock (see
    page 236), more if
    needed
1 small bunch fresh
    cilantro with roots,
    washed and chopped
1 ounce bittersweet
    chocolate
Salt to taste
Maple syrup to taste
Fresh lime juice to taste

Submerge chilies in hot water in a small bowl. Set aside.

Heat 2 tablespoons sesame oil in a medium sauté pan over medium heat. When hot, add almonds, pistachios, sesame seeds, and pumpkin seeds. Stirring constantly, sauté for 3 to 4 minutes or until light brown. Do not burn. Remove nuts from pan and reserve.

Heat 2 more tablespoons sesame oil in a large saucepan over medium heat. Add onion and sauté for 8 minutes or until browned. Add shallots and garlic and continue browning for 2 to 3 minutes. Remove onion mixture from pan and reserve.

Add remaining sesame oil to the same saucepan over medium heat. Stir in plantains, pineapple, mango, and papaya and, stirring constantly, sauté for 10 minutes or until fruit is caramelized but not burnt. Drain chilies, then add to caramelized fruit along with nuts and onion mixture. Stir in tomato, tomatillos, mustard seeds, coriander, cumin, clove, cinnamon stick, 4 cups chicken stock, and cilantro and bring to a boil. Lower heat and simmer 40 minutes.

Remove from heat. Discard cinnamon stick and purée, small amounts at a time, in a food processor.

In a large saucepan, bring purée to a boil over high heat, then reduce heat. Slowly stir in chocolate and adjust consistency of sauce. If too thick, thin with chicken stock. If too thin, simmer until desired thickness is reached.

Strain through a medium strainer. Season with salt, maple syrup, if too bitter, and lime juice to taste.

PICO DE GALLO RICE

1 cup uncooked Texmati
   rice (or white rice)
1³/₄ cups chicken stock (see
   page 236)
2 tomatoes, peeled, cored,
   seeded, and diced
1 small onion, peeled and
   cut into ¹/₄-inch dice

2 serrano chilies, finely
   chopped
1 clove garlic, peeled and
   minced
1 tablespoon chopped fresh
   cilantro
Juice of 2 limes
Salt to taste

Combine rice and stock in a medium saucepan over high heat. Bring to a boil and stir once. Cover and lower heat. Simmer for 25 to 30 minutes. Remove from heat. Reserve and keep warm.

In a medium bowl, combine tomatoes, onion, serranos, garlic, cilantro, lime juice, and salt. Cover and let stand for at least 20 minutes. Stir into rice and mix thoroughly.

TRIANGLE TORTILLA CHIPS

2 cups vegetable oil
16 round corn tortillas
   (preferably 4 ancho
   chili, 4 blue corn,

and 4 yellow corn),
   cut into 1-inch
   equilateral triangles
Salt to taste

Heat oil to 350° on a food thermometer in a medium saucepan with high sides over medium-high heat. Cook tortilla triangles in small batches for 1 to 2 minutes or until crisp. Remove from oil and drain on paper towel. Season with salt.

Jalapeño–Smoked Chicken Fajita with Grilled Onion Guacamole and Watermelon Pico de Gallo

SERVES 4

Chef Jody Denton and I worked together for years at The Mansion on Turtle Creek. Before Jody left to join Wolfgang Puck in Los Angeles, I begged him for this recipe. On his last day in Dallas, he finally handed me a folded-up piece of paper that looked like it had been through the wash a couple of times, leaving me to decipher the ingredients. I did, and the recipe is a winner.

4 whole boneless, skinless chicken breasts
1 large onion, peeled and sliced
2 shallots, peeled and chopped
2 cloves garlic, peeled and minced
3 jalapeño chilies, 2 seeded, all 3 finely chopped
1 small bunch fresh cilantro, chopped

1 1/2 teaspoons crushed black pepper
1/8 teaspoon cayenne pepper
2 teaspoons salt or to taste
1 1/2 cups dark beer
1/2 cup corn oil
Grilled Onion Guacamole
Watermelon Pico de Gallo
8 warm Flour Tortillas
Fresh salsa, grated cheddar cheese, and sour cream (optional)

In a medium bowl, combine chicken breasts, onion, shallots, garlic, jalapeños, cilantro, black and cayenne peppers, salt, beer, and oil. Marinate for 2 hours at room temperature.

Prepare smoker for cold smoke (see page 230). Remove chicken from marinade and cold smoke with as little heat as possible for 15 to 20 minutes. Then return to marinade for another hour.

Prepare grill. Make sure grates are clean and lightly rubbed or brushed with oil.

Remove chicken from marinade and place on hot grill. Cook for 4 minutes. Turn and grill other side for 3 minutes or until chicken is cooked through. When cooked, cut into small strips.

Place a julienned chicken breast, Grilled Onion Guacamole, and Watermelon Pico de Gallo on each of four serving plates. Pass warm Flour Tortillas. You may also serve as condiments fresh salsa, grated cheddar cheese, and sour cream.

Jalapeño–Smoked Chicken Fajita with Grilled Onion Guacamole and Watermelon Pico de Gallo

GRILLED ONION GUACAMOLE

2 tablespoons corn oil
2 tablespoons fresh lemon
juice
1 tablespoon red wine
vinegar
1 teaspoon crushed black
pepper
1 teaspoon ground whole
cumin seeds
³/₄ teaspoon salt

1 large red onion
3 avocados, peeled, seeded,
and cut into ¹/₂-inch
dice
1 large tomato, diced
2 cloves garlic, minced
3 serrano chilies, chopped
1 small bunch fresh
cilantro, chopped
Fresh lime juice to taste

In a small bowl, combine oil, lemon juice, vinegar, pepper, cumin, and salt. Mix thoroughly.

Peel and slice onion ¹/₄ inch thick and pour marinade over top. Marinate for 1 hour. Drain off liquid and lay the onion slices on a hot grill. Grill for 3 minutes per side. When done, combine with remaining ingredients in a medium bowl until thoroughly mixed. Taste for seasoning, and keep at room temperature until ready to serve.

WATERMELON PICO DE GALLO

1/2 cup diced jicama
1 1/2 cups 1/4-inch-dice
  watermelon, no seeds
1/4 cup 1/4-inch-dice
  honeydew melon
1/4 cup 1/4-inch-dice
  cantaloupe
1/4 cup 1/4-inch-dice red
  onion

1 jalapeño chili, chopped
2 tablespoons fresh lime
  juice
1/2 cup chopped fresh
  cilantro leaves
1/2 teaspoon salt or to taste

Combine all ingredients in a medium bowl and mix lightly so as not to break up the watermelon. Serve immediately.

FLOUR TORTILLAS

MAKES 10 TO 12 TORTILLAS

2 cups sifted all-purpose
  flour
1 teaspoon baking powder
1/2 teaspoon salt
1/2 teaspoon sugar

1 tablespoon cold vegetable
  shortening
1/2 cup warm water,
  approximately

In a mixing bowl, sift together flour, baking powder, salt, and sugar. Cut in shortening until flour looks as though it has small peas in it. Add enough warm water to make a soft dough. Mix well and knead on a well-floured board for 3 to 5 minutes or until shiny and elastic. Cover dough and let rest out of draft for 30 minutes.

Form dough into balls 2 to 2 1/2 inches in diameter. On a lightly floured board, roll into circles 7 inches in diameter and 1/4 inch thick. Cook on a hot, ungreased griddle for 2 minutes or until slightly brown at the edges. Turn and cook on other side for 1 minute or until edges are brown. Keep warm, tightly wrapped in foil, until ready to serve (or reheat, tightly wrapped in foil, in a preheated 300° oven for 10 to 15 minutes or until heated through).

Oven-Roasted Free-Range Chicken with Sherry-Achiote Glaze

SERVES 4

2 3-pound free-range
  chickens
Salt to taste
Ground black pepper to
  taste

2 tablespoons vegetable oil
Sherry-Achiote Glaze

Preheat oven to 400°.

Remove wings from chickens and reserve for another use. On each chicken, starting at keel bone, run the tip of a boning knife between breast meat and bone back to the thigh so that the boneless breast and thigh meat separate in one piece. Leave skin on. Cutting from underside, remove thigh and leg bones. You now have 4 boneless chicken halves. Season with salt and pepper.

Heat oil over medium heat in a large sauté pan. When hot, place chicken halves in pan in a single layer. Sauté chicken, skin side down, for about 5 minutes or until a light brown crust has formed, being careful not to burn. Turn halves skin side up and place on a baking sheet in preheated oven. Roast for 8 minutes. Remove from oven and brush with Sherry-Achiote Glaze. Return to oven for 5 minutes. Remove, check for doneness, and serve immediately.

SHERRY-ACHIOTE GLAZE

1 tablespoon corn oil
1 onion, peeled and sliced
2 cloves garlic, chopped
1 serrano chili, seeded and
  chopped
2 ancho chilies, seeded and
  chopped
1 tomato, cored, seeded,
  and chopped
2 ounces achiote paste* (or
  3 tablespoons annatto
  seeds soaked in 1/3 cup
  chicken stock for 1
  hour, then puréed)

1/4 cup dry sherry
1/2 cup chicken stock (see
  page 236)
1/4 cup fresh orange juice
1 tablespoon chopped fresh
  cilantro
1/4 cup pecans
Salt to taste
Ground black pepper to
  taste
Fresh lime juice to taste

Heat oil in a small saucepan over medium heat. Add onion, garlic, and chilies and sauté for 5 minutes or until onion is translucent. Add tomato, achiote paste, sherry, chicken stock, and orange juice. Cook for 10 minutes or until reduced by one-third. Pour into a blender and process until smooth. Add cilantro and pecans and continue processing until smooth. Season with salt, pepper, and lime juice.

* Found in Mexican specialty stores.

MEAT AND GAME

"Carne Asada" Strip Sirloin with Southwest Stuffed Baby Baked Potatoes

SERVES 4

This recipe can be made with chicken, fish, lamb, or game. Whatever you use, you will always taste the great flavors of *carne asada*.

4 8-ounce sirloin strip steaks, trimmed of fat and silver skin
¹/₂ cup olive oil
1 onion, peeled and thinly sliced
3 cloves garlic, peeled and finely chopped
3 serrano chilies, seeded and finely chopped

2 tablespoons chopped fresh cilantro
Juice of 3 limes
Salt to taste
Ground black pepper to taste
Southwest Stuffed Baby Baked Potatoes

Place steaks in a glass dish in a single layer. In a small bowl, combine oil, onion, garlic, serranos, cilantro, and lime juice and pour over steaks. Cover and marinate at a cool temperature for at least 2 hours, turning steaks occasionally.

Prepare grill. Make sure grates are clean and lightly rubbed or brushed with oil.

Remove steaks from marinade, let excess marinade drip off, and season with salt and pepper. Place on hot grill and cook for 4 to 5 minutes. Turn and cook for 3 to 4 minutes for medium-rare, or until cooked to the desired degree of doneness. Remove from grill.

Place 1 steak on each of four hot serving plates and place 2 Southwest Stuffed Baby Baked Potatoes beside it. Serve immediately.

SOUTHWEST STUFFED BABY BAKED POTATOES

8 baby baking potatoes, approximately 3 inches long
1 tablespoon corn oil
1/3 cup cooked, chopped chorizo sausage
2/3 cup grated jalapeño jack cheese
1 tablespoon chopped fresh cilantro
1 tablespoon chopped fresh chives
2 tablespoons sour cream
Salt to taste
Fresh lime juice to taste

Preheat oven to 375°.

Place potatoes on a baking sheet and brush skin with oil. Place in preheated oven and bake for 30 minutes or until cooked. Remove from oven and cool until able to handle. Do not turn off oven.

Cut center top off of each potato, about 1/4 inch down and about 2 inches across. With a spoon, scoop potato out into a medium bowl, scraping as close to skin as possible. Return empty shells to baking sheet. Add chorizo, cheese, cilantro, chives, sour cream, salt, and lime juice to the potato and whip until smooth. Adjust seasonings.

Using a teaspoon, heap each potato shell with filling. When stuffed, return to oven and cook for 15 minutes or until light brown and heated through.

Texas Antelope–Pozole Stew in a Flour Tortilla
SERVES 4

2 tablespoons corn oil

1½ pounds tenderloin of antelope (or venison), trimmed of fat and silver skin, cut into ½-inch dice

Salt to taste

Fresh cracked black pepper to taste

3 shallots, peeled and chopped

2 cloves garlic, peeled and minced

1–2 serrano chilies, chopped

½ teaspoon ground cumin

½ teaspoon ground coriander

2 cups veal demi-glace (see page 237)

1 tablespoon chopped fresh cilantro

2 teaspoons chopped fresh oregano

1 cup cooked pozole (or rinsed, drained canned hominy)

½ cup cooked, drained black beans

1 small red bell pepper, roasted, peeled, seeded, and cut into ½-inch dice (see page 232)

1 small yellow bell pepper, roasted, peeled, seeded, and cut into ½-inch dice

1 poblano chili, roasted, peeled, seeded, and cut into ½-inch dice

1 ripe tomato, peeled, cored, seeded, and cut into ½-inch dice

½ ripe papaya, peeled, seeded, and cut into ½-inch dice

Fresh lime juice to taste

Flour Tortillas (see page 28)

Heat oil in a stockpot over high heat. Season antelope meat with salt and pepper and place in heated oil. Cook, stirring frequently, for 4 to 5 minutes or until meat is brown on all sides. Lower heat and add shallots, garlic, serranos, cumin, and coriander. Sauté for 1 minute, then add all remaining ingredients except Flour Tortillas. Raise heat and bring to a boil. Lower heat and simmer for 5 minutes. Adjust seasoning if necessary.

Line each of four warm soup bowls with a Flour Tortilla. Ladle stew on top of tortillas and serve immediately.

Texas Antelope–Pozole Stew in a Flour Tortilla

Texas Hunter's Quail Dinner
SERVES 4

Morgan Hull did his extern with us from the Culinary Institute of America. Being from Texas and a hunter, I asked Morgan for a traditional hunter's quail dinner recipe. He assured me that this one is a "family tradition."

8 boneless quail
4 jalapeño chilies, seeded and chopped
4 cloves garlic, peeled and chopped
1 yellow onion, peeled and chopped

Salt to taste
Ground black pepper to taste
8 strips smoked bacon
5 tablespoons peanut oil
Mansion Barbecue Sauce (see page 13)

Preheat oven to 350°.

Rinse quail, then pat dry and set aside.

Combine jalapeños, garlic, and onion. Divide mixture into 8 equal parts and stuff cavities of quail with it. Season with salt and pepper. Wrap a strip of bacon around each quail and secure with a toothpick.

Heat oil in a large ovenproof sauté pan over medium-high heat. Add quail, breast side down, and sauté for 4 minutes or until browned. Turn quail on back and place in preheated oven for 10 minutes. Serve hot with Mansion Barbecue Sauce on the side.

CHAPTER TWO

The American South

MY FAMILY HERITAGE has given me a strong tie to the foods of the South and the incumbent hospitality with which they are offered. My traditions are steeped in the bounty of the land, the warmth of the hearth, and the rich blend of the people of the region. I know that I learned home cooking at its very best.

Oyster and Artichoke Bisque with Corn-Bread Oysters

SERVES 4

1 tablespoon peanut oil
3 cooked fresh artichoke
    hearts with bottoms,
    chopped
1 medium yellow onion,
    peeled and chopped
1 small stalk celery,
    trimmed and sliced
1 clove garlic, peeled and
    chopped
1/2 cup dry white wine
2 tablespoons chopped fresh
    cilantro
1 cup fish stock (see page
    235)

1/3 cup uncooked white rice
4 cups chicken stock (see
    page 236)
8 oysters, shucked and
    drained
1/4 cup heavy cream
Salt to taste
Fresh lemon juice to taste
1 red bell pepper, seeded
    and membranes
    removed, julienned
1 cup shredded fresh
    spinach leaves
Corn-Bread Oysters

Heat oil in a large saucepan over medium-high heat. When hot, add chopped artichokes, onion, celery, and garlic and sauté for 4 minutes or until onion is soft. Do not brown. Add wine, cilantro, and fish stock. Bring to a boil and cook for 4 minutes or until reduced by half. Then add rice and chicken stock. Bring to a boil. Lower heat and simmer for 30 minutes. Add oysters and cream to mixture and pour into blender. Purée until smooth. Strain, and season with salt and lemon juice. Stir in red pepper and spinach leaves.

Pour equal portions into four warm soup bowls and garnish each with 2 Corn-Bread Oysters.

CORN-BREAD OYSTERS

3 cups peanut oil
2 cups yellow cornmeal
1/2 cup flour
2 teaspoons baking powder
1 teaspoon salt
2 large eggs, lightly beaten
1/4 cup bacon fat, melted

1 cup milk
2 teaspoons fresh oyster
    liquor, approximately
8 oysters, shucked and
    drained

Heat oil to 375° on a food thermometer in a deep-sided pot over medium-high heat. Combine cornmeal, flour, baking powder, and salt. Whisk in eggs, bacon grease, milk, and just enough oyster liquor to make mixture the consistency of corn-bread batter. Stir until smooth.

Dip oysters, one at a time, into batter and carefully lower into hot oil. Do not crowd pan; add just enough oysters to form a single layer without touching. Fry for about 3 minutes or until golden brown on both sides. Remove from oil and drain on paper towel. Repeat until all oysters are cooked. Keep warm.

Shrimp Gumbo with Rice

Shrimp Gumbo with Rice

SERVES 4

We love Cajun flavors at The Mansion on Turtle Creek, so nothing could be more appropriate for this book than a good "down-home" gumbo. Be creative and add the kitchen sink.

2 teaspoons peanut oil

12 large peeled and deveined shrimp, shells reserved

1/2 cup diced celery

1/2 cup diced onion

3/4 cup diced green bell pepper

2 cups cooked white rice

1/4 cup flour

1/4 cup unsalted butter, melted

1 large onion, peeled and chopped

1 stalk celery, trimmed and chopped

1 medium green bell pepper, seeded and membranes removed, chopped

2 tablespoons chopped scallion

1 ham bone or smoked ham hock

2 cloves garlic, peeled and chopped

1 teaspoon cayenne pepper

1/2 cup white wine

1 teaspoon Mansion Pepper Mixture (see page 235)

1 bay leaf

1 teaspoon chopped fresh thyme

1 teaspoon chopped fresh basil

1 teaspoon chopped fresh sage

2 tomatoes, peeled, cored, seeded, and chopped

4 cups chicken stock (see page 236)

1 1/2 teaspoons chopped fresh parsley

1 teaspoon Tabasco sauce

1 tablespoon Worcestershire sauce

2 tablespoons gumbo filé powder

1 tablespoon fresh lemon juice

Preheat oven to 350°.

Heat oil in a medium saucepan over high heat. When hot, add shrimp and diced celery, onion, and green pepper. Sauté for 3 minutes or until shrimp are no longer translucent. Stir in rice. Remove from heat and set aside.

Combine flour and butter in a large heavy saucepan over high heat. Cook, stirring constantly, for about 7 minutes or until dark brown. When brown, add chopped onion, celery, green pepper, scallion, and ham bone. Sauté for about 4 minutes or until soft. Add reserved shrimp shells, garlic, and cayenne pepper. Sauté for 1 minute or until shells are red. Add white wine, Mansion Pepper Mixture, bay leaf, thyme, basil, sage, and tomatoes.

Add stock, a little at a time, stirring constantly, until it has all been added and soup is smooth. Add parsley, Tabasco, Worcestershire, filé, and lemon. Simmer 30 minutes or until well blended. Adjust seasonings as desired. Remove from heat. Strain, pushing all the flavor out of the shells.

Place equal portions of shrimp and rice mixture into each of four warm soup bowls. Cover with hot soup and serve immediately.

Brown-Seared Scallops on Whipped Corn Potatoes with Redeye Gravy

SERVES 4

If you grew up in Eastern Kentucky, you can "bet your biscuits" on having redeye gravy more than once in your life. My great-grandma made hers just from the drippings from the iron skillet and black coffee. After the ham slices were fried like shoe leather.

16 large scallops
Sea salt to taste
2 tablespoons corn oil
2 shallots, peeled and chopped
1/2 cup freshly brewed strong coffee
1/4 cup chicken stock (see page 236)
1/4 cup veal demi-glace (see page 237)
Salt to taste
Fresh lemon juice to taste
Whipped Corn Potatoes
Country Green Bean Garnish
Fresh cracked black pepper to taste

Season scallops with sea salt.

Heat 2 tablespoons oil in a large sauté pan over medium-high heat. When hot, place scallops, one by one, in pan. Sear scallops for 4 to 5 minutes or until very brown, but not blackened. Turn each scallop over and repeat process. Remove scallops from pan and place on a warm plate.

Place the scallop pan over medium heat. Add shallots and scrape bottom of pan with a wooden spoon to remove any "fond." Add coffee and cook for about 5 minutes or until pan is dry. Add chicken stock and veal demi-glace and cook for 4 minutes or until reduced to a thin sauce. Season with salt and lemon juice to taste. Strain and keep Redeye Gravy warm.

On each of four hot serving plates, make 4 small mounds of Whipped Corn Potatoes, forming a circle around the rim of each plate. Place a scallop on top of each mound of potatoes, making sure the brownest side is showing. Spoon a small amount of Redeye Gravy over the top of each scallop, making sure it runs off the scallops and potatoes.

Spoon the Country Green Bean Garnish into the middle of each plate. Sprinkle fresh cracked black pepper generously over the top of each scallop and serve immediately.

WHIPPED CORN POTATOES

*3 large baking potatoes,
    peeled and cut into
    chunks*
2 teaspoons corn oil
5 cloves garlic, peeled
1 cup half & half
*2 teaspoons finely chopped
    fresh thyme*

*2 tablespoons unsalted
    butter*
Salt to taste
White pepper to taste
Fresh lemon juice to taste
*Kernels from 2 ears cooked
    sweet corn*

Place potatoes in a large saucepan and cover with water. Bring to a boil over high heat. Lower heat and simmer for about 30 minutes or until potatoes are cooked.

While potatoes are cooking, heat oil in a small sauté pan over medium-low heat. When heated, add whole garlic cloves and sauté for about 10 minutes or until golden brown. (Be sure the pan is not too hot or garlic will blacken and burn.)

Remove garlic from pan and place in a blender. Add half & half and thyme and process until smooth. Reserve.

When potatoes are done, remove from heat and drain well. Place in the bowl of a mixer and add half & half mixture and butter. Whip until smooth. Season with salt, white pepper, and lemon juice. Add corn and mix to incorporate. Keep warm.

COUNTRY GREEN BEAN GARNISH

1 tablespoon corn oil
*¹/₂ pound trimmed and
    blanched green beans*
*¹/₄ pound salt-cured
    country ham, thinly
    sliced and cut into thin
    julienne*
*¹/₂ red bell pepper, seeded
    and membranes
    removed, cut into fine
    julienne*

2 teaspoons molasses
Salt to taste
Cayenne pepper to taste
*Fresh ground black pepper
    to taste*

Heat oil in a large sauté pan over medium heat. Add green beans, ham, and red pepper. Sauté for 3 minutes. Add molasses and incorporate thoroughly. Season with salt, cayenne, and fresh black pepper. Keep warm.

Buttermilk Hot-Water Corn Bread
with Spicy Shrimp and Crabmeat "Newburg"
SERVES 4

This is another twist on that old classic, Newburg, which I have brought up to the modern Southwest times. Included in this recipe is a family favorite, corn bread of any kind!

2 cups yellow cornmeal
1 teaspoon salt
1 teaspoon sugar
1 tablespoon bacon fat
¼ cup buttermilk

1½–2 cups boiling water
Corn oil for frying
Spicy Shrimp and
    Crabmeat "Newburg"
4 sprigs fresh cilantro

In a small mixing bowl, combine cornmeal, salt, and sugar. Add bacon fat, buttermilk, and boiling water and stir to mix well.

In a cast-iron skillet, pour oil to a depth of ½ inch. Heat oil to 325° on a food thermometer

Buttermilk Hot-Water Corn Bread with Spicy Shrimp and Crabmeat "Newburg"

over high heat. Using a large kitchen spoon, scoop up spoonfuls of cornmeal mixture and drop into skillet. Fry for 5 minutes, turning to brown on all sides. Remove from skillet and place on paper towels to drain. Break one apart to check for doneness.

Place a corn bread at the "2," "6," and "10 o'clock" positions of each of four hot serving plates. Ladle the "Newburg" into the middle of each plate, garnish with a sprig of cilantro, and serve immediately.

SPICY SHRIMP AND CRABMEAT "NEWBURG"

1½ cups chicken stock (see page 236)
1½ cups heavy cream
1 tablespoon olive oil
16 large shrimp, peeled and deveined
Salt to taste
½ red bell pepper, seeded and membranes removed, cut into ½-inch dice
½ yellow bell pepper, seeded and membranes removed, cut into ½-inch dice
½ green bell pepper, seeded and membranes removed, cut into ½-inch dice

2 shallots, peeled and chopped
2 cloves garlic, peeled and finely chopped
2 serrano chilies, seeded and finely chopped
2 teaspoons paprika
¼ cup sherry
6 ounces lump crabmeat, picked clean of shell and cartilage
Fresh lemon juice to taste

Combine chicken stock and cream in a small saucepan over high heat. Bring to a boil and cook for 5 to 7 minutes, until reduced to 1½ cups or until thick. Reserve.

Heat oil in a large sauté pan over medium-high heat. Season shrimp with salt and add to hot pan. Quickly sauté for 2 minutes. Add bell peppers and sauté for an additional 2 minutes. Add shallots, garlic, serranos, and paprika and sauté for 1 minute. Add sherry and reduce for 1 minute. Add thickened cream mixture and stir to combine. Stir in crabmeat and lemon juice. Check seasoning. Serve immediately.

Wild Mushroom Ragout with Hill Country Spoon Bread and Texas Mizuna Salad

SERVES 4

Every spring, Robert Del Grande, Stephan Pyles, Anne Greer, and I do a dinner for the Hill Country Food and Wine Festival held in Austin, Texas. It is a fun event involving Texas's own foods and wines. This was my contribution to the 1989 frolic.

1 tablespoon olive oil
1 pound assorted domestic and wild mushrooms, cleaned
2 tablespoons chopped shallots
2 tablespoons Marsala wine
1 cup veal demi-glace (see page 237)

2 teaspoons chopped fresh thyme
Salt to taste
Lemon juice to taste
Texas Mizuna Salad
Hill Country Spoon Bread

Heat oil in a large sauté pan over medium-high heat. When hot, add mushrooms and sauté for 2 minutes. Stir in shallots. Deglaze pan with Marsala and demi-glace and cook for about 3 minutes or until reduced by half. Add thyme and season with salt and lemon juice. Remove from heat and keep warm until ready to serve.

Have ready four serving plates at room temperature. Visually divide each plate into thirds, then place a small pile of Texas Mizuna Salad just off center. Add a scoop of Hill Country Spoon Bread and small ladleful of mushroom ragout in front of salad. Serve immediately.

HILL COUNTRY SPOON BREAD

3 cups milk
1 teaspoon chopped serrano chilies
2 teaspoons chopped garlic
1 tablespoon chopped shallots
1¹/₂ cups cornmeal

3 eggs, well beaten
1 teaspoon salt
1³/₄ teaspoons baking powder
1 tablespoon unsalted butter, melted

Preheat oven to 375°.

Generously butter a 2-quart casserole and set aside.

Combine milk, serranos, garlic, and shallots in a large saucepan over high heat. Bring to a boil, stirring in cornmeal. Cook for about 5 minutes or until very thick, stirring constantly. Remove from heat and allow to cool.

When mixture is cool and very stiff, add eggs, salt, baking powder, and butter. Using an electric mixer, beat for 15 minutes. Pour into prepared casserole and bake in preheated oven for 30 minutes or until light brown. Keep warm until ready to serve.

Wild Mushroom Ragout with Hill Country Spoon Bread and Texas Mizuna Salad

TEXAS MIZUNA SALAD

2 cups mizuna leaves or
 white chicory, loosely
 packed*

1 cup mâche lettuce, loosely
 packed*

¹/₄ cup virgin olive oil

1 tablespoon balsamic
 vinegar

1 shallot, peeled and
 chopped

1 clove garlic, peeled and
 minced

¹/₂ teaspoon minced fresh
 thyme

¹/₂ teaspoon minced fresh
 basil

¹/₂ teaspoon minced fresh
 parsley

¹/₂ teaspoon minced fresh
 chives

Salt to taste

Fresh lemon juice to taste

Pick over and wash greens. Drain well and pat dry. Place in a bowl covered with a damp paper towel.

In a small bowl, combine remaining ingredients and whisk until well combined. Toss in with greens just prior to serving.

* Any delicate fresh salad green may be substituted.

Shrimp and Crabmeat Salad on Sweet Potato Biscuits
SERVES 4

Nothing is better than these Sweet Potato Biscuits. A real treat for
biscuit lovers.

*12 large cooked shrimp,
    peeled, deveined, and
    cut into 1/2-inch dice*
*1/3 pound jumbo lump
    crabmeat, picked clean
    of shell and cartilage*
1 1/2 cups mayonnaise
1/3 cup buttermilk
1/4 cup chopped pecans
*1/2 small red bell pepper,
    seeded and membranes
    removed, cut into
    1/4-inch dice*
*1/2 yellow bell pepper, seeded
    and membranes
    removed, cut into
    1/4-inch dice*
*1 stalk celery, trimmed and
    cut into 1/4-inch dice*

*1 shallot, peeled and finely
    chopped*
*1 clove garlic, peeled and
    minced*
*1 tablespoon chopped fresh
    chives*
1 tablespoon dry mustard
*1/2 tablespoon
    Worcestershire sauce*
*1/4 teaspoon Tabasco sauce
    or to taste*
1/2 teaspoon celery seed
Salt to taste
Fresh lemon juice to taste
Sweet Potato Biscuits
Sprigs of watercress

Combine shrimp and crabmeat in a medium
bowl. Combine remaining ingredients (except
Sweet Potato Biscuits and watercress) in a
small bowl and stir to combine. Pour mixture
over shrimp and crabmeat and toss to blend.
Check for seasoning.

Place a Sweet Potato Biscuit on each of four
serving plates and split it open. Spoon the
salad on the bottom half of the biscuits, and let
it spill off onto the plate. Tilt each biscuit top
toward the back of the plate. Garnish with
sprigs of watercress. Serve.

SWEET POTATO BISCUITS

1 1/2 cups all-purpose flour
4 teaspoons baking powder
3/4 teaspoon salt
2 tablespoons sugar

1/2 cup vegetable shortening
1/4 cup milk
*1 1/2 cups mashed cooked
    sweet potatoes*

Preheat oven to 375°.

Sift dry ingredients into a mixing bowl. Cut
shortening into dry ingredients until the size of
small peas. In a separate bowl, combine milk
and sweet potatoes, then blend into flour mixture until dough just comes together.

Roll out dough on a floured surface to 1/2-
inch thickness. Cut with a 2-inch biscuit cutter
and place biscuits on an ungreased baking
sheet. Place in preheated oven and bake for 12
minutes or until lightly browned. Serve warm.

Shrimp and Crabmeat Salad on Sweet Potato Biscuit.

Pan-Seared Sea Scallops on Creamy Lobster Succotash with Country Ham–Chicory Salad

SERVES 4

I love succotash, but I think some people have bad childhood memories of that dish!

2 tablespoons olive oil
16 large scallops
Sea salt to taste
1 cup Wondra flour (or extra-finely ground cornmeal)

Country Ham–Chicory Salad
Creamy Lobster Succotash

Heat oil in a large cast-iron skillet over medium-high heat.

Season scallops with salt and dredge through flour. Shake excess flour off scallops and place in skillet, round side down. Brown for 2 minutes, then turn over and brown for 2 more minutes or until firm. Remove from skillet and place on paper towel to drain.

Place a small mound of Country Ham–Chicory Salad in the center of each of four hot plates. Spoon a small mound of Creamy Lobster Succotash at the "12," "3," "6," and "9 o'clock" positions of each plate. Lay a scallop up against each mound of succotash and serve immediately.

CREAMY LOBSTER SUCCOTASH

2 1-pound lobsters
2 tablespoons olive oil
1 large onion, peeled and finely chopped
1/2 stalk celery, trimmed and finely chopped
1/2 medium carrot, peeled and finely chopped
2 cloves garlic, peeled and finely chopped
1 serrano chili, seeded and finely chopped
6 sprigs fresh thyme
3 cups chicken stock (see page 236)
1 tablespoon corn starch
1 tablespoon water
1/2 cup heavy cream

2 tablespoons buttermilk
Salt to taste
Fresh lemon juice to taste
1 tablespoon unrefined corn oil
1 cup lima beans, blanched in boiling water, shocked in cold water, and drained
1 cup sweet corn kernels, blanched, shocked, and drained
1/2 cup thin green beans, blanched, shocked, and drained
1/4 cup 1/4-inch-dice red bell pepper, blanched, shocked, and drained

Fill a medium stockpot with lightly salted water and bring to a boil over high heat. Add lobsters and simmer for about 10 minutes or until bright red and fully cooked. Drain and set aside to cool.

When cool, remove meat from lobster tails and claws. Reserve shells for sauce. Cut lobster meat into 1/4-inch dice, cover, and keep cool.

Heat olive oil in a large saucepan over medium heat. When hot, immediately add lobster shells. Stir continuously for 2 minutes. Add onion, celery, and carrot and sauté for 4 minutes, stirring occasionally to prevent sticking. Add garlic and serrano and sauté for 1 minute. Add thyme and chicken stock and bring to a boil.

Mix corn starch and water together and whisk into the boiling stock. When well com-

bined, reduce heat and simmer for 20 minutes.

Strain mixture into a medium saucepan, making sure to press out as much liquid as possible. Add cream and buttermilk and bring to a boil over high heat. Reduce heat to a simmer and cook for about 5 minutes, until sauce coats the back of a spoon. Season with salt and lemon juice. Reserve.

Heat corn oil in a large sauté pan over medium heat. When hot, add remaining vegetables and sauté for 3 minutes. Whisk in reserved lobster meat and cream sauce and bring to a boil, stirring to combine. Adjust seasoning if necessary, and serve immediately.

COUNTRY HAM—CHICORY SALAD

3 tablespoons olive oil

1/3 cup julienned salt-cured country ham

1 shallot, peeled and finely chopped

1 clove garlic, peeled and minced

1 teaspoon minced fresh thyme

2 tablespoons balsamic vinegar

1 small carrot, peeled and cut into very fine julienne

1/2 small head radicchio, trimmed and cut into fine julienne

3 cups baby chicory, picked over and cleaned

Salt to taste

Ground black pepper to taste

Heat 1 tablespoon oil in a small cast-iron skillet over medium heat. When hot, add ham and sauté for 2 minutes. Add shallot and garlic and sauté for 1 minute. Add thyme and vinegar and cook for 1 minute. Add remaining 2 tablespoons oil and remove from fire, stirring constantly.

Combine carrot, radicchio, and chicory in a large bowl. Cover with hot dressing and toss to combine. Season with salt and pepper and serve immediately.

Pan-Fried Trout with Bourbon-Pecan Brown Butter and Fried Spoon Bread

SERVES 4

Fried Spoon Bread may sound traditional, but I believe we invented it or, at least, discovered this method, which I think is a new light version of the hush puppy.

1 cup corn-bread crumbs (see page 233) or cornmeal
Salt to taste
Ground black pepper to taste
4 1-pound trout, cleaned, boned, skinned, heads and tails removed, halved

2 tablespoons vegetable oil
Bourbon-Pecan Brown Butter
Fried Spoon Bread
Buttermilk Leeks

Place crumbs in a glass dish, season with salt and pepper, and press fillets into crumbs to coat on all sides.

Heat oil in a large cast-iron skillet over medium heat. When hot, carefully place fillets in pan and sauté for 2 to 3 minutes or until light brown. Turn each fillet and cook for another 3 minutes or until brown and cooked through. Remove fillets from pan and place on paper towels to drain.

On each of four warm serving plates, form an upside-down *V* with 2 fillets. Spoon Bourbon-Pecan Brown Butter into the middle of each plate. Place two Fried Spoon Breads behind the fish at the top of the plate. Spoon a small portion of Buttermilk Leeks at the bottom. Serve immediately.

BOURBON-PECAN BROWN BUTTER

6 tablespoons unsalted butter
1/4 cup chopped pecans
1 large shallot, peeled and cut into 1/4-inch dice
1 jalapeño chili, seeded and finely chopped
1 tablespoon finely diced red bell pepper

1 tablespoon finely diced yellow bell pepper
1/4 teaspoon minced fresh thyme
Juice of 1 lemon
2 tablespoons Kentucky bourbon or to taste
Salt to taste

Place butter and pecans in a medium sauté pan over medium-high heat. Brown butter for 3 to 4 minutes but do not shake pan until butter is brown around edges. Immediately add remaining ingredients, shaking pan to combine. Check seasoning and serve.

FRIED SPOON BREAD

3 cups milk
1¼ cups cornmeal
3 large eggs, beaten
2 tablespoons unsalted
    butter, melted
1¾ teaspoons baking
    powder

1 teaspoon salt
¼ cup all-purpose flour,
    sifted
5 cups vegetable oil

Bring milk to a boil in a deep saucepan over high heat.

When boiling, stir in cornmeal. Cook for about 5 minutes, stirring frequently, until very thick. Remove from heat and allow to cool. When cool, stir in beaten eggs, butter, baking powder, and salt. Beat with an electric mixer for 15 minutes, then fold in flour.

In a deep pot, heat oil to 350° on a food thermometer. Dip a large spoon into the spoon bread batter and carefully drop batter into the hot oil, a few spoonfuls at a time. Do not overload the pan. Cook each piece for 4 minutes or until done all the way through and golden brown. Remove from oil and drain on paper towel. Serve warm.

BUTTERMILK LEEKS

1 medium leek, white part
    only, cleaned and cut
    into ½-inch dice

3 tablespoons heavy cream
3 tablespoons buttermilk
Salt to taste

Blanch leek in boiling water for 2 minutes. Remove and plunge into ice cold water for 1 minute or until cool. Drain well and pat dry.

Place leek, cream, and buttermilk in a small sauté pan over medium heat. Cook for 3 to 4 minutes or until liquid is thick. Season with salt and keep warm.

POULTRY

Grilled Chicken Breasts with Sweet Corn–Apple Relish and Barbecued Fire-Roasted Onions

SERVES 4

In the summer of 1988, in 106-degree heat, Larry Forgione, Mark Miller, and I prepared a picnic-style State Department dinner honoring George Shultz at the Woodland Plantation in Washington, D.C. This is the dish that I did, and the night was so hot that I swore the chicken cooked itself.

4 whole boneless, skinless chicken breasts
2 tablespoons peanut oil
Salt to taste
Ground black pepper to taste

Sweet Corn–Apple Relish
Barbecued Fire-Roasted Onions

Preheat grill. Make sure grates are clean and lightly rubbed with oil. Brush chicken breasts with 2 tablespoons peanut oil and season with salt and pepper. Place on grill and cook for 5 minutes. Turn and cook for about 5 minutes more or until juices run clear.

Serve 1 breast per person garnished with Sweet Corn–Apple Relish and the Barbecued Fire-Roasted Onions.

SWEET CORN–APPLE RELISH

1 cup diced red apple
1 cup diced Granny Smith apple
3 ears sweet corn
2 tablespoons bacon fat
1 small white onion, peeled and diced
1/4 cup diced red bell pepper

1/4 cup diced green bell pepper
1 tablespoon sweetened rice wine vinegar*
1/2 tablespoon white wine vinegar
Salt to taste
Fresh lemon juice to taste

Place diced apples in lemon water to prevent browning. Set aside.

Using a sharp knife, remove kernels from corn cobs. Reserve kernels. With the back of the knife, scrape pulp from cobs and reserve separately.

Heat bacon fat in a medium sauté pan over medium heat. Add corn kernels and cook, stirring constantly, for about 5 minutes or until they turn a bright yellow. Do not brown. Add onion, bell peppers, and reserved corn pulp and sauté for 5 minutes. Add vinegars and simmer for 4 minutes or until liquid is reduced. Remove from heat. Season with salt and lemon juice. Drain apples well and add to relish. Stir gently to combine. Serve at room temperature.

* Available at Asian markets.

BARBECUED FIRE-ROASTED ONIONS

12 medium onions, peeled
1 cup ketchup
4 tablespoons
*   Worcestershire sauce*
1 tablespoon malt vinegar
2 tablespoons molasses
2 teaspoons Creole mustard
1 teaspoon Tabasco sauce
1 clove garlic, peeled and
*   minced*

Salt to taste
Ground black pepper to
*   taste*
Juice of ½ lemon or to taste
2 tablespoons meat
*   drippings from smoker*
*   (if available) or 2*
*   tablespoons chicken*
*   stock (see page 236) or*
*   beef stock*

Preheat grill. Make sure grates are clean and lightly brushed or rubbed with vegetable oil. Place onions on grill. Grill them slowly, turning gradually until lightly charred on all sides, about 15 minutes.

Preheat oven to 375°. Place onions in a small roasting pan. Combine remaining ingredients and pour over onions. Cover and bake in preheated oven for 30 minutes. Carefully turn onions once halfway through cooking time. Remove pan from oven and keep warm.

MEAT

Pan-Seared Veal Chops with Apple-Bourbon Sauce and East Texas Onion Pudding

SERVES 4

Jim Mills is our executive sous-chef at The Mansion on Turtle Creek, plus a terrific "partner in crime" with me in the daily operation of the restaurant. Jim, from Beaumont, Texas, has added his family recipe of East Texas Onion Pudding to the ante. I think it wins hands down. He always has a wild card up his sleeve.

4 8-ounce center-cut veal
    chops with rib bone
    attached
Salt to taste

3 tablespoons peanut oil
Apple-Bourbon Sauce
East Texas Onion
    Pudding

Preheat oven to 375°.

Using a very sharp knife, completely clean rib bone of all meat.

Season chops with salt. Heat oil in a large ovenproof sauté pan over medium-high heat until small wisps of smoke appear. Carefully place chops in pan, with side to be presented down. Cook for about 4 minutes or until crusty and brown. Turn chops and place pan in preheated oven. Cook for 10 to 12 minutes or until chops reach desired degree of doneness. Remove pan from oven and place chops on warm platter until ready to serve.

Ladle Apple-Bourbon Sauce in the center of each of four hot serving plates. Place 1 chop on each plate and spoon a portion of East Texas Onion Pudding behind the bone. Serve immediately.

APPLE-BOURBON SAUCE

1 pound veal shank bones, cut into small pieces (your butcher can do this for you)
2 tablespoons peanut oil
1 medium onion, peeled and sliced
4 large white mushrooms, cleaned and sliced
4 shallots, peeled and roughly chopped

3 Granny Smith apples, cored and sliced
³/₈ cup Kentucky bourbon
4 sprigs fresh thyme
3 sprigs fresh sage
4 cups chicken stock (see page 236)
2 teaspoons cracked black pepper
Salt to taste
Fresh lemon juice to taste

Preheat oven to 375°.

Place bones in a roasting pan and sprinkle with 1 teaspoon peanut oil. Roast in preheated oven, stirring once during roasting, about 12 minutes or until bones are a deep golden brown. When done, remove from oven and set aside.

Heat remaining 1²/₃ tablespoons oil in a large saucepan over medium heat. When hot, add onion and sauté for 10 minutes or until browned. Add mushrooms, shallots, and 2 apples and sauté for 3 minutes. Add ¹/₄ cup bourbon and stir well, scraping the bottom of the pan to incorporate any bits of vegetables stuck there.

Add the browned bones, thyme, sage, chicken stock, and pepper. Bring to a boil. Lower heat; skim carefully and gently simmer for 30 minutes. Remove bones from sauce and add remaining apple. Cook for an additional 10 minutes.

Pour into a blender and blend for 10 to 15 seconds. Strain through a coarse strainer, pressing well to allow as much pulp as possible to pass through. Add remaining ¹/₈ cup bourbon and season with salt and lemon juice. Keep warm until ready to serve.

EAST TEXAS ONION PUDDING

3 tablespoons peanut oil
4 yellow East Texas
    Noonday onions, peeled
    and sliced
6 Vidalia onions, peeled
    and sliced
1 cup heavy cream

4 large eggs
2 cloves garlic, peeled and
    minced
Salt to taste
Cayenne pepper to taste
Fresh lemon juice to taste
Tobacco Onions

Preheat oven to 300°.

Heat oil in a large sauté pan over medium heat. When hot, add onions and sauté for 10 to 12 minutes or until completely transparent but not brown. Remove from heat and allow to cool.

In a medium mixing bowl whip cream, eggs, and garlic. Add onions and season with salt, cayenne, and lemon juice. Pour into an 8-inch square ceramic baking dish and place on center rack of preheated oven. Cook for approximately 20 minutes or until top begins to set. Sprinkle Tobacco Onions evenly over pudding and return to oven. Cook for about 20 minutes more or until center is completely set. Cover loosely with aluminum foil if onions begin to get too brown.

Remove pudding from oven and allow to rest for 10 minutes before serving.

Tobacco Onions

5 cups peanut oil (or other
    light oil)
2 large yellow or sweet
    onions, peeled and
    sliced crosswise ⅛ inch
    thick

1 cup all-purpose flour
1 teaspoon paprika
1 teaspoon salt
1 teaspoon black pepper
½ teaspoon cayenne pepper

Heat oil to 350° on a food thermometer in a deep saucepan over medium heat. Combine remaining ingredients in a medium bowl and carefully toss to coat onions.

Remove onion slices from flour mixture, shaking to remove excess. Fry a few slices at a time for about 10 minutes or until crisp and golden brown. Repeat until all onions are fried. Drain on paper towel.

Baked Ham with Cornmeal Glaze and Apple-Ginger Sauce, Served with Succotash Casserole

SERVES 4

The technique for making this traditional-type glaze was taught to me by a lady who worked for my father for years and years. I will never forget the first time I tasted her ham when I was a young boy—embedded in my memory as the best thing I've ever tasted.

1 8-pound smoked, cured ham with bone
2 tablespoons vegetable oil
2 onions, peeled and cut into 1-inch dice
1 large stalk celery, trimmed and cut into 1-inch dice
1/4 large carrot, peeled and cut into 1-inch dice
2 cups chicken stock (see page 236)

3 tablespoons brown sugar
3 tablespoons molasses
4 tablespoons Dijon mustard (or yellow mustard)
4 tablespoons cornmeal
1/2 cup pineapple juice
Succotash Casserole
Apple-Ginger Sauce

Preheat oven to 325°.

Trim ham of its skin, leaving the fat. Wash ham and pat dry. With a small knife, make long diagonal slashes 1/4 inch deep and 1 inch apart across the surface of the ham. At a 90° angle to these slashes, make additional slashes to form a diamond pattern across top of ham.

Heat oil in a roasting pan over medium-high heat. When hot, add onions, celery, and carrot and sauté for 5 minutes or until light golden brown. Place ham on top of vegetables. Place in preheated oven and cook for 10 to 15 minutes per pound or until cooked through to the bone. Baste ham every 10 minutes with 1 tablespoon chicken stock, reserving unused stock to mix with pan drippings. When ham is done, remove to a large platter. Keep warm.

Raise oven to 400°.

Heat roasting pan with vegetables over medium-high heat and sauté until all liquid has evaporated and vegetables are brown, scraping bottom of pan as you sauté. Do not allow to burn. Add reserved stock and stir to combine. When well combined, strain through a fine sieve, pressing hard to extract as much liquid as possible. Reserve for use in Apple-Ginger Sauce.

Place ham back into the same roasting pan. In a medium bowl, place brown sugar, mo-

lasses, mustard, cornmeal, and pineapple juice and stir to combine. Brush one half of mixture over ham. Place in 400° oven and cook for 10 minutes. Glaze ham with remaining cornmeal mixture and finish cooking for an additional 10 minutes.

Place ham on carving board and with a very sharp knife cut 4 to 5 thin slices per person. Fan out slices between the "3" and "9 o'clock" positions on each of four hot serving plates. Spoon the Succotash Casserole above the ham in the center of the plate and ladle the Apple-Ginger Sauce over all. Serve immediately.

APPLE-GINGER SAUCE

1 tablespoon vegetable oil
3 Granny Smith apples, peeled, cored, and cut into small pieces
3 shallots, peeled and chopped
1 clove
1 cinnamon stick
Pinch of mace
Pinch of cayenne pepper
Pinch of ground coriander
¹/₂ teaspoon cracked whole white peppercorns

¹/₂ teaspoon curry powder
1 tablespoon finely grated fresh ginger
5 sprigs fresh thyme
¹/₂ cup veal demi-glace (see page 237)
¹/₂ cup fresh orange juice
1 cup drippings from ham roasting pan
Salt to taste
Fresh lemon juice to taste

Heat oil in a medium saucepan over medium-high heat. When hot, add apples and cook for about 10 minutes or until caramelized. Reduce heat and stir in shallots. Sauté for 2 minutes. Add clove, cinnamon, mace, cayenne, coriander, white pepper, curry powder, and ginger. Stir to combine and cook for 3 minutes. Add thyme, demi-glace, orange juice, and ham drippings. Bring to a boil. Lower heat and simmer for 30 minutes. Strain sauce through a coarse sieve, pressing to extract as much liquid as possible. Season with salt and lemon juice and keep warm.

SUCCOTASH CASSEROLE

1³/₄ cups cooked, drained
    lima beans
³/₄ cup cooked sweet corn
    kernels
¹/₂ cup cooked thinly sliced
    green beans
¹/₃ cup diced red bell pepper
1¹/₂ tablespoons vegetable
    oil (or bacon fat)
1 onion, peeled, halved,
    and cut into ¹/₄-inch
    dice
1 clove garlic, peeled and
    minced
Pinch of cayenne pepper

Pinch of fresh cracked black
    pepper
1 tablespoon all-purpose
    flour
1¹/₂ cups milk
1¹/₂ teaspoons minced fresh
    thyme
1 tablespoon finely grated
    Romano cheese
Salt to taste
Fresh lemon juice to taste
1¹/₂ cups corn-bread
    crumbs (see page 233)
Tobacco Onions (see pages
    55, 176)

Preheat oven to 350°.

In a medium bowl, combine lima beans, corn, green beans, and red pepper.

Heat oil in a small saucepan over medium heat. When hot, add onion and sauté for 4 minutes or until transparent. Add garlic, cayenne, and black pepper and sauté for 1 minute. Stir in flour. Reduce heat and, stirring constantly, cook 4 to 5 minutes or until roux has the smell of hazelnuts. Slowly whisk in milk, beating constantly to incorporate. Bring to a boil. Lower heat, add thyme, and cook for 15 minutes, stirring occasionally. Remove from heat and whisk in cheese. Whip to incorporate, and season with salt and lemon juice.

Stir the white sauce into the lima bean mixture until well combined. Check seasoning. Press corn-bread crumbs into the bottom of a 1¹/₂-quart casserole. Pour in lima bean mixture. Top with Tobacco Onions, pressing down slightly. Cover tightly with foil. Place in preheated oven and cook for 20 to 25 minutes or until bubbling around the edges. Remove foil during the last 5 minutes of cooking to lightly brown top. Serve immediately.

Roast Loin of Pork with Henry Bain Sauce and Great Grandma Wright's Fried Corn

SERVES 6

Henry Bain was a waiter at the Pendennis Club in Louisville, Kentucky, in the 1880s. He invented this sauce, which would be very popular for years to come. My father taught me how to make it long before I ever thought of being a saucier.

2 tablespoons vegetable oil
1 6-rib center-cut pork loin, trimmed of all fat and silver skin, bone attached
Tabasco sauce to taste
Salt to taste
Mansion Pepper Mixture to taste (see page 235)

2 tablespoons yellow mustard
½ cup corn-bread crumbs (see page 233)
Henry Bain Sauce
Great Grandma Wright's Fried Corn
Sprigs of watercress

Preheat oven to 450°.

Heat oil in a large cast-iron skillet over medium-high heat. Rub pork with Tabasco and season with salt and Mansion Pepper Mixture. When oil is hot, lay loin, meat side down, into hot pan. Cook for about 5 minutes, searing to a golden brown, slowly turning meat to brown all sides. Turn meat over with rib end down to form a rack. Place in preheated oven and cook for 10 minutes. Lower oven to 350° and cook loin for 20 minutes per pound, trimmed weight. Fifteen minutes before removing meat from oven, brush loin with mustard and sprinkle crumbs over mustard coating. Finish cooking. Remove loin from pan and let rest for 10 minutes before slicing.

Place loin on cutting board and, with a sharp knife, cut down between the bones to produce 6 portions. Lay 1 chop on each of six hot plates and cover a small portion of the meat with Henry Bain Sauce spilling over onto the plate. Spoon a portion of Great Grandma Wright's Fried Corn behind each bone. Garnish with watercress and serve immediately.

HENRY BAIN SAUCE

1 12-ounce bottle chili sauce
1 14-ounce bottle ketchup
1 11-ounce bottle A-1 sauce
1 10-ounce bottle Worcestershire sauce

1 1-pound, 1-ounce bottle mango chutney
Tabasco sauce to taste
Chopped watercress (optional)

Mix all ingredients together. If chutney contains large pieces of mango, chop fine. Serve at room temperature. (Any leftover sauce may be stored, covered and refrigerated, for up to 3 months.)

GREAT GRANDMA WRIGHT'S FRIED CORN

8 ears sweet corn, shucked and cleaned
3 tablespoons bacon fat
1 onion, peeled and cut into ¼-inch dice

Salt to taste
Ground black pepper to taste

Cut kernels from corn and set aside. With the back of a French knife, scrape down rows of corn cobs, collecting as much pulp as possible. Reserve pulp separately from corn kernels.

Heat bacon fat in a medium cast-iron skillet over medium heat. When hot, add kernels and cook for 10 to 12 minutes, stirring occasionally. Add onion and cook for 5 minutes, stirring occasionally. Add corn pulp, salt, and pepper and, stirring continuously, cook for about 5 minutes or until mixture has thickened. Remove from heat and check seasoning. Keep warm until ready to serve.

CHAPTER THREE

The Asian Connection

THE FOODS of the Orient have had the greatest impact on the New Alliance at The Mansion on Turtle Creek. Lightly cooked with little fat, Asian foods remain crunchy, flavorful, high in nutrition, and beautiful on the plate. Design, color, and quantity have as large a role in serving as taste does. However, the flavors must always play evenly and a harmony and balance must prevail.

Many of the flavorings and ingredients used in the following recipes are now widely available at supermarkets throughout the United States as well as at Oriental and other specialty food stores.

Oriental Chicken Consommé

SERVES 6

1 bunch scallions, trimmed
  and chopped
1 medium onion, peeled
  and coarsely chopped
2 cloves garlic, peeled and
  coarsely chopped
1 medium leek, cleaned
  and coarsely chopped
1 1-inch piece ginger,
  peeled and grated
¼ cup coarsely chopped
  fresh cilantro
2 serrano chilies, seeded
  and chopped
2 tamarind pods, peeled,
  seeded, and chopped
  (optional)
1 tablespoon black soy sauce
1 tablespoon sansho
  Japanese pepper
¼ cup mirin
½ cup sweetened rice wine
  vinegar

1 tablespoon oyster sauce
1 tablespoon sambal chili
  paste or hot sauce
6 egg whites
8 cups chicken stock (see
  page 236)
Salt to taste
Maple syrup, if necessary
1 medium red bell pepper,
  seeded and membranes
  removed, cut into fine
  julienne
1 medium yellow bell
  pepper, seeded and
  membranes removed,
  cut into fine julienne
1 red onion, peeled and cut
  into fine julienne
10 snow peas, julienned
6 leaves fresh mint
6 leaves fresh cilantro

Using a food grinder with a medium disc, grind chopped scallions, onion, garlic, leek, ginger, cilantro, serranos, and tamarind, catching all juices as you grind. (A food processor may also be used.)

Combine ground vegetables in a large bowl. Add black soy sauce, Japanese pepper, mirin, rice vinegar, oyster sauce, sambal paste, and egg whites, whisking until eggs are foamy. Pour into a stockpot (preferably one with a spigot) along with chicken stock, stirring briskly. Bring to a slow boil over medium-high heat, stirring occasionally to prevent sticking.

When raft (the congealed vegetables that rise to the top) is completely formed and floating on top of stock, reduce heat to a simmer. Do not stir stock. Simmer for 1 hour, moistening raft with stock from a medium hole you poke in center of raft. After 1 hour, strain stock carefully through damp cheesecloth or a coffee filter, then season with salt. If soup is slightly bitter, add a few drops of maple syrup. If using a stockpot without a spigot, avoid breaking up raft by dipping soup out with a ladle. Keep warm.

Place ice and water in a medium bowl. Place bell peppers, red onion, and snow peas in ice water for 20 minutes or until crisp. When crisp, drain vegetables and fold into warm soup. Pour equal portions into six warm bowls. Garnish with mint and cilantro leaves and serve immediately.

Oriental Chicken Consommé

Crab-Eggdrop Soup

SERVES 4

3 live crabs
1 tablespoon sesame oil
2 tablespoons vegetable oil
1 onion, peeled and
　chopped
2 cloves garlic, peeled and
　chopped
2 shallots, peeled and
　chopped
2 jalapeño chilies, seeded
　and chopped
2 stalks fresh lemon grass,
　chopped
4 scallions, chopped
3 tablespoons grated fresh
　ginger with juice
4 sprigs fresh cilantro
3 tablespoons fish sauce
1/4 cup sweetened rice wine
　vinegar
1/4 cup soy sauce
1 teaspoon sambal chili
　paste

1 tablespoon sansho
　Japanese pepper
1 tablespoon oyster sauce
3 tablespoons brown sugar
2 tablespoons ketchup
8 cups chicken stock (see
　page 236)
1 tablespoon corn starch
1 tablespoon water
4 large egg whites, lightly
　beaten
4 ounces jumbo lump
　crabmeat, well cleaned
　of shell and cartilage
1 red bell pepper, seeded
　and membranes
　removed, cut into fine
　julienne
1/2 cup enoki mushrooms
1/4 cup 1/2-inch-long fresh
　chive pieces
Salt to taste

With a large cleaver, cut bodies of crabs into small pieces. Heat sesame and vegetable oils in a large stockpot over medium-high heat. Sauté crab pieces for 3 minutes or until shells start to change color. Add onion, garlic, shallots, jalapeños, and lemon grass. Sauté for 3 minutes or until onion is transparent. Add scallions, ginger, cilantro, fish sauce, rice vinegar, soy sauce, sambal paste, Japanese pepper, oyster sauce, brown sugar, ketchup, and chicken stock. Bring to a boil. Mix corn starch and water together and add to soup, stirring lightly. Lower heat and simmer for 30 minutes. Strain. Pour back into large stockpot and bring to a boil. Lower heat and in a small stream, pour egg whites into soup mixture without stirring, allowing whites to slowly congeal in soup. Add crabmeat, red pepper, mushrooms, and chives. Season with salt, pour into four warm soup bowls, and serve immediately.

Ginger Duck Spring Rolls with Red Chili "Voodoo" Sauce

SERVES 4

Chef Robert Del Grande makes the best "Voodoo" Sauce, but he always leaves out a few ingredients when he gives me the recipe. He thinks I'm going to bottle his recipe.

1 medium red bell pepper, seeded and membranes removed, cut into coarse julienne
1 medium yellow bell pepper, seeded and membranes removed, cut into fine julienne
1 medium green bell pepper, seeded and membranes removed, cut into fine julienne
1 cup julienned daikon

1 cup enoki mushrooms, stems removed
1 cup julienned Napa cabbage
4 tablespoons oyster sauce
8 tablespoons black soy sauce
Ginger Duck
8 7-×-7-inch wonton wrappers
6 cups vegetable oil
Red Chili "Voodoo" Sauce

Add all bell peppers, daikon, enoki mushrooms, Napa cabbage, oyster sauce, and half the black soy sauce to a large bowl with Ginger Duck. Toss to combine.

Separate wonton wrappers individually and place on a table side by side. Spread the reserved black soy sauce around the edges. Portion a small amount of duck mixture in the center of each wrapper. Fold in two opposite corners of each wrapper so they meet in the center of the duck mixture, repeat with the third corner, and continue rolling up into a small cylinder shape.

Heat oil to 350° degrees on a food thermometer in a large stockpot over high heat. Fry 2 spring rolls at a time and cook for 4 minutes or until wrapper is crisp and light brown. Remove from fryer and place on paper towel to drain. Repeat process until all spring rolls are completely cooked.

Serve two spring rolls per person, cutting on the bias through the middle of each spring roll. Spoon Red Chili "Voodoo" Sauce onto each plate and serve.

GINGER DUCK

1 5-pound duck
1 cup fresh orange juice
1 cup pineapple juice
4 cups water
$1/2$ cup packed brown sugar
$1/2$ cup honey
2 sticks whole cinnamon
1 tablespoon whole white
   peppercorns
3 tablespoons grated fresh
   ginger
1 bay leaf
1 teaspoon cloves
1 fresh shallot, peeled and
   chopped

1 small clove garlic, peeled
   and chopped
1 teaspoon fennel seeds
1 teaspoon star anise
1 teaspoon pickling spice
1 tablespoon chopped fresh
   cilantro
1 teaspoon thyme
1 teaspoon chopped fresh
   basil
1 teaspoon whole cumin
   seeds

Wash duck. Dry and set aside.

Combine remaining ingredients in a large bowl. Stir to combine. Add duck and marinate for 12 to 24 hours, turning frequently.

Preheat oven to 325°.

Place duck in preheated oven on a rack in a baking pan and cook for $1\frac{1}{2}$ hours. Remove from oven and cool. Debone duck and julienne into fine strips. Reserve.

RED CHILI "VOODOO" SAUCE

1 tablespoon sesame oil
4 red bell peppers, seeded
   and chopped
2 onions, peeled and
   chopped
3 cloves garlic, peeled and
   chopped
2 ancho chilies, seeded
2 serrano chilies, chopped
2 Thai red chilies or dried
   red chilies, chopped
2 ripe tomatoes, chopped
1 mango, peeled, seeded,
   and chopped

2 tablespoons brown sugar
2 tablespoons grated fresh
   ginger
1 cup sweetened rice wine
   vinegar
1 cup chicken stock (see
   page 236) or water
$1\frac{1}{2}$ cups fresh orange juice
1 tablespoon fish sauce
1 tablespoon soy sauce
Salt to taste
Fresh lime juice to taste

Heat oil in a large saucepan over medium heat. When hot, add red peppers, onions, garlic, and all chilies. Sauté for 3 to 4 minutes or until onions are transparent. Add tomatoes, mango, brown sugar, ginger, rice vinegar, chicken stock, and orange juice, and bring to a boil. Turn heat down to simmer and cook for 30 minutes. Pour mixture into a blender and process until smooth. Strain and add fish sauce and soy sauce and season with salt and lime juice. Store any leftover sauce in a sealed container in the refrigerator.

Sesame Chicken Breast with Scallion Dipping Sauce

SERVES 4

2 whole boneless, skinless
   chicken breasts, cut
   into ¹/₄-inch-thick
   strips
¹/₂ cup coconut milk
2 shallots, peeled and
   chopped
1 clove garlic, peeled and
   chopped
1 teaspoon grated fresh
   ginger
1 teaspoon curry powder

1 tablespoon chopped fresh
   cilantro
Juice of 1 lime
2 eggs, well beaten
5 cups vegetable oil
2 tablespoons black sesame
   seeds
2 tablespoons white sesame
   seeds
1¹/₂ cups dry bread crumbs
Salt to taste
Scallion Dipping Sauce

In a medium bowl, combine chicken with coconut milk, shallots, garlic, ginger, curry powder, cilantro, lime juice, and eggs. Marinate, refrigerated, for 2 hours.

Heat oil to 350° on a food thermometer in a large stockpot over high heat. Blend black and white sesame seeds with bread crumbs.

Remove chicken from marinade. Roll into bread crumb mixture until each piece is coated. Place chicken pieces in hot oil and fry for about 4 minutes or until golden brown. Remove from oil and drain on paper towel. Season with salt. Serve warm with Scallion Dipping Sauce.

SCALLION DIPPING SAUCE

¹/₂ cup sour cream
2 tablespoons sweetened rice
   wine vinegar
2 tablespoons mushroom soy
   sauce
1 teaspoon grated fresh
   ginger
1 shallot, peeled and finely
   chopped
1 clove garlic, peeled and
   finely chopped

1 serrano chili, finely
   chopped
³/₄ cup finely chopped
   scallions
1 tablespoon chopped fresh
   mint
1 tablespoon chopped fresh
   cilantro
Salt to taste
Fresh lime juice to taste

Purée all ingredients in a blender until smooth.

Shrimp Pot Stickers

SERVES 4

¹/₂ pound uncooked shrimp,
    shelled and deveined,
    tails removed
1 tablespoon grated fresh
    ginger
2 cloves garlic, peeled and
    minced
2 scallions, white part only,
    sliced very thin
2 tablespoons chopped fresh
    cilantro
1 serrano chili, seeded and
    minced
1 egg white

1 tablespoon mirin
2 teaspoons corn starch
¹/₂ teaspoon salt or to taste
¹/₂ teaspoon dry mustard
24 7-×-7-inch wonton
    wrappers
1 egg, beaten
2 teaspoons dark sesame oil
¹/₃ cup chicken stock (see
    page 236)
2 tablespoons soy sauce
Thai Sweet Chili Sauce
    (see page 79)

In a food processor fitted with a metal blade, purée shrimp with ginger, garlic, scallions, and cilantro. Pulse motor until smooth. Do not run continuously. When mixture is smooth, add serrano, egg white, mirin, corn starch, salt, and mustard. Turn out into a bowl; cover and chill.

Lightly brush one side of a wonton wrapper with beaten egg. Place 2 teaspoons chilled shrimp filling in the center of each square. Fold lower edge up over filling, then fold sides in and roll up egg roll style. Lay the dumplings seam side down on a sheet of wax paper sprinkled with corn starch.

Heat sesame oil in a 9-inch cast-iron skillet over medium-high heat. When small puffs of white smoke appear, carefully arrange dumplings in pan. Lower heat and cook dumplings for 30 seconds. Combine the chicken stock and soy sauce, add to skillet, and raise heat.

When liquid boils, lower heat, cover, and steam for 2 minutes. Uncover pan and let stock evaporate. Do not turn or move dumplings. When they begin to fry again, remove to a warm serving plate with crisp side up. Serve with Thai Sweet Chili Sauce.

Stir-Fried Rice Noodles with Shiitake Mushrooms, Eggplant, and Bean Sprouts, Served with Two Sauces: Thai Red Curry and Mango

SERVES 4

We do quite a few vegetarian dishes as daily specials at The Mansion on Turtle Creek. This shows how complex and beautiful our vegetarian dishes can get. Serve as an appetizer or an entrée.

1 13-ounce package linguine-style rice noodles
¼ cup tamari sauce
1 tablespoon honey
1 tablespoon corn starch
2 tablespoons sesame oil
8 large shiitake mushrooms, stems removed, sliced

1 carrot, peeled and julienned
1½ cups peeled and julienned eggplant
1 cup bean sprouts
1 cup small broccoli florets
Thai Red Curry Sauce
Mango Sauce

Soak rice noodles in warm water for about 15 minutes or until pliable. Drain and reserve.

In a small bowl, combine tamari, honey, and corn starch. Mix well until corn starch dissolves. Reserve.

Heat oil in a large wok or sauté pan over high heat. When hot, add mushrooms, carrot, eggplant, sprouts, and broccoli. Stir-fry for 2 minutes. Add reserved noodles and stir-fry for 1 minute. Add reserved tamari mixture and stir for about 1 minute or until just incorporated.

Portion stir-fry mixture in the middle of four hot salad plates. Surround half of each plate with Thai Red Curry Sauce and the other half with Mango Sauce. Serve immediately.

THAI RED CURRY SAUCE

1 tablespoon sesame oil
5 shallots, peeled and chopped
3 cloves garlic, peeled and chopped
2 dried red chilies
2 red bell peppers, seeded and membranes removed, chopped
1 tablespoon grated fresh ginger
1 clove
1 cinnamon stick
1 teaspoon fennel seeds

1 teaspoon ground cumin
1 teaspoon black peppercorns
¼ cup sweetened rice wine vinegar
¼ cup water or vegetable stock (see page 238)
1 cup coconut milk
1 tablespoon black soy sauce
¼ cup chopped fresh cilantro
Salt to taste
Fresh lime juice to taste

Heat oil in a medium saucepan over medium heat. When hot, add shallots, garlic, chilies, and red bell peppers. Sauté for 1 minute. Add ginger, clove, cinnamon, fennel seeds, cumin, black peppercorns, rice vinegar, water or vegetable stock, and coconut milk. Bring to a boil. Lower heat and simmer for 30 minutes. Pour mixture into a blender with black soy sauce and cilantro and purée until very smooth. Strain through a fine sieve. Season with salt and lime juice. Keep warm.

MANGO SAUCE

*2 very ripe mangoes, peeled
and seeded*
*1 tablespoon grated fresh
ginger*
*1 cup water or vegetable
stock (see page 238)*

2 sprigs fresh basil
Fresh lime juice to taste
Salt to taste

In a medium saucepan over medium heat, place mangoes, ginger, and water or vegetable stock. Bring to a boil. When boiling, immediately pour into a blender and purée until very smooth. Pour mixture back into saucepan. Add basil and steep for 10 minutes. Remove basil and strain through a fine sieve. Season with lime juice and salt. Keep warm.

Hacked Chicken Salad with Black Sesame Seed Vinaigrette and Tempura Pickled Vegetables

SERVES 4

I love this salad even if shredding the chicken takes a little patience and time. Once you taste the combination of flavors, you'll forget everything except to enjoy it.

4 large boneless, skinless chicken breast halves

1 tablespoon dark sesame oil

2 shallots, peeled and cut into 1/8-inch dice

2 cloves garlic, peeled and minced

1 tablespoon finely grated fresh ginger

2 Thai red chilies or 2 serrano chilies, very finely chopped

1/4 cup sweetened rice wine vinegar

1 tablespoon Thai fish sauce

1/4 cup chicken stock (see page 236)

1/2 tablespoon oyster sauce

2 tablespoons black soy sauce

1 teaspoon dried shrimp powder

1 teaspoon minced fresh cilantro

1 teaspoon minced fresh basil

1 teaspoon minced fresh mint

Juice of 1/2 lime

2 tablespoons black sesame seeds or toasted white sesame seeds

1/4 red bell pepper, seeded and membranes removed, cut into very thin julienne

1/2 yellow bell pepper, seeded and membranes removed, cut into very thin julienne

1/2 cup finely julienned jicama or apple

1/2 cup finely julienned carrot

1/2 cup finely julienned ripe mango

8 small center leaves romaine lettuce, washed and dried

1/4 cup 1-inch-long pieces fresh chive

1/2 cup chopped roasted peanuts

Tempura Pickled Vegetables

Preheat oven to 300°.

Place chicken breasts on a rack in a small roasting pan. Use 2 teaspoons sesame oil to brush tops of each breast. Place roasting pan in preheated oven and cook for about 12 minutes or until chicken is done. Remove breasts. Let sit until cool enough to handle. Pick up breasts and, starting with the skin side up, use your fingers to pull off a small piece of meat and shred it with the grain. The result should be a thin thread of chicken breast meat. Repeat for all breasts. Place shredded meat in a medium bowl and keep cool.

Whisk remaining 1 teaspoon sesame oil with shallots, garlic, ginger, chilies, rice vinegar, fish sauce, chicken stock, oyster sauce, black soy sauce, shrimp powder, cilantro, basil, mint, lime juice, and 1 tablespoon of sesame seeds.

Add the bell peppers, jicama, carrot, and mango to the reserved chicken pieces. Slowly pour a small amount of the black sesame seed dressing over the top. Use the tips of your fingers to gently toss and incorporate the dressing. Repeat until chicken meat is seasoned and salad is well dressed.

Place 2 romaine leaves on each of four salad plates in a *V* shape coming out from the middle of the plate. Mound a small amount of the salad where the *V* comes to a point. Do not mash the salad down. Sprinkle chives over the top of each hacked salad; then sprinkle nuts and remaining sesame seeds over the bottom

Hacked Chicken Salad with Black Sesame Seed Vinaigrette and Tempura Pickled Vegetables

of each plate. Drizzle remaining vinaigrette over the bottom of each plate, especially covering the greens. In front of the hacked salad, attractively scatter a portion of hot Tempura Pickled Vegetables. Serve immediately.

TEMPURA PICKLED VEGETABLES

2 carrots, peeled, cut on the bias into 1/4-inch slices
1 sweet potato, peeled, cut on the bias into 1/4-inch slices
2 lotus roots, cut on the bias into 1/4-inch slices
8 medium cauliflower florets
1 cup sweetened rice wine vinegar
1/2 cup sugar
1/2 cup saki
1 tablespoon finely grated fresh ginger
2 dried red chilies
1 small bunch fresh cilantro, tied together
6 cups corn oil
Tempura Batter

Place vegetables, rice vinegar, sugar, saki, ginger, chilies, and cilantro in a medium saucepan over medium heat. Bring to a simmer. Immediately remove from heat and pour into a bowl. Allow vegetables to marinate for at least 20 minutes.

Heat oil to 350° on a food thermometer in a large saucepan over high heat. Prepare Tempura Batter. Dredge pickled vegetables, a few at a time, through batter and drop in hot oil. Cook for 2 minutes or until golden brown. Remove and place on paper towel to drain. Repeat process until all vegetables are cooked. Serve immediately.

Tempura Batter

2 egg whites
1 cup beer
1/2 cup corn starch
1 cup rice flour
Salt to taste

Beat egg whites and beer. Whisk in corn starch. When well combined, add rice flour, whipping constantly until a smooth batter forms. Season with salt.

Japanese Soba Noodle Salad with Shiitake Mushrooms and Crabmeat

SERVES 4

The Asian gift to pasta salads—soba noodles.

1 tablespoon vegetable oil
8 large shiitake
    mushrooms, stems
    removed, thinly sliced
1/2 pound soba noodles
    (Japanese buckwheat
    noodles)
1/2 pound jumbo lump
    crabmeat, picked clean
    of shell and cartilage
1/2 red bell pepper, seeded
    and membranes
    removed, cut into fine
    julienne
1/2 yellow bell pepper, seeded
    and membranes
    removed, cut into fine
    julienne
10 snow peas, julienned
1/4 cup soy sauce

1/4 cup chicken stock (see
    page 236)
1/4 cup sweetened rice wine
    vinegar
1 tablespoon tamari sauce
1 teaspoon sesame oil
1 shallot, finely chopped
1 serrano chili, finely
    chopped
1/2 tablespoon finely chopped
    fresh ginger
1 tablespoon finely chopped
    fresh cilantro
3 tablespoons sliced scallions
Salt to taste
Fresh lime juice to taste
4 cups mixed salad greens,
    such as chicory,
    mizuna, etc. (optional)

Heat oil in a small skillet over medium heat. Add mushrooms and sauté for 4 minutes. Remove to mixing bowl.

Bring 2 quarts water to a boil in a large saucepan. Add soba noodles and cook for 5 minutes or until *al dente*. Drain in a colander, and rinse under cold running water. Drain well and toss in with mushrooms.

Add crabmeat, bell peppers, and snow peas and toss to combine. In a small bowl, combine remaining ingredients, except mixed greens. Whisk and check seasoning. Pour over noodles and toss gently but thoroughly. Served on four chilled plates over mixed greens, if desired.

Japanese Soba Noodle Salad with Shiitake Mushrooms and Crabmeat

FISH

Snapper with Orange-Horseradish Crust and Thai Shrimp Salad
SERVES 4

1 cup dry bread crumbs
2 tablespoons finely grated
    fresh horseradish
1½ tablespoons finely
    grated orange peel
1 clove garlic, peeled and
    minced

4 7-ounce snapper fillets,
    trimmed of skin, bones,
    and dark membrane
Salt to taste
3 tablespoons peanut oil
1 teaspoon sesame oil
Thai Shrimp Salad

Preheat oven to 375°.

Combine crumbs, horseradish, orange peel, and garlic. Spread on a small plate or piece of wax paper. Season snapper fillets lightly with salt, then press each fillet into crumb mixture, making sure both sides are completely covered.

Heat oils over medium heat in an ovenproof

saute pan large enough to hold fillets in a single layer. Place fillets in hot pan carefully so as not to knock off crumbs. Sauté for 1 minute or until crust is light brown but not blackened. When all fillets are brown on one side, arrange them, uncooked side down, in sauté pan and place in preheated oven. Bake for about 5 minutes or until fish is just firm in the middle.

Place a snapper fillet on each of four warm dinner plates. Place Thai Shrimp Salad alongside fish, allowing 4 shrimp halves per serving. Dressing from salad should spread to cover the bottom of the plate. Serve immediately.

THAI SHRIMP SALAD

¹/₄ red bell pepper, seeded and membranes removed, cut into fine julienne

¹/₂ yellow bell pepper, seeded and membranes removed, cut into fine julienne

1 cup finely julienned red onion

¹/₄ cup loosely packed very small fresh mint leaves

¹/₄ cup fresh basil leaves

¹/₄ cup loosely packed fresh cilantro leaves

1 clove garlic, peeled and minced

2 shallots, peeled and minced

1¹/₂ tablespoons finely grated fresh ginger

2 Thai red chilies, minced

¹/₄ cup Thai fish sauce

¹/₄ cup sweetened rice wine vinegar

¹/₄ cup chicken stock (see page 236)

1 teaspoon sesame oil

1 teaspoon black soy sauce

Salt to taste

Juice of 1 lime or to taste

1 tablespoon dark sesame oil

8 medium shrimp, peeled and deveined

Place bell peppers, red onion, mint, basil, and cilantro in a large bowl, in iced water to cover, for at least 30 minutes. This is to ensure that the vegetables stay crisp.

In a medium bowl, combine garlic, shallots, ginger, chilies, fish sauce, rice vinegar, chicken stock, sesame oil, and soy sauce, whisking to blend. Season with salt and lime juice. Cover and set aside.

Heat dark sesame oil in a large sauté pan over medium-high heat. When hot, add shrimp and season with salt. Stir-fry shrimp for about 2 minutes or until just firm and no longer translucent. Remove from pan and slice in half lengthwise. Keep warm.

Drain vegetables and herbs and dry thoroughly. Place in a large bowl. Add shrimp and pour dressing over all. Toss lightly to combine and coat ingredients. Serve immediately.

Snapper with Orange-Horseradish Crust and Thai Shrimp Salad

Wood-Grilled Salmon with Thai Sweet Chili Sauce and Stir-Fried Rice Stick Noodles

SERVES 4

When I visited Bangkok with our assistant maître d', Alex Jureeratana, many restaurants had their own version of a sweet and sour chili sauce which I couldn't live without the whole time we were there. Alex got so sick of eating the same style sauce, he finally asked a chef in his native language how he composed the sauce. The chef wouldn't tell him so I had to figure it out myself.

4 6–7-ounce salmon fillets,
    trimmed of skin and
    bones
3 tablespoons vegetable oil
Salt to taste

Thai Sweet Chili Sauce
Stir-Fried Rice Stick
    Noodles
Fried Basil Leaves

Prepare grill for grilling over a wood fire. Make sure grates are clean and lightly rubbed or brushed with oil just before putting fish on grill.

Brush fillets with 3 tablespoons oil and place on preheated grill, skin side up. Season skin side with salt. Grill salmon about 3 minutes. Turn each fillet over and grill for 4 to 5 minutes depending on the thickness of the fillets. Do not overcook. The fish should be very moist.

Place a fillet on each of four hot dinner plates, presentation side up. Ladle Thai Sweet Chili Sauce over one half of the fillet, letting it run onto the plate. Curl a mound of the Stir-Fried Rice Stick Noodles beside each fillet. Place 2 Fried Basil Leaves between the salmon and the Rice Stick Noodles, fanning outward on each plate. Serve immediately.

THAI SWEET CHILI SAUCE

*1 large red bell pepper,
seeded and membranes
removed, cut into ¹/₄-
inch dice (preserve
scraps)*

*1 large yellow bell pepper,
seeded and membranes
removed, cut into ¹/₄-
inch dice (preserve
scraps)*

*1 large poblano chili or
green bell pepper,
seeded and membranes
removed, cut into ¹/₄-
inch dice (preserve
scraps)*

*3 jalapeño chilies, seeded
and cut into ¹/₄-inch
dice*

2 Thai red chilies, minced

*3 shallots, peeled and cut
into ¹/₄-inch dice*

*1 tablespoon minced fresh
basil, stems reserved*

*1 tablespoon minced fresh
mint, stems reserved*

*1 tablespoon minced fresh
cilantro, stems reserved*

2 teaspoons dark sesame oil

*3 cloves garlic, peeled and
finely chopped*

*5 shallots, peeled and finely
chopped*

2 scallions, finely chopped

*1¹/₂ cups chicken stock (see
page 236)*

*1 tablespoon Thai fish
sauce*

*2 tablespoons sweetened rice
wine vinegar*

1 tablespoon black soy sauce

1 tablespoon brown sugar

*1 tablespoon chopped fresh
lemon grass*

*1 tablespoon grated fresh
ginger*

*1 teaspoon dried shrimp
powder*

1 tablespoon ketchup

2 tablespoons corn starch

2 tablespoons water

Juice of 1 lime

Salt to taste

In a medium bowl, combine diced bell peppers, chilies, shallots, and herbs. Set aside.

Heat oil in a medium saucepan over medium heat. Add bell pepper and chili scraps, and chopped garlic, shallots, and scallions. Sauté for 3 minutes. Add chicken stock, fish sauce, rice vinegar, soy sauce, brown sugar, lemon grass, ginger, shrimp powder, ketchup, and reserved herb stems. Bring to a boil. Dissolve corn starch in water and add to sauce, stirring lightly. Reduce heat and simmer for about 20 minutes or until slightly thickened.

Strain into a fresh saucepan and add reserved bell peppers, chilies, shallots, and herbs. Place over high heat and bring sauce almost to a boil. Immediately remove from heat. Season with lime juice and salt. Keep warm.

STIR-FRIED RICE STICK NOODLES

1 tablespoon Thai fish
   sauce
1 tablespoon chicken stock
   (see page 236)
1 tablespoon brown sugar
1 tablespoon black soy sauce
1/2 tablespoon grated fresh
   ginger
1/2 tablespoon finely chopped
   fresh lemon grass
2 cloves garlic, peeled and
   finely chopped
1 shallot, peeled and finely
   chopped
1 Thai red chili, minced
1 teaspoon finely grated
   lemon rind
Juice of 1 lime
1 tablespoon dark sesame
   oil

2 scallions, cut on the bias
   into 1/4-inch pieces
1/4 cup bean sprouts
1/4 cup finely julienned red
   cabbage
1/4 cup finely julienned
   skinless, seedless
   cucumber
1/4 cup finely julienned
   green mango
1/2 package rice stick
   noodles, submerged in
   warm water for 20
   minutes
2 teaspoons chopped fresh
   cilantro
1 large egg, beaten

In a small bowl, combine fish sauce, chicken stock, brown sugar, soy sauce, ginger, lemon grass, garlic, shallot, chili, lemon rind, and lime juice. Reserve.

Heat sesame oil in a large sauté pan over medium-high heat. When pan starts to smoke, add scallions, sprouts, cabbage, cucumber, and mango. Stir mixture for 30 seconds. Drain noodles well and add to sauté pan. Stir-fry for another 30 seconds. Add sauce and cook down 1 minute or until sauce coats noodles.

Add cilantro to beaten egg. Pour egg mixture in a thin stream around the outside of the sauté pan. Allow egg to congeal, then gently fold into noodles. Remove from fire and serve immediately.

FRIED BASIL LEAVES

3 cups peanut oil

8 large basil leaves

Heat oil to 350° on a food thermometer in a medium saucepan over high heat. Add basil leaves, one at a time, and fry for 10 seconds or until just crisp. Drain on paper towel.

Grilled Sesame Chicken with Orange Cashew Sauce

SERVES 4

4 whole boneless chicken
  breasts
1/4 cup sesame oil
1/4 cup fresh orange juice
1/4 cup sweetened rice wine
  vinegar
1 tablespoon honey
1 tablespoon soy sauce
1 tablespoon finely grated
  fresh ginger
2 shallots, peeled and
  minced

2 cloves garlic, peeled and
  minced
2 Thai red chilies, minced
1 tablespoon finely chopped
  fresh mint
1 tablespoon finely chopped
  fresh cilantro
1 tablespoon finely chopped
  fresh basil
Salt to taste
Orange Cashew Sauce
4 sprigs fresh cilantro

Combine chicken with sesame oil, orange juice, rice vinegar, honey, soy sauce, ginger, shallots, garlic, chilies, mint, cilantro, basil, and salt. Cover and marinate for 2 hours, stirring chicken frequently.

Prepare grill. Brush or rub grates lightly with oil.

Remove chicken from marinade and allow excess marinade to drip off. Place on low heat and grill, skin side down, for about 10 minutes or until skin is crisp but not blackened. Turn and finish cooking for an additional 5 minutes or until chicken is cooked through.

Ladle Orange Cashew Sauce on each of four warm plates. Place 1 piece of grilled chicken in the center and garnish with a cilantro sprig. Serve immediately.

ORANGE CASHEW SAUCE

1 cup fresh orange juice,
  plus more if needed
1/2 cup chicken stock (see
  page 236)
1/2 cup sweetened rice wine
  vinegar
1 tablespoon Thai fish
  sauce
1 tablespoon soy sauce
1 tablespoon finely
  julienned fresh ginger
1 tablespoon finely
  julienned fresh lemon
  grass
1 shallot, peeled and cut
  into 1/8-inch dice
1 clove garlic, peeled and
  minced

1/2 small red bell pepper,
  seeded and membranes
  removed, cut into 1/8-
  inch dice
2 tablespoons corn starch
2 tablespoons water
1 tablespoon minced fresh
  mint
1 tablespoon minced fresh
  cilantro
1 tablespoon minced fresh
  basil
Salt to taste
Juice of 1/2 lime or to taste
1/2 cup chopped unsalted
  cashews

Combine orange juice, chicken stock, rice vinegar, fish sauce, soy sauce, ginger, lemon grass, shallot, garlic, and red pepper in a medium saucepan over medium heat. Bring to a boil. Dissolve corn starch in water and whisk into sauce. Lower heat and simmer for 20 minutes. If sauce gets too thick, add additional orange juice a bit at a time.

When done, add remaining ingredients and serve hot.

Black Soy–Seared Beef Medallions with Green Curry Sauce

SERVES 4

1/4 cup black soy sauce
1/4 cup molasses
1/4 cup Thai fish sauce
3 tablespoons sesame oil
8 3 1/2-ounce beef
    tenderloins, trimmed of
    all fat and silver skin

Salt to taste
Ground black pepper to
    taste
Green Curry Sauce

In a small bowl, mix together soy sauce, molasses, and fish sauce until well combined. Reserve.

Heat oil in a large sauté pan over medium-high heat. When hot, season tenderloins with salt and pepper and place in pan. Sauté for 3 minutes, then turn and sauté for 2 minutes. Add reserved soy sauce mixture to pan and stir to deglaze, coating each tenderloin entirely.

On each of four warm serving plates, place 2 beef medallions, one overlapping the other. Surround with Green Curry Sauce. Serve hot.

GREEN CURRY SAUCE

6 shallots, peeled and
    chopped
3 cloves garlic, peeled and
    chopped
2 green bell peppers, seeded
    and membranes
    removed, chopped
3 serrano chilies, seeded
    and chopped
1 Thai red chili or 1 dried
    red chili, chopped
1 tablespoon grated fresh
    ginger
1/4 cup chopped fresh
    cilantro
1 tablespoon chopped fresh
    mint
1 tablespoon chopped fresh
    basil

2 cloves
1 teaspoon cumin seed
1 teaspoon coriander seed
1 teaspoon fennel seed
1 teaspoon black
    peppercorns
3 tablespoons sesame oil
1 cup chicken stock (see
    page 236)
1/2 cup coconut milk
1/2 cup veal demi-glace (see
    page 237)
1/4 cup sweetened rice wine
    vinegar
1 tablespoon Thai fish
    sauce
Fresh lime juice to taste
Salt to taste

Put the shallots, garlic, green peppers, chilies, ginger, herbs, and spices in a blender and purée until smooth.

Heat oil in a large saucepan over medium-high heat. When hot, stir in blended mixture and cook for 8 minutes, stirring constantly. Add chicken stock, coconut milk, demi-glace, rice vinegar, and fish sauce and bring to a boil. Lower heat and simmer for 30 minutes.

Pour mixture into blender and process until smooth. Season with lime juice and salt. Keep warm until ready to serve.

Black Soy–Seared Beef Medallions with Green Curry Sauce

Grilled Teriyaki Steak with Tempura Green Beans

SERVES 4

A steak can be just a steak, but a Teriyaki Steak is totally different. Marinating the meat with the soy mixture brings the flavor to new heights. It is not necessary to serve the meat with a sauce.

4 10-ounce strip sirloin steaks, trimmed of all fat and silver skin
1/2 cup soy sauce
1/4 cup fresh pineapple juice
1/4 cup fresh orange juice
1 tablespoon sweetened rice wine vinegar
1 tablespoon tamari sauce
1 tablespoon honey
2 teaspoons wasabi mustard

1 shallot, peeled and chopped
1 clove garlic, peeled and minced
1 tablespoon finely grated fresh ginger
1 teaspoon sesame oil
3 tablespoons peanut oil
Salt to taste
Tempura Green Beans

Place steaks in a glass bowl. Combine soy sauce, pineapple juice, orange juice, rice vinegar, tamari sauce, honey, wasabi mustard, shallot, garlic, ginger, and sesame oil. Pour over steaks. Cover and marinate for 2 hours, turning frequently.

Prepare grill. Lightly brush or rub grates with oil.

Remove steaks from marinade, brush with peanut oil, and season with salt. Grill steaks over medium heat for 5 minutes per side or until cooked to desired degree.

Place steaks on four warm serving plates. Serve immediately with Tempura Green Beans.

TEMPURA GREEN BEANS

5 cups corn oil
1/2 pound thin green beans, picked and cleaned

Tempura Batter (see page 73)
Salt to taste

Heat oil to 350° on a food thermometer in a large stockpot over high heat. Individually dredge green beans through batter and drop in hot oil. Fry for 30 seconds or until golden brown. Remove from oil. Drain on paper towel. Season with salt. Serve immediately.

PART TWO

The New Alliance

THE NEW ALLIANCE includes and expands on everything we've learned about Mexican, Southern, and Asian cuisines. We think the result is a distinctive and distinctively American style of cookery. At its heart, of course, are our hybrid sauces: light but intense sauces, rich with flavor, made with the healthiest possible components—free of large amounts of butter, cream, liquor, and demi-glace. These complex sauces, neither heavy nor cloying, enhance the flavors of each recipe. Our philosophy is to use the freshest ingredients we can find for our recipes, and not everything will be available in every region of the country. So be creative, use what's produced locally—and have fun!

CHAPTER ONE
Soups

Lima Bean–Ancho Chili Soup with Cornmeal Meringues

SERVES 4

1 pound dried lima beans
5 ancho chilies
1 tablespoon bacon fat or oil
2 onions, peeled and cut into ¼-inch dice
2 stalks celery, trimmed and cut into ¼-inch dice
½ red bell pepper, seeded and membranes removed, cut into ¼-inch dice
½ yellow bell pepper, seeded and membranes removed, cut into ¼-inch dice

½ green bell pepper, seeded and membranes removed, cut into ¼-inch dice
1 carrot, peeled and cut into ¼-inch dice
7 cups chicken stock (see page 236)
1 smoked ham hock
1 small sprig fresh epazote or cilantro
2 jalapeño chilies, seeded and finely chopped
Salt to taste
Cornmeal Meringues

Place lima beans in a stockpot with enough cold water to cover by 2 inches. Allow to soak at least 8 hours. Drain and set aside.

Seed anchos and place in warm water to cover for 20 minutes. Drain well, then cut into ¼-inch dice. Set aside.

Heat bacon fat in a large stockpot over medium heat. When hot, add onions, celery, bell peppers, and carrot and sauté for 3 minutes or until soft. Add lima beans, anchos, chicken stock, ham hock, epazote, and jalapeños. Bring to a boil. Lower heat and simmer for approximately 1 hour or until lima beans are tender but not mushy. Remove ham hock and epazote. Season with salt and pour into warm soup bowls. Serve immediately with Cornmeal Meringues.

CORNMEAL MERINGUES

1½ cups chicken stock (see page 236) or water
5 tablespoons white (or yellow) cornmeal

¼ teaspoon salt
4 egg whites, stiffly beaten

Preheat oven to 300°.

Bring stock to a boil in a small saucepan over high heat. Stir in cornmeal and return to a boil, beating for 3 to 4 minutes or until smooth.

Remove from heat and allow to cool. Beat in salt. Fold beaten egg whites into cornmeal mixture until well combined. Drop from the end of a tablespoon onto a greased cookie sheet. Place in preheated oven and bake for 30 minutes or until outside is golden brown and center is cooked through.

Remove from heat and serve immediately.

Cheddar Cheese and Poblano Chili Soup with Crisp Pecan Crackers

SERVES 4

Cheddar cheese soup has probably been my favorite since my early childhood. This is a spin-off of a great American classic that took a vacation in the Southwest.

1 tablespoon bacon fat
1 onion, peeled and
    chopped
3 shallots, peeled and
    chopped
1 clove garlic, peeled and
    chopped
1 jalapeño chili, seeded and
    chopped
1/2 tablespoon chili powder
2 tablespoons chopped fresh
    cilantro
1 tablespoon chopped fresh
    epazote, or 1 teaspoon
    dried

Pinch of cumin seeds
3/4 cup beer
7 cups chicken stock (see
    page 236)
1/4 cup unsalted butter,
    softened
1/4 cup all-purpose flour
2 poblano chilies, seeded
    and cut into 1/4-inch
    dice
4 cups shredded cheddar
    cheese
Salt to taste
Fresh lime juice to taste
Crisp Pecan Crackers

Heat bacon fat in a large sauté pan over medium heat. When hot, add onion, shallots, garlic, jalapeño, and chili powder and sauté for 2 minutes or until soft. Add cilantro, epazote, cumin seeds, and beer and bring to a boil. Boil for about 5 minutes or until liquid has reduced by half. Add chicken stock and bring to a boil, skimming foam from top. Knead butter and flour together, then slowly whisk into boiling soup, mixing until smooth. Lower heat and simmer for about 40 minutes.

Prepare smoker for cold smoke (see page 230). Smoke poblanos for 10 to 12 minutes. Reserve.

Remove from heat and immediately stir in cheese. Pour into blender and process until smooth. Add reserved poblanos and season with salt and lime juice. Pour into warm soup bowls and serve immediately with Crisp Pecan Crackers on the side.

CRISP PECAN CRACKERS

1 cup grated sharp cheddar
    cheese
1/2 cup shredded Parmesan
    cheese
1/2 cup unsalted butter,
    softened
1 teaspoon Tabasco sauce

1 teaspoon Worcestershire
    sauce
2 large eggs
2 1/2 cups all-purpose flour
2 tablespoons minced fresh
    chives
1/2 cup chopped pecans

In a large bowl, cream cheeses and butter until smooth. Stir in Tabasco, Worcestershire, and eggs. Blend in flour, chives, and pecans. When well combined, roll mixture into logs 1/2 inch in diameter. Wrap in wax paper or clear plastic wrap and place in freezer for about 1 hour or until hard enough to slice paper-thin.

Preheat oven to 350°.

When well chilled, slice logs paper-thin and place on lightly greased baking sheet. Bake in preheated oven until golden brown. Remove from oven and cool until crisp.

Lobster–White Cheddar Soup
SERVES 6

Why does the addition of cheese to a soup transform it into the best thing that anybody has ever tasted? Now picture the addition of lobster to the cheese and this soup becomes the world's greatest.

2 1-pound live lobsters
1 tablespoon peanut oil
1 onion, peeled and diced
1 leek, white part only, cleaned and sliced
2 cloves garlic, peeled and minced
1 cup white port wine
6 cups chicken stock (see page 236)
4 sprigs fresh thyme
4 sprigs fresh Italian parsley

3 tablespoons unsalted butter
3 tablespoons all-purpose flour
3 russet potatoes
1 red bell pepper
2 cups grated white cheddar cheese
1/4 cup heavy cream
3/4 teaspoon Tabasco sauce
Salt to taste
Juice of 1 lemon or to taste

Carefully holding the lobsters by the body, insert the point of a sharp knife at the top of the head just behind the eyes. Pull claws and tails from body. Chop heads coarsely. Steam or boil tails and claws for 5 minutes or until just cooked. Cool quickly. Remove meat from shells, cut into small dice, and reserve.

Heat oil in a large stockpot over medium-high heat. When it smokes, add chopped lobster heads. Sauté one minute or until shells turn bright red. Add onion, leek, and garlic and sauté 2 more minutes. Add port and cook for 5 minutes or until reduced by half. Add chicken stock and herbs and bring to a boil. Lower heat and simmer.

Heat butter in a small saucepan over medium-low heat. When sizzling stops, add flour. Cook, stirring constantly, for 5 minutes. Do not allow flour to brown. Whisk roux into simmering soup and continue to cook for 40 minutes.

Peel potatoes. Cut into 1/4-inch dice and place in a small saucepan in cold water to cover. Over high heat, bring to a boil and cook for 2 minutes or until just barely cooked. Drain and reserve.

Core, seed, and remove membranes from red pepper. Cut into 1/4-inch dice and place in a small saucepan in cold water to cover. Over high heat, bring to a boil and cook for 1 minute or until just barely cooked. Drain and reserve.

Strain soup through a coarse sieve into a blender, being careful not to overfill. Add cheese and heavy cream. Cover and purée until

smooth. Strain back into clean saucepan, and whisk in Tabasco. Season with salt and lemon juice. Add potatoes and red pepper and stir to combine. Ladle into warm soup bowls and serve immediately.

Artichoke-Corn Chowder

SERVES 6

5 large artichokes
3 strips smoked bacon, finely julienned
1½ medium onions, peeled and cut into ¼-inch dice
2 stalks celery, trimmed and cut into ¼-inch dice
4 cups chicken stock (see page 236)
1 large potato, peeled and cut into ¼-inch dice

Kernels from 2 uncooked medium ears of corn
1 cup heavy cream
3 dashes of Tabasco sauce
2 dashes of Worcestershire sauce
Salt to taste
Ground black pepper to taste
Fresh lemon juice to taste

Bring a large pot of salted water to boil over high heat. Add artichokes and simmer, covered, for 30 minutes or until bottom is easily pierced by the point of a knife. Cool under cold running water for 15 minutes. When cool, remove all leaves and reserve for another use. With a small spoon, dig out the short fibers, or choke, to expose the heart. Cut artichoke hearts into ¼-inch dice and set aside.

Fry bacon in a medium saucepan over medium-low heat for 5 minutes or until brown. Add onions and celery and cook for 3 minutes or until onions become translucent but not brown. Add chicken stock and bring to a boil. Lower heat and simmer for 10 minutes, skimming fat from surface from time to time. Add potato, corn, and artichokes and simmer for 10 minutes or until potato is cooked. Add cream and bring to a boil. When boiling, add Tabasco and Worcestershire, and season with salt, pepper, and lemon juice. Remove from heat, pour into warm soup bowls, and serve immediately.

Roast Chicken–Almond Soup with Dried-Fruit Polenta

SERVES 4

Scott Davenport was our morning sous-chef at The Mansion on Turtle Creek. Most of the soups in this book were created by him. It was a great feeling to know that in the early morning hours, while I was still sleeping, Scott and his crew were preparing a delicious soup that I would be tasting at lunch.

1 tablespoon vegetable oil
1 large onion, peeled and chopped
2 stalks celery, trimmed and chopped
1/2 cup chopped toasted almonds
3 cloves garlic, peeled and chopped
1 tablespoon chopped fresh thyme
1 tablespoon chopped fresh parsley
3/4 cup uncooked rice

1 cup white port wine
8 cups chicken stock (see page 236)
1/3 cup honey
1/2 cup heavy cream
Salt to taste
Ground black pepper to taste
Fresh lemon juice to taste
1 cup diced roasted, skinless, boneless chicken breast
Dried-Fruit Polenta

Heat 1 tablespoon oil in a large heavy saucepan over medium heat. Add onion, celery, and almonds and cook, stirring frequently, for about 5 minutes or until vegetables are golden brown. Add garlic and cook, stirring frequently, for 2 minutes or until garlic is soft. Stir in thyme, parsley, rice, and port. Cook, stirring frequently so that rice does not stick, for 5 minutes or until port is reduced by half. Raise heat and add chicken stock. Bring to a boil, then lower heat and simmer for 45 minutes, skimming fat from surface from time to time.

Heat a heavy saucepan over high heat until very hot. Add honey and cook for about 4 minutes, until large bubbles form or just before honey begins to burn. Whisk into the simmering soup with heavy cream.

Remove from heat. Pour into a blender and process until smooth. Strain through a fine sieve and season with salt, pepper, and lemon juice. Divide diced chicken meat among four warm soup bowls, pour soup over chicken, and immediately add squares of Dried-Fruit Polenta. Serve.

DRIED-FRUIT POLENTA

1 cup milk
Salt to taste
¹/₂ cup yellow cornmeal
¹/₄ cup raisins
¹/₄ cup chopped dried cherries
¹/₄ cup chopped dried apricots

¹/₄ cup chopped dried pineapple
¹/₄ cup chopped dried pears
¹/₄ cup chopped dried apples
3 tablespoons salted butter, softened

Heat milk and salt in a heavy saucepan over medium heat. When milk begins to boil, gradually whisk in cornmeal. Lower heat and simmer, stirring constantly, for 10 minutes or until very thick. Immediately stir in all the dried fruit.

Smoothly spread polenta out onto a lightly greased baking tray and allow to cool. When cool, cut into 1-inch squares.

Melt butter in a heavy sauté pan over medium heat. When hot, add polenta squares, a few at a time, and fry 4 minutes per side or until lightly browned. Keep warm until ready to serve.

Spicy Pumpkin Chowder with Crispy Crayfish

SERVES 4

Daniel O'Leary, a good friend who is chef at The Crescent Court, our
sister hotel in Dallas, gave me this recipe on the promise that I wouldn't
take full credit for it.

1 1–1¹/₂ pound pumpkin
1 red onion, peeled and cut
    into ¹/₂-inch dice
2 cloves garlic, peeled and
    minced
2 serrano chilies, seeded
    and finely chopped
1 tablespoon olive oil
¹/₄ teaspoon minced fresh
    oregano
¹/₄ teaspoon minced fresh
    sage
¹/₄ teaspoon minced fresh
    thyme
4 cups chicken stock (see
    page 236)
1 cup heavy cream

1 red bell pepper, seeded
    and membranes
    removed, cut into
    ¹/₄-inch dice
1 green bell pepper, seeded
    and membranes
    removed, cut into
    ¹/₄-inch dice
1 medium carrot, peeled
    and cut into ¹/₄-inch
    dice
1 large Idaho potato,
    peeled and cut into
    ¹/₄-inch dice
Salt to taste
Fresh lemon juice to taste

Preheat oven to 350°.

Cut pumpkin in half, remove seeds, and
place on a baking sheet in preheated oven.
Bake for 45 minutes or until soft. Remove
from oven, peel off skin, and cut into a rough
dice.

In a large saucepan over medium-high heat,
sweat onion, garlic, and serranos in oil for 3
minutes or until soft but not brown. Add
pumpkin, herbs, and chicken stock. Bring to a
boil. Lower heat to medium and simmer 45
minutes, stirring occasionally. Remove pumpkin mixture from heat and place in a blender.
Purée until smooth. Return to heat. Add heavy
cream, bell peppers, carrot, and potato and
simmer for 5 minutes or until carrot is cooked.
Season with salt and lemon juice.

Pour equal portions into four warm soup
bowls. Sprinkle with Crispy Crayfish and serve
immediately.

CRISPY CRAYFISH

1¹/₂ cups all-purpose flour
1 teaspoon salt
1 teaspoon cayenne pepper

¹/₂ cup crayfish tails, well
    cleaned
2 cups vegetable oil

Mix together flour, salt, and cayenne. Toss
crayfish in flour mixture until well coated.
Shake off extra flour.

Heat oil in a small deep-sided heavy sauté
pan over medium heat. When hot, add floured
crayfish, a few at a time, and fry for 4 minutes
or until crisp. Drain on paper towel.

CHAPTER TWO
Appetizers

Lobster with Smoked Pepper–Cheddar Cheese Sauce and Crisp Cornmeal Waffles
SERVES 4

Who says you can't eat waffles except at breakfast? These cornmeal waffles can be eaten any time—breakfast, lunch, or dinner. A true Southern tradition, try them with warm molasses and butter, also.

2 tablespoons corn oil
2 shallots, peeled and chopped
2 cloves garlic, peeled and minced
2 serrano chilies, finely chopped
1 cup chicken stock (see page 236)
1¹/₂ cups heavy cream
1¹/₂ cups finely grated cheddar cheese
3 cups diced cooked lobster meat
¹/₃ cup cold-smoked ¹/₄-inch-dice red bell pepper (see page 230)
¹/₃ cup cold-smoked ¹/₄-inch-dice yellow bell pepper
¹/₃ cup ¹/₄-inch-dice peeled, cored, seeded tomatoes
¹/₂ tablespoon chopped fresh basil
¹/₂ tablespoon chopped fresh cilantro
Salt to taste
Fresh lime juice to taste
Crisp Cornmeal Waffles

Heat oil in a medium saucepan over medium heat. When hot, add shallots, garlic, and serranos and sauté for 2 minutes. Add chicken stock and bring to a boil. Boil for 4 minutes or until reduced by half. Add cream. Bring to a boil and cook for 5 minutes or until reduced by half. Stir in cheddar cheese. Lower heat and cook, stirring constantly, until smooth.

Stir in lobster, smoked peppers, tomatoes, basil, and cilantro until well combined. Bring to a boil, then immediately remove from heat. The sauce should be slightly thick. Season with salt and lime juice.

Cut waffles into fourths. On each of four hot serving plates, place 2 pieces of waffle overlapping each other. Spoon lobster and cheddar cheese mixture over the middle of the waffles, allowing the sauce to make pools on both sides. Serve immediately.

Lobster with Smoked Pepper–Cheddar Cheese Sauce and Crisp Cornmeal Waffles

CRISP CORNMEAL WAFFLES

3/4 cup white cornmeal
2 tablespoons all-purpose
    flour
1 teaspoon sugar
1/2 teaspoon baking powder
1/3 teaspoon salt

1/4 teaspoon baking soda
2 large eggs
1 cup buttermilk
1/4 cup unsalted butter (or
    mixture of bacon fat
    and lard), melted

Preheat waffle iron.

Combine dry ingredients in a medium bowl. Stir in eggs. Gradually add buttermilk, beating to prevent lumps. Beat in melted butter until well incorporated. Make waffles following manufacturer's instructions. Serve hot.

Littleneck Clams Ragout with Penne Pasta and Pumpernickel Croutons
SERVES 4

24 2¹/₂–3-inch littleneck
    clams
¹/₂ cup white wine
5 shallots, peeled and
    minced
4 cloves garlic, peeled and
    minced
1 tablespoon minced fresh
    thyme
1 cup chicken stock (see
    page 236)
2 cups ¹/₂-inch-dice peeled,
    cored, and seeded
    yellow tomatoes
3 tablespoons olive oil

1¹/₂ cups cleaned, trimmed
    chanterelle mushrooms
    (or any other wild
    mushroom)
Salt to taste
4 cups cooked, drained
    penne pasta
5 large leaves fresh basil,
    cut into very fine strips
¹/₄ cup freshly grated aged
    Romano cheese
Ground black pepper to
    taste
Pumpernickel Croutons

Scrub the littleneck clams under cold water. Drain well. Place wine, shallots, garlic, and thyme in a medium saucepan over high heat. When liquid comes to a boil, immediately add clams. Cover with a tight-fitting lid and simmer for 5 minutes or until clams have all opened. Do not overcook or clams will be tough.

Remove clams with a slotted spoon, reserving liquid in pan. Cool clams. When cool, remove clams from shells and reserve.

Return reserved liquid to a boil over high heat, scraping shallots, garlic, and thyme from the sides back down into the liquid. Add chicken stock and tomatoes. Lower heat and simmer for 15 minutes.

Heat oil in a medium sauté pan over medium-high heat. When hot, stir in mushrooms and sauté, stirring constantly, for 4 minutes. Scrape into yellow tomato sauce and season with salt.

Stir pasta, basil, cheese, and clams into sauce until well combined. Place equal portions of pasta on four hot serving plates. Sprinkle top with fresh pepper and Pumpernickel Croutons, allowing some croutons to surround the pasta on the plate. Serve immediately.

PUMPERNICKEL CROUTONS

3 tablespoons olive oil
5 slices pumpernickel
* bread, crust removed*
* and cut into ¼-inch*
* dice*

1 clove garlic, peeled and
* minced*
Salt to taste

Preheat oven to 300°.

Heat oil in a large sauté pan over medium heat. When hot, toss in diced pumpernickel, shaking pan constantly. Sprinkle garlic over bread and continue shaking pan. Lightly season with salt. Sauté for 4 to 5 minutes or until crisp. A spoon may be used to help move croutons around.

Remove croutons from pan. Place on a baking sheet and put in preheated oven for 5 minutes or until dry. Remove from oven and drain on paper towel.

Venison Chili in Tortilla Cups
with Mango-Corn Relish
SERVES 4

This is a great hors d'oeuvre that may be passed at a party or used to start a multi-course dinner.

4 pasilla chilies, seeded
2 ancho chilies, seeded
1 chili de Arbol, seeded
1¹/₂ cups chicken stock (see page 236), more if needed
2 corn tortillas, quartered
6 tablespoons corn oil
1¹/₂ pounds venison stew meat, cut into ¹/₂-inch cubes
1 large yellow onion, peeled and minced
4 cloves garlic, peeled and minced

2 tablespoons ground cumin
1¹/₂ cups dark beer
4 cups chicken stock (see page 236) or beef stock
1 cinnamon stick
8 sprigs fresh cilantro tied in a bundle
Fresh lime juice to taste
Salt to taste
Ground black pepper to taste
Tortilla Cups
Mango-Corn Relish

Combine chilies and 1¹/₂ cups chicken stock in a medium saucepan over high heat. Bring to a boil, then lower heat and simmer for 10 minutes, stirring twice, or until chilies are soft. Cool slightly. Pour into a blender. Add tortillas and purée until smooth. Chili mixture should be quite thick, with just enough liquid to purée. You may need to add a bit of additional stock.

Heat oil in a large sauté pan over medium-high heat. When oil smokes, add venison cubes and cook, stirring frequently, for 5 minutes or until just brown. Remove meat with a slotted spoon and set aside.

While oil is still hot, stir in onion and cook for 5 minutes or until well browned. When brown, add garlic and cumin and cook for 1 minute. Add chili purée and fry for about 7 minutes or until thick and very dark, stirring often to keep from scorching.

When thick, add meat, beer, and 4 cups chicken stock, stirring well. Lower heat and simmer, uncovered, for 1 hour or until very thick and reduced by half. Remove from heat and stir in the cinnamon and cilantro bundle. Let stand, without stirring, for 15 minutes. Remove cinnamon and cilantro and stir in lime juice. Season with salt and pepper.

Spoon chili into Tortilla Cups and top with Mango-Corn Relish, allowing 4 per person. Serve immediately.

Venison Chili in Tortilla Cups with Mango-Corn Relish

TORTILLA CUPS

*8 corn tortillas,
approximately*

6 cups corn oil

With a 2-inch round biscuit cutter, cut 16 small tortillas.

Heat oil to 325° on a food thermometer in a deep pot over medium heat.

Float a circle of tortilla on top of the oil. Then, with a small ladle held in the center, push tortilla below the surface and hold for about 30 seconds or until a crisp cup forms. Immediately remove and place on paper towel to drain.

MANGO-CORN RELISH

2 ears corn, unshucked
1 mango, peeled, seeded,
  and cut into ¼-inch
  dice
2 tablespoons finely diced
  red onion
2 tablespoons finely diced
  red bell pepper

1 tablespoon finely chopped
  fresh cilantro
1 teaspoon fresh lime juice
1 teaspoon maple syrup
Salt to taste

Preheat oven to 350°.

Place unshucked ears of corn on a baking sheet in preheated oven for 20 minutes. Remove and allow to cool. Shuck and remove silk. Cut kernels from cob, avoiding the chewy heart alongside the cob.

Combine corn with remaining ingredients and let stand for 1 hour before serving.

Dean's Six O'Clock Pasta

SERVES 4

This is a great simple dish to make after fighting the traffic jam for 1½ hours coming home. It uses a one-pot method and can be made in minutes.

3 tablespoons olive oil
1 onion, peeled and
  julienned
5 button mushrooms,
  cleaned and thinly
  sliced
½ cup julienned green
  cabbage
1–2 serrano chilies,
  julienned
2 cloves garlic, peeled and
  minced
½ cup chicken stock (see
  page 236)
1 teaspoon chopped fresh
  thyme

1 teaspoon chopped fresh
  basil
½ teaspoon chopped fresh
  sage
½ teaspoon chopped fresh
  oregano
3 cups al dente cooked
  penne pasta
Salt to taste
Ground black pepper to
  taste
⅓ cup finely grated
  Romano cheese
Hot crusty bread with lots
  of virgin olive oil

Heat oil in a medium saucepan over medium-high heat. When hot, add onion and sauté for 4 to 5 minutes or until lightly browned. Add mushrooms and cabbage and sauté for 2 minutes. Add serrano and garlic and sauté for 1 minute, stirring constantly. Add stock and herbs and bring to a boil. When boiling, add pasta and cook, stirring constantly, until hot. Season with salt.

Remove from fire and place equal portions on each of four warm serving plates. Sprinkle with fresh black pepper and freshly grated cheese. Serve with hot crusty bread with lots of virgin olive oil to dip it in.

Southwest Clams Casino Streaked with Cilantro Tartar Sauce

SERVES 4

Even if clams are not indigenous to the Southwest, I always have a craving for those little morsels. The compound butter mixture adds a nice zing.

24 littleneck clams, washed and drained (you may want a few extra to allow for unusable clams)

2 tablespoons cornmeal

1 cup salted butter, softened

1 tablespoon Dijon mustard

1 tablespoon chopped fresh cilantro

2 tablespoons 1/4-inch-dice cold-smoked red bell pepper (see page 230)

2 tablespoons 1/4-inch-dice cold-smoked yellow bell pepper

2 tablespoons diced, cooked smoked slab bacon

2 shallots, peeled and cut into 1/4-inch dice

1 clove garlic, peeled and minced

1–2 serrano chilies, minced

Salt to taste

Fresh lime juice to taste

3/4 cup corn-bread crumbs (see page 233)

Cilantro Tartar Sauce

Preheat oven to 450°.

Place clams in kitchen sink and cover with 4 inches cold water.

Add cornmeal and stir until well mixed. After about 10 minutes, the clams will slowly start to eat cornmeal, which will plump up their bodies. After 15 additional minutes, open clams, leaving them on half shell. Discard top shell and any clams that are tightly shut.

While clams are soaking, combine butter, mustard, cilantro, bell peppers, bacon, shallots, garlic, serranos, salt, and lime juice in a medium bowl. Mix until well combined. Check seasoning.

Place clams on a baking tray with sides and spoon a portion of butter mixture over top of each. Generously sprinkle corn-bread crumbs on top and bake in preheated oven for 5 to 7 minutes or until butter is very hot and corn-bread crumbs are brown.

Carefully place 6 clams per person on each of four serving plates. Streak Cilantro Tartar Sauce in a zigzag design over top of each clam. Serve immediately (with hot crusty bread to soak up the excess butter in shells, if desired).

CILANTRO TARTAR SAUCE

¹/₂ cup mayonnaise
1 tablespoon chopped fresh cilantro
¹/₂ tablespoon chopped fresh parsley
¹/₂ tablespoon chopped fresh basil
1 tablespoon finely chopped onion
1 tablespoon finely chopped dill pickles
¹/₂ tablespoon finely chopped capers
Salt to taste
Fresh lemon juice to taste

Place all ingredients in a blender and process until smooth. Strain. Check seasoning.

Pour mixture into a plastic squeeze bottle like those used for mustard and set aside until ready to use.

Southwest Beef "Tartare" on Chipotle Corn Cakes

SERVES 4

This is another classic dish that took a trip to the Southwest. The chipotle corn cakes are a great addition to anything. Mark Miller of the Coyote Cafe in Santa Fe let me "borrow" his recipe for the cakes.

¹/₂ pound center-cut beef tenderloin, trimmed of fat, sinew, and silver skin
4 ancho chilies, seeded
1 jalapeño chili, seeded and chopped
1 serrano chili, chopped
2 shallots, peeled and chopped
2 cloves garlic, peeled and chopped
1 tablespoon chopped fresh cilantro root
¹/₄ teaspoon ground cumin
¹/₂ cup chicken stock (see page 236)
¹/₄ cup fresh orange juice
Salt to taste

2 tablespoons fresh lime juice or to taste
Maple syrup to taste
4 tablespoons cooked, drained black beans
4 tablespoons cooked sweet corn kernels
2 tablespoons ¹/₄-inch-dice red bell pepper, cold smoked for 10 minutes (see page 230)
2 tablespoons ¹/₄-inch-dice yellow bell pepper, cold smoked for 10 minutes
12 Chipotle Corn Cakes
¹/₂ cup julienned jicama
1 tablespoon ground toasted pumpkin seeds
10 leaves fresh cilantro

With a sharp knife, slice center-cut tenderloin into very thin slices. Stack meat and cut into long thin strips. Do a quarter turn and cut strips into ¹/₈-inch dice. Cover and reserve in refrigerator.

Combine chilies, shallots, garlic, cilantro root, cumin, chicken stock, and orange juice in a small saucepan over medium heat. Bring to a boil. Lower heat and simmer for 15 minutes or until chilies are very soft. Pour into a blender and purée until smooth. Season with salt, lime juice, and maple syrup. Set aside to cool.

When cool, pour 4 tablespoons chili purée over diced meat. Add black beans, corn, and smoked bell peppers and toss to combine. Adjust seasonings.

Place 3 hot Chipotle Corn Cakes on each of four warm plates. Spoon an equal portion of tartare onto each cake. Sprinkle julienned jicama on top of the tartare, then ground pumpkin seeds. Place a cilantro leaf on top of each tartare and serve immediately.

CHIPOTLE CORN CAKES

3 chipotle chilies, seeded
¼ cup chicken stock (see page 236)
1 tablespoon chopped fresh cilantro
1 extra-large egg, separated
½ cup yellow cornmeal
½ cup all-purpose flour
½ teaspoon baking powder

¼ cup milk
½ cup unsalted butter, melted
¼ cup minced onions
2 cloves garlic, peeled and minced
Salt to taste
Juice of 1 lime
1–2 tablespoons unrefined corn oil

Place chipotles and chicken stock in a small saucepan over high heat. Bring to a boil. Lower heat and simmer for 10 minutes or until chipotles are soft. Add cilantro and pour into blender. Purée for 2 minutes or until smooth.

Beat egg white until soft peaks form. In a medium bowl, combine chipotle purée, cornmeal, flour, baking powder, egg yolk, milk, butter, onions, garlic, salt, and lime juice. Fold in beaten egg white. The batter should be the consistency of thin pancake batter.

Heat 1 tablespoon corn oil in a large sauté pan over medium heat. When hot, ladle silver-dollar-size corn cakes into pan. Cook for 1 minute or until brown on bottom. Turn each cake over and cook for 1 minute. Remove from pan, add oil as needed, and repeat until all batter is used. Keep cakes warm until ready to serve.

Cornmeal-Crusted Oysters on Jicama "Tortillas" with Smoked Red and Yellow Bell Pepper Creams

SERVES 4

Jicama "Tortillas" is a play on the word *tortilla*—we simply cut the jicama to simulate the look of tortillas.

8 medium-to-large fresh
   oysters
2 cups dried corn-bread
   crumbs (see page 233)
1 serrano chili, seeded and
   minced
1 clove garlic, peeled and
   minced
1 teaspoon cayenne pepper
1 teaspoon ground black
   pepper
1/2 cup peanut oil
1 large jicama, about 1
   pound
1 cup water
Juice of 2 large limes
3 pinches of cayenne pepper
   or to taste
Salt to taste

1/2 pound green cabbage
1/2 cup peanut oil
3 tablespoons white wine
   vinegar
1 tablespoon fresh lime
   juice
1 1/2 tablespoons finely
   chopped fresh cilantro
1 clove garlic, peeled and
   minced
1 shallot, peeled and
   minced
1 serrano chili, seeded and
   finely chopped
Smoked Red Bell Pepper
   Cream
Smoked Yellow Bell Pepper
   Cream

Preheat oven to 300°.

Shuck oysters and reserve in a small bowl with their juice.

In a small bowl, combine crumbs, serrano, garlic, cayenne, and black pepper, mixing well.

Lift oysters out of their juice, one at a time, and dredge in crumb mixture until heavily coated. Lay breaded oysters on a sheet of wax paper until ready to fry.

Heat oil in a large sauté pan over medium heat. When hot, carefully place oysters in pan, one at a time. Fry for 2 minutes or until light brown. Turn and fry other side for 2 minutes or until light brown. Do not overcook. Remove and drain on paper towel. Keep warm.

Cut jicama lengthwise into 1/4-inch-thick slices. With a 3-inch pastry cutter, cut 8 round circles from jicama slices. Place circles in a medium bowl and add water, lime juice, and cayenne pepper. Gently mix and season with salt. Marinate for at least 15 minutes.

Remove dark outer leaves and core of cabbage. Removing each leaf separately, cut out the large center vein in a *V* shape. Stack leaves 4 high. Roll stacked leaves into a cigar shape. Using a sharp knife, start at one end of the cigar roll and cut 1/8-inch-thick strips. Carefully unroll cabbage strips into a large bowl. Repeat with remaining cabbage. Set aside.

Whisk remaining ingredients, except Red and Yellow Bell Pepper Creams, together. Season with salt and set aside.

Remove jicama from marinade and place 2 circles side by side on each of four ovenproof

Cornmeal-Crusted Oysters on Jicama "Tortillas" with Smoked Red and Yellow Bell Pepper Creams

plates. Place plates in preheated oven for 2 minutes.

Combine vinaigrette with julienned cabbage and toss to coat. Remove plates from oven and place a small mound of cabbage on top of each circle. Place one oyster on top of every cabbage mound. Streak Red Bell Pepper Cream over one and Yellow Bell Pepper Cream over the other, allowing streak to form an attractive pattern on the plate. Serve immediately.

SMOKED RED BELL PEPPER CREAM

1 cold-smoked red bell pepper, seeded (see page 230)
2 tablespoons very cold heavy cream

¹/₄ cup sour cream
Salt to taste
Fresh lime juice to taste

In a food processor, using a steel blade, purée smoked red pepper until very smooth. Add cream and sour cream. Process briefly to combine. Season with salt and lime juice. Strain through a fine sieve. Pour pepper cream into a squeeze bottle like those used for mustard. Set aside.

SMOKED YELLOW BELL PEPPER CREAM

1 cold-smoked yellow bell pepper, seeded (see page 230)
2 tablespoons very cold heavy cream

¹/₄ cup sour cream
Salt to taste
Fresh lime juice to taste

In a food processor, using a steel blade, purée smoked yellow pepper until very smooth. Add cream and sour cream. Process briefly to combine. Season with salt and lime juice. Strain through a fine sieve. Pour pepper cream into a squeeze bottle like those used for mustard. Set aside.

Wood-Grilled Gulf Shrimp with a Serrano Chili–Mint Sauce and Bulgur Wheat Salad

SERVES 4

The Bulgur Wheat Salad used in this dish could stand alone as a lunch item or as an accompaniment for other salads.

16 large shrimp, peeled and deveined, tails intact
2 tablespoons vegetable oil
Salt to taste

Bulgur Wheat Salad
Serrano Chili–Mint Sauce
2 tablespoons ¼-inch-dice yellow bell pepper
4 sprigs fresh cilantro

Prepare grill for grilling over a wood fire. Lightly brush or rub grates with oil.

Brush shrimp with 2 tablespoons vegetable oil and season with salt.

Skewer 8 shrimp on 2 wooden skewers to ease handling when grilling. Place skewers on hot grill and cook shrimp for 3 minutes. Turn and finish cooking for 2 minutes or until shrimp are done.

Spoon a mound of Bulgur Wheat Salad in the middle of each of four serving plates. Ladle small pools of Serrano Chili–Mint Sauce at the "2," "4," "8," and "10 o'clock" positions of each plate. Lay 1 shrimp in the middle of each pool of sauce, with its tail leaning on the Bulgur Wheat Salad. Sprinkle diced yellow bell pepper around each plate and garnish with a cilantro sprig.

SERRANO CHILI–MINT SAUCE

1½ cups chopped fresh mint leaves, tightly packed
¼ cup peeled and chopped shallot
1 clove garlic, peeled and chopped
1–2 serrano chilies, chopped
1 tablespoon shelled, seeded, and chopped tamarind

2 teaspoons finely grated fresh ginger
2 teaspoons sugar
⅓ teaspoon ground cumin
⅓ teaspoon ground coriander
⅓ cup water
Salt to taste
Fresh lime juice to taste

Place all ingredients in a food processor fitted with a metal blade and process until smooth. You may need to add additional water if sauce seems too thick. Recheck seasonings.

BULGUR WHEAT SALAD

1 cup bulgur wheat
1 cup defatted chicken stock (see page 236) or water
1 ripe tomato, peeled, cored, seeded, and cut into 1/4-inch dice
1/4 cup 1/4-inch-dice peeled and seeded cucumber
1 serrano chili, minced

1 shallot, peeled and minced
2 tablespoons minced fresh Italian parsley
1 tablespoon minced fresh cilantro
2 tablespoons olive oil
1 tablespoon fresh lime juice
Salt to taste

Combine bulgur wheat and chicken stock and soak for 15 minutes. Drain thoroughly if any liquid remains. Stir in remaining ingredients until well combined.

Crisp Tostada of Grilled Lobster, Chayote, and Jalapeño Jack Cheese with Papaya and Toasted Garlic

SERVES 4

2 1-pound uncooked
    lobsters
5 cloves garlic
2 tablespoons olive oil
Salt to taste
Black Bean Purée
4 crisply fried corn tortillas
1 chayote, peeled and cut
    into thin julienne

1 cup finely grated
    jalapeño jack cheese
3 tablespoons whole fresh
    cilantro leaves
1 ripe papaya, peeled,
    seeded, and cut into
    1/4-inch dice

Preheat grill, making sure grates are clean and rubbed or brushed with oil.

With a sharp knife, split the heads of the lobsters in the middle, 1 inch behind the eyes. Allow lobsters to drain.

Place lobsters on hot grill, legs down, and cook for 5 minutes. Turn and grill for another 5 minutes or until firm and cooked through. Remove from grill and let stand until cool enough to handle. Remove meat from lobster and cut into 1/2-inch dice.

Peel and thinly slice garlic cloves. Heat oil in small sauté pan over medium-low heat. When hot, add sliced garlic and sauté, stirring constantly, for 2 to 4 minutes or until light brown. Remove from heat and drain on paper towel. Season with salt.

Preheat oven to 350°.

Carefully spread Black Bean Purée over entire surface of each fried tortilla. Place on baking sheet and sprinkle lobster meat and chayote evenly over top. Generously sprinkle cheese over each tostada. Place baking sheet in preheated oven and bake for 4 minutes or until cheese has melted. Place each tostada on a hot serving plate and sprinkle top with cilantro leaves, papaya, and toasted garlic. Serve hot.

BLACK BEAN PURÉE

1 cup dried black beans
3 1/2 cups chicken stock (see
    page 236), more if
    needed
1 onion, peeled and
    chopped
2 cloves garlic, peeled and
    chopped

2–3 slices smoked bacon,
    chopped
2 serrano chilies, chopped
1 sprig fresh epazote
Salt to taste

Place black beans in a heavy saucepan and cover with cold water. Allow to soak for 8 hours, if possible. Drain well.

Combine beans with remaining ingredients in a large saucepan over high heat. Bring to a boil. Lower heat and simmer for 1 hour or until beans are tender. Place in a food processor and purée until smooth. If consistency is too thick, add additional chicken stock. Recheck seasoning.

CHAPTER THREE
Salads

Smoked Chicken Salad with Southwest Vegetables, Crisp Tortilla Strips, and Ancho-Honey Dressing

SERVES 4

2 cups julienned smoked chicken (see page 229)
½ carrot, peeled and cut into fine julienne
½ small zucchini (only part with green skin attached), cut into fine julienne
½ yellow squash (only part with yellow skin attached), cut into fine julienne
1 red bell pepper, seeded and membranes removed, cut into fine julienne

1 green bell pepper, seeded and membranes removed, cut into fine julienne
1 yellow bell pepper, seeded and membranes removed, cut into fine julienne
½ cup cooked, drained black beans
½ cup roasted corn kernels
Cilantro Mayonnaise
Ancho-Honey Dressing
Crisp Tortilla Strips

Toss chicken, vegetables, and Cilantro Mayonnaise together in a mixing bowl. (Add mayonnaise a little at a time until chicken and vegetables are finely coated.)

Ladle about 2 tablespoons Ancho-Honey Dressing onto each of four cold salad plates, spreading thinly to cover. Place equal portions of chicken and vegetables in the center of each plate with small piles of each kind of tortilla strip around the salad. Serve immediately.

CILANTRO MAYONNAISE

⅔ cup chopped cilantro
1 large egg yolk
1 tablespoon Dijon mustard
1 shallot, peeled and chopped
1 clove garlic, peeled and chopped

1 serrano chili, chopped
1½ cups peanut oil
Salt to taste
1 tablespoon fresh lime juice or to taste

Place cilantro, egg yolk, and mustard in a food processor fitted with a metal blade (or blender) and process until smooth. Add shallot, garlic, and serrano and process until well incorporated. With machine running, slowly add oil in a thin steady stream until oil is incorporated. Blend in salt and lime juice.

110

CRISP TORTILLA STRIPS

2 blue corn tortillas*
2 ancho corn tortillas*
2 corn tortillas

5 cups vegetable oil,
   approximately
Salt to taste

Cut tortillas in half, then into thin strips, keeping colors separate.

Heat vegetable oil to 350° on a food thermometer in a deep sauté pan over high heat.

Deep-fry tortilla strips, a few at a time, for about 45 seconds or until just crisp. Do not allow them to turn brown. Drain on paper towel. Season with salt.

* Use ordinary corn tortillas if others are unobtainable.

ANCHO-HONEY DRESSING

4 ancho chilies, seeded
2 shallots, peeled and
   chopped
2 cloves garlic, peeled and
   chopped
¼ cup chopped fresh
   cilantro

2 cups water
⅓ cup honey
¼ cup white wine vinegar
½ cup peanut oil
Juice of ½ lime
Salt to taste

Combine anchos, shallots, garlic, and cilantro in a small saucepan and cover with water. Place over medium heat and bring to a boil. Boil for about 10 minutes or until reduced by two-thirds.

Pour into a blender and purée until very smooth. Add honey and vinegar and process until well incorporated.

With blender running, slowly add oil in a thin steady stream until oil is incorporated. Add lime juice and season with salt.

Barbecued Oysters on Spinach–Red Onion Salad with Bacon–Blue Cheese Dressing

SERVES 4

Our night sous-chef Randall Warder developed this salad, which has become one of our evening best-sellers. You must eat each oyster with the combination of everything for the full flavor effect.

20 large fresh oysters
Mansion Barbecue Spice
    Mix (see page 234)
1 tablespoon all-purpose
    flour

1 cup peanut oil
Spinach–Red Onion Salad
Bacon–Blue Cheese
    Dressing
Ancho Chili Mayonnaise

Shuck oysters and drain liquid. Combine Mansion Barbecue Spice Mix and flour. Dredge oysters in mixture. Shake off excess.

Heat ¼ cup oil in a small sauté pan over medium heat. Fry oysters, 5 at a time, for 1 minute per side or until golden. Wipe pan and use fresh oil for each batch. Drain on paper towel. Keep warm.

On each of four salad plates, arrange 5 little mounds of Spinach–Red Onion Salad, allowing about 2 tablespoons per mound, around the outside of each plate. Drizzle Bacon–Blue Cheese Dressing in the center of each plate. Place an oyster on each salad mound, then streak about ½ teaspoon Ancho Chili Mayonnaise on top of each oyster. Serve immediately.

SPINACH–RED ONION SALAD

1½ cups packed fresh
    spinach leaves, washed
    and dried
1 small carrot
1 red onion

¼ cup sweetened rice wine
    vinegar
1 tablespoon sugar
Pinch of salt

Stack spinach leaves together, 5 or 6 leaves thick. Roll into a log shape and cut into thin slices. You will have spinach threads. Set aside.

Peel carrot and cut into very thin julienne. Toss with spinach in a medium bowl and set aside.

Peel onion. Cut in half and slice into very thin half-moon shapes. Put in a small bowl and set aside.

Heat rice vinegar and sugar in a small saucepan over medium heat, stirring constantly. When sugar dissolves, remove from heat. Add pinch of salt and pour over onion. When cool, drain onion and pour over spinach and carrot and toss to combine.

BACON—BLUE CHEESE DRESSING

4 slices bacon
3 shallots, peeled and minced
1 clove garlic, peeled and minced
2 tablespoons white wine vinegar
1/4 cup heavy cream
1/4 cup chicken stock (see page 236)

1 cup fresh buttermilk
1 tablespoon corn starch
1 tablespoon water
Salt to taste
Fresh cracked black pepper to taste
1/4 cup blue cheese, crumbled

Julienne bacon across grain into short strips. Place in a medium sauté pan over medium heat and sauté for 6 minutes or until bacon is crisp. Remove and drain on paper towel. Pour off half of bacon fat from pan. Add shallots and garlic and sauté for 2 minutes. Stir in white wine vinegar. Bring to a boil, stirring constantly, then add cream, chicken stock, and buttermilk. Return to a boil.

Dissolve corn starch in water. When dressing returns to a boil, stir in corn starch little by little until dressing is slightly thickened. Season with salt and pepper. Add blue cheese and bacon strips. Keep warm.

ANCHO CHILI MAYONNAISE

4 ancho chilies, seeded
1 large egg yolk
1 tablespoon Dijon mustard
2 tablespoons balsamic vinegar

1 cup corn oil
Juice of 1 lime or to taste
Salt to taste

Soak chilies in hot water for about 20 minutes or until soft. Place in a blender and purée until smooth. Add egg yolk, Dijon mustard, and balsamic vinegar. Process until well incorporated. With blender running, slowly add oil in a thin, steady stream. When well combined, blend in lime juice. Season to taste. Pour mixture into a plastic ketchup bottle and set aside until ready to use.

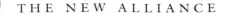

Grilled Barbecued Glazed Quail with Tortilla Salad and Roast Corn–Molasses Vinaigrette

SERVES 4

This is an unusual salad because we serve a warm demi-glace base sauce with the salad as a vinaigrette. I love the combination of cold and hot together.

*4 5-ounce boneless quail,
  wings removed*
*¼ cup Mansion Barbecue
  Spice Mix (see page
  234)*
*8 slices pickled jalapeño
  chili*
*¼ cup Mansion Barbecue
  Sauce (see page 13)*
Tortilla Salad
*Roast Corn–Molasses
  Vinaigrette*
4 large sprigs fresh cilantro

Preheat grill, making sure grates are clean and rubbed or brushed with oil.

Sprinkle quail with Mansion Barbecue Spice Mix, making sure to coat the whole bird. Place 2 slices of pickled jalapeño chili in each quail cavity. Grill quail, breast side down, for 4 minutes. Turn quail and brush with Mansion Barbecue Sauce, coating the whole side. Grill for 3 to 4 minutes or until done. Remove quail from grill and place on cutting board to rest for 4 to 5 minutes.

Place a mound of Tortilla Salad at the "12 o'clock" position on each of four large salad plates. Ladle Roast Corn–Molasses Vinaigrette to the front of the Tortilla Salad at the "6 o'clock" position on each plate. Cut each quail in half lengthwise. Place quail with the breast toward the "6 o'clock" position and legs crisscrossed coming down off the Tortilla Salad. Place a sprig of cilantro by each quail and serve immediately.

TORTILLA SALAD

8 corn tortillas
8 blue corn tortillas*
8 ancho corn tortillas*
5 cups corn oil
*½ cup cooked, drained
  black beans*
½ cup ¼-inch-dice jicama
*½ cup ¼-inch-dice red bell
  pepper*
*½ cup ¼-inch-dice yellow
  bell pepper*
3 tablespoons corn oil
*1½ tablespoons fresh lime
  juice or to taste*
*1 tablespoon finely chopped
  fresh cilantro*
*2 serrano chilies, seeded
  and finely chopped*
Salt to taste

Make 3 tortilla stacks and cut each stack in half. Restack tortillas, forming 3 half-moon stacks. Starting at one end of each tortilla stack, cut ⅛-inch threads across the half moon. With the tips of your fingers, separate each piece. Combine all three colors of tortillas into one big pile.

Heat 5 cups corn oil to 325° on a food thermometer in a medium deep-sided stockpot or deep fryer. When hot, add one-third of the tortillas. Stirring constantly, fry for 35 seconds

Grilled Barbecued Glazed Quail with Tortilla Salad and Roast Corn–Molasses Vinaigrette

or until crisp. Do not overcook or tortillas will lose their color and burn. Remove from oil and place tortillas on paper towel to drain. Repeat process for remaining tortillas. Reserve.

In a large bowl, combine beans, jicama, bell peppers, 3 tablespoons corn oil, lime juice, cilantro, chilies, and salt and toss to mix. Adjust seasoning.

Gently toss in reserved tortilla threads, being careful not to break but making sure they are well coated with dressing. Serve immediately.

* Use ordinary corn tortillas if others are unobtainable.

ROAST CORN–MOLASSES VINAIGRETTE

2 large ears sweet corn
1 tablespoon corn oil
1 medium onion, peeled and cut into ¼-inch dice
2 cloves garlic, peeled and chopped
2 teaspoons chopped fresh thyme
1 teaspoon cracked black pepper
½ cup veal demi-glace (see page 237)
¼ cup chicken stock (see page 236)
⅓ cup molasses
2 tablespoons balsamic vinegar
1 tablespoon cider vinegar
1 tablespoon Kentucky bourbon
Salt to taste

Preheat oven to 450°.

Leave corn in husks, dip in water, and place in preheated oven. Bake for 15 minutes. Remove from oven and let cool. Shuck and clean silk from corn. With a sharp knife, remove kernels. Using the dull side of the knife, scrape the cobs for pulp. Combine kernels and pulp and reserve.

Heat oil in a medium saucepan over medium heat. When hot, add onion. Sauté for 4 minutes, stirring constantly. Add garlic and sauté for 1 minute. Add thyme, pepper, demi-glace, and chicken stock. Bring to a boil. Lower heat and simmer for 5 to 7 minutes, until reduced by one-third or until slightly thickened.

Heat a small saucepan over high heat. When hot, slowly pour in molasses. Allow the molasses to bubble for 3 minutes, shaking the pan constantly. Do not allow molasses to burn. Add vinegars and bourbon and cook for 3 to 4 minutes or until slightly reduced. Stir molasses mixture into demi-glace mixture and return to a boil. Immediately add reserved corn and stir to combine. If vinaigrette does not coat back of a spoon, lower heat and simmer until it reaches the proper consistency. Season with salt and keep warm.

Wilted Spinach and Smoked Duck Salad with Potato-Corn Cakes

SERVES 4

1 tablespoon hot chili oil
2 tablespoons bacon fat, melted
2 tablespoons virgin olive oil
4 tablespoons balsamic vinegar
1 tablespoon malt vinegar
3 cloves garlic, peeled and finely chopped
3 large shallots, peeled and finely chopped
2 teaspoons finely chopped fresh thyme
1 tablespoon finely chopped fresh chives
2 teaspoons cracked black pepper

Salt to taste
Fresh lemon juice to taste
1 pound fresh spinach, stems removed, picked clean, and washed 3 times
2 smoked duck breasts (see page 229), thinly sliced
1 roasted red bell pepper (see page 232), skinned and seeded, cut into very fine julienne
1 roasted yellow bell pepper, skinned and seeded, cut into very fine julienne
Potato-Corn Cakes

In a small bowl, whisk together chili oil, bacon fat, olive oil, vinegars, garlic, shallots, herbs, pepper, salt, and lemon juice until well combined. Set aside.

Wilt spinach in a large sauté pan over medium-high heat. Keep turning spinach with a pair of tongs. While wilting, add reserved dressing a little at a time, turning spinach until thoroughly coated with dressing. Reserve some of the dressing.

When well coated, quickly remove spinach from heat and place in a medium salad bowl. Add duck and roasted peppers. Toss to combine.

Divide the salad among four warm dinner plates, making sure equal amounts of duck and peppers are in each serving. Drizzle any extra dressing over the top of each spinach salad, letting a little of the dressing spill out onto the plate. Place 4 hot Potato-Corn Cakes at the "12," "3," "6," and "9 o'clock" positions on each plate. Serve immediately.

POTATO-CORN CAKES

3 large baking potatoes
2 ears sweet corn
3 shallots, peeled and finely chopped
1 serrano chili, finely chopped

1 tablespoon chopped fresh chives
Salt to taste
3 tablespoons corn oil, plus more if needed

Peel and grate potatoes. Set aside.

Shuck and clean corn of silk. With a sharp knife, cut kernels from each ear, then scrape off pulp with the dull side of the blade. Set aside.

Combine potatoes, kernels, pulp, shallots, chili, and chives. Add salt to taste and mix thoroughly.

Form into sixteen 1½-inch cakes, using the palms of your hands to firmly press into shape. Heat oil in a large cast-iron skillet over medium-high heat. When hot, place 8 cakes into pan. Fry for about 5 minutes or until golden brown and crisp. Turn and brown other side. Remove from heat and keep warm. Cook remaining cakes, using additional oil if necessary. Serve hot.

Barbecued Loin of Rabbit on Country Fried Corn–Mâche Salad with Sweet Potato Confetti

SERVES 4

If rabbit is not available, don't bypass this recipe. Just cut skinless and boneless chicken breasts into long, thick strips, then proceed with the recipe. You will not regret it; the combinations in this salad taste great.

4 rabbit loins, trimmed of fat and silver skin
Mansion Barbecue Spice Mix (see page 234)

2 tablespoons vegetable oil
Country Fried Corn–Mâche Salad
Sweet Potato Confetti

Prepare smoker for cold smoke (see page 230).

Roll loins in Mansion Barbecue Spice Mix until well coated. Place loins on smoker rack and put in smoker. Smoke for 10 to 12 minutes. Remove from smoker.

Preheat oven to 350°.

Heat oil in a medium ovenproof sauté pan over medium heat. When hot, add loins and sear for about 4 minutes or until all sides are brown. Place pan in preheated oven and roast for about 8 minutes or until done. Do not overcook.

Remove loins from heat and place on a warm platter. Set aside.

Place a mound of Country Fried Corn–Mâche Salad (make sure to keep the salad loose and alive, not mashed down) in the center of four large salad plates. Slice each loin, lengthwise, into long, thin strips. Using one loin per plate, arrange strips around the mound of salad. Place a small mound of Sweet Potato Confetti on opposite sides of the salad. Serve immediately.

Barbecued Loin of Rabbit on Country Fried Corn–Mâche Salad with Sweet Potato Confetti

COUNTRY FRIED CORN–MÂCHE SALAD

3 large ears sweet corn
2 tablespoons bacon fat (or olive oil)
1 medium onion, peeled and cut into ¹/₄-inch dice
2 cloves garlic, peeled and finely minced
2 tablespoons cider vinegar
Salt to taste
¹/₄ cup Mansion Vinaigrette (see page 234)

3 cups mâche lettuce (or any other delicate salad green), picked clean and washed
2 cups long strands of picked clean and washed baby white chicory

Shuck and clean each ear of corn. With a sharp knife, remove kernels from each ear. Scrape off pulp with the other side of the blade, keeping pulp separate from kernels.

Heat fat in a medium cast-iron skillet over medium heat. When hot, add corn kernels. Sauté for 10 minutes, stirring constantly. Do not burn. Add onion and sauté for 4 minutes, stirring constantly. Add corn pulp and garlic and sauté for 4 minutes, stirring constantly. Add vinegar and stir to incorporate. Cook for 2 minutes. Remove pan from fire and season with salt. Pour corn into a medium bowl to cool slightly.

After 15 minutes, add Mansion Vinaigrette and whisk to thoroughly incorporate. Adjust seasoning. In a large bowl, combine mâche and chicory. Add corn vinaigrette a little at a time and gently toss until fully coated. Serve immediately.

SWEET POTATO CONFETTI

1 large sweet potato, peeled   *3 cups vegetable oil*

Slice sweet potato into very thin julienne. Pat dry.

Heat oil to 300° on a food thermometer in a medium deep-sided stockpot. Add sweet potatoes, in small batches, stirring constantly with a slotted spoon. Fry for 4 minutes or until bright orange in color and fully cooked.

Immediately remove with a slotted spoon and spread out on paper towel to dry. Repeat with remaining potatoes, being careful not to pile newly fried potatoes on top of already fried ones. Serve immediately.

Crisp Ginger Fried Lobster on a Salad of Sticky Rice, Plum, and Watercress with Soy-Lime Dressing

SERVES 4

One of the reasons I love Asian-style salads is the colorful hues that can be obtained by using different products and combinations that wouldn't normally go together. This salad is a good example.

3 1-pound lobsters
3¹/₂ cups Tempura Batter
    (see page 73)
¹/₂ tablespoon finely grated
    fresh ginger
5 cups vegetable oil
1¹/₂ cups cooked sushi rice
2 cups stemmed watercress,
    picked clean and
    washed
¹/₂ red bell pepper, seeded
    and membranes
    removed, cut into very
    fine julienne

¹/₂ yellow bell pepper, seeded
    and membranes
    removed, cut into very
    fine julienne
5 large ripe red plums, pit
    removed, thinly sliced
Soy-Lime Dressing
1 tablespoon black sesame
    seeds

Fill a large stockpot with lightly salted water and bring to a boil over high heat. Add lobsters and cook for 8 minutes. Drain well. Allow lobsters to cool slightly. When cool enough to handle, remove meat from tails and claws, being careful not to tear meat apart. Cut meat into thin medallions (or larger-sized dice if meat breaks apart).

Combine Tempura Batter and ginger. Mix well.

Heat oil to 350° on a food thermometer in a medium stockpot over medium-high heat. Coat lobster meat in batter. Place in hot oil, a few pieces at a time, and cook for 4 minutes or until crisp. Remove and drain on paper towel.

In a large bowl, combine rice, watercress, bell peppers, plums, and Soy-Lime Dressing. Toss to blend.

Place a tall mound of salad in the middle of each of four salad plates, allowing the excess dressing to flow onto the plate. Surround salad with equal portions of lobster. Sprinkle entire plate with black sesame seeds. Serve immediately.

Crisp Ginger Fried Lobster on a Salad of Sticky Rice, Plum, and Watercress with Soy-Lime Dressing

SOY-LIME DRESSING

¹/₄ cup chicken stock (see page 236)
¹/₄ cup sweetened rice wine vinegar
3 tablespoons soy sauce
¹/₂ tablespoon dark sesame oil
3 tablespoons fresh lime juice
1 tablespoon tamari sauce
1 shallot, peeled and finely chopped

1 clove garlic, peeled and minced
1 Thai red chili (or serrano), finely chopped
2 teaspoons grated fresh ginger
1 teaspoon chopped fresh mint
Salt to taste

Whisk all ingredients together in a small bowl and allow to marinate 10 minutes before serving.

Warm Squab Salad with Dried Cherry–Sorghum Dressing and Sweet Potato Confetti

SERVES 4

4 squabs, wings and
　wishbone removed
Salt to taste
Mansion Pepper Mixture
　(see page 235)
1 tablespoon vegetable oil
1 small head Bibb lettuce,
　leaves separated,
　rinsed, and dried
3 bunches mâche lettuce
　(or any other delicate
　salad green), leaves
　separated, rinsed, and
　dried
1/2 small head baby chicory,
　yellow and white leaves
　only, rinsed and dried

12–16 small leaves
　mizuna, rinsed and
　dried
2 tablespoons sherry
　vinegar
2 tablespoons virgin olive
　oil
2 tablespoons peanut oil
Salt to taste
Ground black pepper to
　taste
Dried Cherry–Sorghum
　Dressing
Sweet Potato Confetti (see
　page 119)

Preheat oven to 375°.

Season squabs well with salt and Mansion Pepper Mixture, coating both inside the cavity and the skin.

Heat oil in a medium ovenproof sauté pan over medium-high heat. When hot, add birds and cook on all sides, turning frequently, for 4 minutes or until all sides are a golden brown. Place pan in preheated oven and roast birds for 15 minutes, basting often, or until cooked medium-rare. Remove from oven.

Cut legs from squabs using the sharp tip of a knife. Remove breast meat from carcass. Reserve legs and breast halves. Keep warm. Reserve carcass for Dried Cherry–Sorghum Dressing.

Combine lettuces, chicory, and mizuna in a large bowl. Set aside. Whisk together sherry vinegar, oils, salt, and pepper until well combined. Pour over salad greens and toss to combine.

Place equal portions of dressed salad greens toward the "12 o'clock" position on each of four salad plates. Thinly slice the squab breasts on the bias. Fan out each breast half in front of salad. Place squab legs in a crisscross pattern beside one end of the sliced breasts. Spoon Dried Cherry–Sorghum Dressing in front of the breasts, covering the front part of the plate. Mound a small portion of Sweet Potato Confetti on the other end of the breast. Serve immediately.

DRIED CHERRY–SORGHUM DRESSING

Reserved squab carcasses,
  chopped
2 cups veal demi-glace (see
  page 237)
1/2 cup dried cherries
1/2 cup brandy
1/2 cup sorghum
2 tablespoons hazelnut oil
  (or other nut oil)

2 shallots, peeled and cut
  into 1/4-inch dice
2 tablespoons white wine
  vinegar
1/2 teaspoon fresh cracked
  black pepper
2 teaspoons Dijon mustard
Salt to taste

Combine squab carcasses with demi-glace in a small saucepan over high heat. Bring to a boil. Lower heat and simmer for 15 minutes. Strain and keep warm. Reserve.

Combine cherries and brandy in a small saucepan over high heat. Bring to a boil. Immediately remove from heat and pour into a small bowl. Allow to marinate for at least 1/2 hour.

Heat sorghum in a small saucepan over medium-high heat. Allow to come to a boil, and boil hard for 4 minutes to caramelize syrup, shaking pan back and forth to prevent burning. Remove from heat and carefully pour into marinating cherries.

Heat oil in a small saucepan over medium heat. Add shallots and sauté for 1 minute. Add white wine vinegar and pepper and cook for about 3 minutes or until pan is dry. Add marinated cherries with brandy and cook for about 5 minutes or until pan is dry. Add reserved demi-glace and bring to a boil. Immediately remove from heat and stir in mustard. Season with salt and keep warm until ready to use.

Smoked "Chili Cured" Coho Salmon on White Chicory–Roast Pepper Salad with Corn-Cilantro Pesto
SERVES 4

"Chili Cured" in this recipe is the same as a technique used to make gravlax. It is very easy so don't be afraid to be adventurous.

4 baby coho salmon fillets, trimmed of skin and bones
1 cup salt
2 cups sugar

2 jalapeño chilies, sliced thin
White Chicory–Roast Pepper Salad
Corn-Cilantro Pesto

Prepare smoker for cold smoke (see page 230).

Place fillets on rack in smoker. Cold smoke for 12 minutes, making sure the fillets do not begin to cook. (This step is optional.)

Combine salt and sugar. Pour a third of the mixture into the bottom of an 8-inch-square glass dish. Lay the smoked fillets on top and cover each fillet with jalapeño slices. Pour remaining salt-sugar mixture over the top of each fillet, making sure they are fully covered. Tightly wrap in clear plastic and refrigerate for 24 hours.

After 24 hours, unwrap and wipe fish clean of jalapeños and salt-sugar mixture. Using a sharp knife, cut fillets into triangle shapes. Reserve.

Place a mound of White Chicory–Roast Pepper Salad in the center of each of four salad plates. Spoon Corn-Cilantro Pesto around each salad, making irregular thin and thick pools. Arrange salmon triangles around each salad. Serve immediately.

WHITE CHICORY–ROAST PEPPER SALAD

3 cups baby chicory leaves,
    rinsed and dried
1/2 cup finely julienned
    carrot
1 roasted red bell pepper
    (see page 232),
    skinned, seeded, and
    finely julienned
1 roasted yellow bell pepper,
    skinned, seeded, and
    finely julienned

1/2 tablespoon fresh lemon
    juice
1 tablespoon balsamic
    vinegar
3 tablespoons olive oil
1 tablespoon finely chopped
    fresh chives
Salt to taste
Ground black pepper to
    taste

Combine chicory leaves and carrot. Set aside.

Combine roasted peppers, lemon juice, balsamic vinegar, oil, chives, salt, and pepper until well mixed. Check seasonings. Pour over salad and toss to combine.

CORN-CILANTRO PESTO

2 ears sweet corn
3 tablespoons corn oil
1 small bunch fresh
    cilantro
1 shallot, peeled and
    chopped
1 clove garlic, peeled and
    chopped

1 ounce cream cheese
1 tablespoon chicken stock
    (see page 236)
1 tablespoon chopped pecans
Juice of 1 lime
Salt to taste
Maple syrup to taste, if
    needed

Shuck corn and clean silk off. Using a sharp knife, remove kernels from cobs. With the other side of the blade, scrape off pulp, keeping separate from kernels.

Heat 1 tablespoon oil in a small cast-iron skillet over medium heat. Add corn kernels and sauté for 5 minutes, stirring often. Add pulp and continue cooking for 5 minutes, stirring constantly.

Pour into a blender and add remaining ingredients. Process until smooth. (If corn is not naturally sweet, bring up natural sweetness with maple syrup.)

CHAPTER FOUR

Fish and Shellfish

Jalapeño Smoked Shrimp with Tamale Spoon-Bread Sticks and Pinto Bean "Ranchero" Sauce

SERVES 4

Once you have tried the Jalapeño Smoked Shrimp you will probably never eat a plain shrimp dish again. Eaten along with this unusual sauce, the combination of flavors is rustic and earthy.

24 large Gulf shrimp
3 jalapeño chilies, finely chopped
1/4 cup finely chopped pickled jalapeño chilies
1/4 cup juice from pickled jalapeños
3 shallots, peeled and finely chopped
3 cloves garlic, peeled and finely chopped
2 tablespoons finely chopped fresh cilantro

1 tablespoon finely chopped fresh epazote
3 tablespoons fresh lime juice
2 tablespoons unrefined corn oil (or olive oil)
Salt to taste
Tamale Spoon-Bread Sticks
Pinto Bean "Ranchero" Sauce
4 sprigs fresh cilantro

Peel shrimp, leaving tails on. Clean and devein. In a medium bowl, combine shrimp with all jalapeños, jalapeño juice, shallots, garlic, cilantro, epazote, and lime juice. Coat shrimp and allow to marinate for at least 2 hours, turning occasionally.

Prepare smoker for cold smoke (see page 230).

Drain shrimp well. Place on smoking rack and place in smoker for 15 minutes. Shrimp should still be raw with no evidence of cooking. Remove shrimp from smoker.

Heat 1 tablespoon oil in a large sauté pan over medium-high heat. Season shrimp with salt and place half of them into hot pan. Sauté for about 6 minutes or until shrimp are no longer translucent. Remove shrimp to a large warm platter, add remaining tablespoon oil to pan, and cook remaining shrimp as above.

Crisscross 2 Tamale Spoon-Bread Sticks at the "12 o'clock" position on each of four hot serving plates. Ladle a small portion of Pinto Bean "Ranchero" Sauce at the "6 o'clock" position, making sure not to cover the entire plate. Lay the shrimp, tails up, on top of sauce. Place a sprig of cilantro in the center of each plate between the spoon bread and the shrimp. Serve immediately.

Jalapeño Smoked Shrimp with Tamale Spoon-Bread Sticks and Pinto Bean "Ranchero" Sauce

TAMALE SPOON-BREAD STICKS

2 cups milk
1 cup masa harina
¹/₄ cup yellow cornmeal
2 tablespoons vegetable oil
¹/₂ large onion, peeled and sliced
1 teaspoon chopped garlic
¹/₄ cup diced red bell pepper
1 jalapeño chili, chopped
2 tablespoons diced Anaheim chili

¹/₄ pound cooked ground chorizo sausage
¹/₄ cup unsalted butter, softened
4 large eggs
1 teaspoon baking powder
¹/₄ cup grated jalapeño jack cheese
¹/₄ cup grated cheddar cheese
1 teaspoon salt or to taste

Place milk in a heavy saucepan and bring to a boil over high heat. Remove from heat.

Place masa harina in a blender and, with the motor running, pour in half the hot milk. Process until thoroughly blended. Pour into hot milk in the saucepan and return to medium heat. Whisk in cornmeal, whisking continuously to keep masa from sticking. Lower heat and simmer, stirring constantly, for 5 minutes. Remove from heat.

Heat oil in a medium sauté pan over medium heat. When hot, add onion, garlic, bell

pepper, and chilies and sauté until tender, then stir into masa mixture along with cooked chorizo. Beat in butter, then allow to cool to room temperature. When cool, beat in eggs, baking powder, cheeses, and salt.

Preheat oven to 325°.

Butter 2 hot corn-stick pans (or cast-iron skillets). Fill each section with spoon-bread batter. Place in preheated oven and bake for 20 minutes or until set and light brown, checking periodically. If spoon-bread sticks begin to get too brown, cover with foil. Serve hot.

PINTO BEAN "RANCHERO" SAUCE

1 cup pinto beans, picked clean

2 tablespoons unrefined corn oil

1 medium onion, peeled and cut into ¼-inch dice

1 stalk celery, trimmed and cut into ¼-inch dice

1 small green bell pepper, seeded and membranes removed, cut into ¼-inch dice

3 cloves garlic, peeled and minced

1 serrano chili, minced

4 cups chicken stock (see page 236)

2 tomatoes, peeled, cored, seeded, and cut into ¼-inch dice

½ teaspoon ground cumin

½ teaspoon ground coriander

1 tablespoon black peppercorns

½ bay leaf

1 small bunch fresh thyme

1 small bunch fresh oregano

1 small roasted red bell pepper (see page 232), skinned, seeded, and cut into ¼-inch dice

1 small roasted yellow bell pepper, skinned, seeded, and cut into ¼-inch dice

1 roasted poblano chili, skinned, seeded, and cut into ¼-inch dice

Tabasco to taste

Salt to taste

Fresh lime juice to taste

Cover beans with 8 cups cold water and allow to soak at least 8 hours if possible, changing water twice. Rinse and drain well before using.

Heat oil in a medium saucepan over medium-high heat. When hot, add onion, celery, and green pepper and sauté for 4 minutes or until onion is transparent. Add garlic and serrano and sauté for 1 minute. Add drained beans, chicken stock, and tomatoes. Tie spices and herbs into a cheesecloth bag, add to beans, and bring to a boil. Lower heat and simmer, stirring occasionally, for 1 hour or until beans are soft and sauce is thick.

Remove cheesecloth bag. Stir in roasted peppers and poblano. Season with Tabasco, salt, and lime juice and keep warm until ready to serve.

Crabmeat-Stuffed Gulf Shrimp with Ancho Chili Sauce and Lime Custard

SERVES 4

20 large Gulf shrimp, heads intact

6 blue corn tortillas*

6 ancho corn tortillas*

3 ounces fresh uncooked shrimp, peeled and deveined

2 tablespoons cooked chorizo sausage

¹/₄ red bell pepper, seeded and membranes removed

2 sprigs fresh cilantro

1 clove garlic, peeled

¹/₂ small onion, peeled and chopped

3 ounces jumbo lump blue crabmeat, picked clean of shell and cartilage

2 teaspoons extra-fine dried bread crumbs

Tabasco sauce to taste

Worcestershire sauce to taste

Salt to taste

1 cup milk

4 large eggs

2 cups all-purpose flour

2 tablespoons peanut oil

Lime Custard

Ancho Chili Sauce

Remove heads and shells from Gulf shrimp, leaving tails on. Reserve heads and shells for sauce. Butterfly shrimp by splitting up the center on the underside. Remove vein. Set aside and keep cool.

Cut tortillas in half and then in half again lengthwise. Cut across the quarters to form very fine tortilla shavings. Set aside in a shallow pan.

In a food processor fitted with a metal blade, finely chop the 3 ounces raw shrimp, chorizo, red pepper, cilantro, garlic, and onion. When chopped, remove from processor bowl and combine in a medium bowl with crabmeat, bread crumbs, Tabasco, Worcestershire, and salt. Keep cool.

In a medium bowl, whisk milk and eggs until well combined. Set aside in a shallow dish.

Place flour in a shallow pan and line up alongside the milk-egg mixture and the tortilla shavings. Place 1 tablespoon crabmeat stuffing on the open underside of each shrimp, patting it into the shrimp to secure. Roll the stuffed shrimp into the flour, shaking gently to remove excess. Then dip floured shrimp into the egg-milk mixture and finally roll in the tortilla shavings. Shrimp will not be completely coated. (You may refrigerate, at this point, until ready to cook.)

Preheat oven to 350°.

Heat 2 tablespoons oil in a large ovenproof skillet over medium-high heat. When just hot, add shrimp, a few at a time, and fry for about 3 minutes per side or until tortilla breading is set. When all shrimp have been fried, return to skillet and place in preheated oven. Turn

shrimp after 2 minutes, then bake an additional 3 minutes. Remove from oven and place shrimp on paper towel to drain.

Unmold 1 Lime Custard into the center of each of four warm serving plates. Arrange 5 shrimp around each custard, like spokes on a wheel. Spoon a small portion of Ancho Chili Sauce into the spaces between the shrimp. Serve immediately.

* Use ordinary corn tortillas if others are unobtainable.

ANCHO CHILI SAUCE

1 tablespoon olive oil
Shells and heads from
   shrimp
2 shallots, peeled and diced
1 clove garlic, peeled and
   sliced
4 ancho chilies, seeded and
   chopped
1 tomato, cored and
   chopped

2 sprigs fresh cilantro,
   chopped
1 serrano chili, seeded
2 cups fish stock (see page
   235)
1 tablespoon masa harina
1 teaspoon fresh lime juice
1/2 teaspoon honey
Salt to taste

Heat oil in a small saucepan over high heat. When it just begins to smoke, add shrimp shells and heads and sauté for 1 minute, stirring constantly, or until bright pink in color. Add shallots, garlic, and anchos. Lower heat and cook, stirring constantly, for about 4 minutes or until shallots, garlic, and anchos are lightly toasted.

Add tomato, cilantro, and serrano. Raise heat to medium and cook 2 minutes. Add stock. Lower heat and simmer gently for 15 minutes. Do not reduce. Pour into a blender and purée until smooth. Mix masa harina with enough cold water to make a paste. Then, with the motor running, add to the purée in the blender. Strain through a fine sieve and stir in lime juice, honey, and salt. Keep warm until ready to use.

LIME CUSTARD

2 large eggs
1/2 cup heavy cream
Grated zest of 1 lime,
   blanched and drained

1 teaspoon fresh lime juice
1/2 teaspoon honey
Pinch of salt

Preheat oven to 350°.

In a medium bowl, whisk all ingredients together until well combined. Pour into 4 buttered 3-ounce custard cups. Place filled cups in a shallow baking dish filled with hot water to a level halfway up the cups.

Place in preheated oven and bake for 30 minutes or until set. Remove from pan, cover, and keep warm until ready to serve.

Achiote-Glazed Red Snapper with Green Mole and Orange–Red Onion Pico de Gallo

SERVES 4

Achiote is a paste flavored mainly by the annatto seed, from a Central American plant. The seeds themselves are often used as a coloring agent in cheddar cheese.

4 7-ounce red snapper fillets, trimmed of skin and bones
Salt to taste
4 tablespoons peanut oil

Achiote Paste
Green Mole
Orange–Red Onion Pico de Gallo
4 sprigs fresh cilantro

Preheat oven to 350°.

Season snapper fillets with salt. Heat oil in a large ovenproof skillet over medium heat. When hot, add fillets and fry, flesh side up, for 4 minutes or until a heavy crust forms, being careful not to burn. Turn fillets and spread approximately 1 tablespoon Achiote Paste over each one. Place pan in oven and continue cooking, allowing no more than 5 minutes total cooking time for each 1/2 inch of thickness at the thickest part of the fillet. *Do not overcook* as the fish should remain moist.

Cover half the surface of each of four warm dinner plates with Green Mole. Place a fillet in the center of each plate. Beside each fillet, on the unsauced side of the plate, place 2 teaspoons Orange–Red Onion Pico de Gallo and a cilantro sprig. Serve immediately.

ACHIOTE PASTE

¹/₂ cup annatto seeds*
2 teaspoons olive oil
1 onion, peeled and
　chopped
4 cloves garlic, peeled and
　minced
2 serrano chilies, seeded
　and membranes
　removed, finely diced

¹/₂ cup fresh orange juice
¹/₄ cup fresh grapefruit
　juice
1 teaspoon fresh cracked
　black pepper
¹/₂ teaspoon salt or to taste
Juice of 1 lime or to taste

Place 1¹/₂ cups water in a small saucepan over high heat. When boiling, add annatto seeds. Remove from heat and allow to soak for 15 minutes. Drain and set aside.

Heat oil in a medium saucepan over medium heat. When hot, add onion and sauté for 4 minutes or until golden. Add garlic and serranos and cook for 3 minutes. Add drained annatto seeds, fruit juices, and black pepper. Season with salt. Bring to a boil. Lower heat and simmer for about 10 minutes or until remaining liquid is about 2 tablespoons. Add lime juice and remove from heat. Place in a blender and purée until smooth.

* Found in ethnic markets.

GREEN MOLE

1 tablespoon olive oil
2 medium onions, peeled
　and diced
2 serrano chilies, seeded
　and membranes
　removed, diced
2 cloves garlic, peeled and
　chopped
2 cups diced fresh tomatillos
¹/₂ tablespoon ground
　cumin
¹/₂ tablespoon ground
　coriander
2 cups chicken stock (see
　page 236)

2 crisply fried corn tortillas,
　crumbled
¹/₂ cup toasted green
　pumpkin seeds
¹/₂ cup diced mango or
　papaya
1 bunch fresh cilantro,
　stems removed
¹/₂ cup tightly packed
　chopped fresh spinach
Salt to taste
Fresh lime juice to taste

Heat oil in a large saucepan over medium heat. When hot, add onions and sauté for 5 minutes or until golden. Add serranos, garlic, tomatillos, and spices, and sauté for 6 minutes or until mixture is fairly dry and vegetables begin to brown slightly.

Add chicken stock, tortillas, pumpkin seeds, and mango. Bring to a boil. Lower heat and simmer for 15 minutes or until mixture equals 2 cups.

Pour into a blender. Add cilantro, spinach, salt, and lime juice and purée until smooth. Cover and keep warm until ready to serve.

ORANGE–RED ONION PICO DE GALLO

1 large red onion, peeled and cut into ¹/₂-inch dice

1 tablespoon olive oil

¹/₂ teaspoon balsamic vinegar

1 teaspoon brown sugar

1 large or 2 small oranges, peeled, pith and center white core removed

1 serrano chili, seeded and membranes removed, finely minced

1 clove garlic, peeled and finely minced

¹/₂ tomato, cored and cut into ¹/₂-inch dice

¹/₂ avocado, peeled, seeded, and cut into ¹/₂-inch dice

4 sprigs fresh cilantro, chopped

Salt to taste

Juice of 2 limes

Toss onion with oil, balsamic vinegar, and brown sugar. Place in a heavy sauté pan over medium-high heat and sauté for 5 minutes or until translucent and sugar begins to caramelize. Remove from heat.

Slice orange, crosswise, about ¹/₂ inch thick. Remove any seeds and cut into ¹/₂-inch dice.

Combine all ingredients. Cover and set aside for 10 to 15 minutes to allow flavors to blend before serving.

Wood-Grilled Red Snapper with Mango–Black Bean Sauce and Tomatillo Rice

SERVES 4

This dish uses a terrific example of our Southwestern-style hybrid sauce. The smoked red bell pepper adds great flavor and gives the sauce complexity.

4 7-ounce red snapper fillets, trimmed of skin and bones
3 tablespoons corn oil

Salt to taste
Mango–Black Bean Sauce
Tomatillo Rice
4 sprigs fresh cilantro

Prepare grill for grilling over a wood fire. Make sure grates are clean and lightly brushed or rubbed with oil.

Thoroughly coat fillets with 3 tablespoons corn oil and season with salt. Place fillets on hot grill, skin side up. Grill for about 3 minutes. Turn fillets and grill about 2 minutes or until fish feels firm. Do not overcook.

Place a fillet in the center of each of four hot serving plates. Ladle Mango–Black Bean Sauce on one side of the fillet and a portion of Tomatillo Rice on the other side, coming out from under the fish. Garnish with a sprig of cilantro and serve immediately.

MANGO–BLACK BEAN SAUCE

1 tablespoon corn oil
2 large yellow onions,
 peeled and chopped
1 small carrot, peeled and
 chopped
2 poblano chilies, seeded
 and chopped
2 serrano chilies, finely
 chopped
3 cloves garlic, peeled and
 finely chopped
1 pinch of ground cumin
1 pinch of ground
 coriander
1 pinch of chili powder
1 small bunch fresh
 cilantro

3 cups chicken stock (see
 page 236), more if
 needed
2 tablespoons corn starch
2 tablespoons water
1 ripe mango, peeled,
 seeded, and cut into
 ¹/₂-inch dice
1 cup cooked, drained black
 beans
2 tablespoons cold-smoked
 ¹/₂-inch-dice red bell
 pepper (see page 230)
1 tablespoon chopped fresh
 cilantro
Salt to taste
Fresh lime juice to taste

Heat oil in a large saucepan over medium heat. When hot, add onions, carrot, chilies, garlic, and spices. Sauté for 4 minutes. Stir in cilantro and chicken stock and bring to a boil.

Dissolve corn starch in water and pour in a thin stream, stirring constantly, into the boiling chicken stock until slightly thickened.

Lower heat and simmer for 20 minutes. Strain through a fine sieve. If sauce is too thick, add additional chicken stock. Keep warm.

Just before serving, stir in mango, beans, red pepper, and chopped cilantro. Bring to a boil over high heat, then immediately remove from heat. Season with salt and lime juice. Serve hot.

TOMATILLO RICE

8 husked tomatillos, well
 scrubbed
3 cloves garlic, peeled and
 chopped
2 serrano chilies, chopped
1 small bunch fresh
 cilantro, chopped

5 leaves fresh spinach,
 washed, dried, and
 chopped
Salt to taste
Fresh lime juice to taste
4 cups hot cooked rice

Process tomatillos, garlic, serranos, cilantro, and spinach in a blender until smooth. Season with salt and lime juice.

Pour tomatillo mixture into hot rice and mix thoroughly. Serve immediately.

Wood-Grilled Red Snapper on Corn Purée Streaked with Three Sauces: Black Bean, Papaya, and Red Chili

SERVES 4

Have fun creating your own designs with these sauces by streaking different patterns. I personally like the "Indian blanket" effect made by using the three colors in a tight formation.

4 7-ounce red snapper
  fillets, trimmed of skin
  and bones
3 tablespoons peanut oil
Salt to taste
	Black Bean Sauce
	Papaya Sauce
	Red Chili Sauce
	Corn Purée
	Jicama-Tomatillo Relish

Prepare grill for grilling over a wood fire. Make sure grates are clean and lightly brushed or rubbed with oil.

Coat fillets in 3 tablespoons peanut oil and place on hot grill, skin side up. Season with salt. Grill for about 2 minutes. Turn fillets and grill another 2 minutes or until fish is firm. Do not overcook as fillets should remain moist.

Starting with Black Bean Sauce, squirt thin lines on each of four hot serving plates, from one side to the other. Repeat the pattern on another angle using Papaya Sauce, and repeat again with the Red Chili Sauce. Place about 2 tablespoons Corn Purée slightly off center on each plate and a fish fillet in the center. Garnish with a tablespoon of Jicama-Tomatillo Relish and serve immediately.

CORN PURÉE

2 ears sweet corn 2 tablespoons bacon fat 1 tablespoon chopped shallot	2 teaspoons chopped garlic Fresh lemon juice to taste Salt to taste

Shuck corn and remove silk. With a paring knife, cut down the center of each corn row, then scrape down cob with the back of a French knife, retaining all liquid and pulp.

Heat bacon fat in a medium sauté pan over medium-high heat. When hot, add corn, shallot, and garlic. Lower heat and simmer for 15 minutes, stirring often. Season with lemon juice and salt. Keep warm until ready to serve.

Wood-Grilled Red Snapper on Corn Purée Streaked with Three Sauces: Black Bean, Papaya, and Red Chili

BLACK BEAN SAUCE

1 cup cooked, drained black beans
1 serrano chili, seeded and chopped
1 shallot, peeled and chopped

1 clove garlic, peeled and chopped
1 tablespoon chopped fresh cilantro
1/2 cup chicken stock (see page 236)

Combine all ingredients in a small saucepan over high heat. Bring to a boil. Lower heat and simmer for 15 minutes. Pour into a blender and process until smooth. Pour into a plastic squirt bottle such as those used for mustard or ketchup. Set aside.

PAPAYA SAUCE

1 ripe papaya, peeled, seeded, and chopped
2 teaspoons grated fresh ginger

1/4 cup chicken stock (see page 236)
Fresh lime juice to taste
Salt to taste

Combine papaya, ginger, and chicken stock in a heavy saucepan over high heat. Bring to a boil. Lower heat and simmer for about 15 minutes or until papaya is soft and liquid has reduced by half. Season with lime juice and salt. Pour into a blender and process until smooth. Strain and pour into a plastic squirt bottle such as those used for mustard or ketchup. Set aside.

RED CHILI SAUCE

2 red bell peppers, seeded and membranes removed, chopped
1 shallot, peeled and chopped
1 clove garlic, peeled and chopped

1 red chili, chopped
1/4 cup chopped fresh cilantro
1/4 cup chicken stock (see page 236)
Fresh lime juice to taste
Salt to taste

Combine all ingredients except lime juice and salt in a medium saucepan over high heat. Bring to a boil. Lower heat and simmer for 15 minutes. Pour into a blender and purée until smooth. Strain through a fine sieve and season with lime juice and salt. Pour into a plastic squirt bottle such as those used for mustard or ketchup. Set aside.

Jicama-Tomatillo Relish

2 cups ¹/₄-inch-dice peeled
  jicama
4 large tomatillos, husked
  and cut into ¹/₄-inch
  dice
1 teaspoon chopped shallot
1 teaspoon minced garlic
¹/₂ red bell pepper, seeded
  and membranes
  removed, cut into ¹/₄-
  inch dice

¹/₂ yellow bell pepper, seeded
  and membranes
  removed, cut into ¹/₄-
  inch dice
1 poblano chili, seeded and
  cut into ¹/₄-inch dice
¹/₄ cup sweetened rice wine
  vinegar
¹/₄ cup peanut oil
Salt to taste
Fresh lime juice to taste

Mix all ingredients together, then check seasoning.

Pasta-Crusted Salmon with Roast Vegetable Sauce and Griddled Shallot Croutons

SERVES 4

The crust on this salmon is of a unique breed. When you coat the fish with fresh pasta, then sauté and bake it, the pasta becomes crisp and adds great texture with lots of crunch.

1 cup finely minced fresh linguine pasta (use as many different flavors as possible)
4 8-ounce salmon fillets, trimmed of skin and bones

Salt to taste
2 tablespoons olive oil
Roast Vegetable Sauce
Oven-Roasted Vegetables
Griddled Shallot Croutons

Preheat oven to 350°.

Place minced pasta in a medium bowl. Season fillets with salt, then press one side of the fillets in pasta mixture, coating that side heavily, and set aside. Heat oil in a heavy ovenproof sauté pan over medium heat. When hot, add fillets, pasta side down, and fry for 1 minute or until golden brown. Turn each fillet over. Place pan in oven (pasta side up) and cook for 5 minutes or until fish is cooked.

Ladle Roast Vegetable Sauce over the surface of each of four warm serving plates. Place a salmon fillet in the center of each plate. Arrange the Oven-Roasted Vegetables around the salmon on top of the sauce. Place 2 Griddled Shallot Croutons to the side of the fish. Serve immediately.

OVEN-ROASTED VEGETABLES

3 tablespoons olive oil
1 cup pearl onions, peeled
1 small leek, cleaned and cut into triangle shapes
1 stalk celery, peeled and cut into triangle shapes

1 carrot, peeled and cut into triangle shapes
Salt to taste

Preheat oven to 350°.

Bring a medium ovenproof sauté pan to medium heat. When hot, add oil and all the vegetables. Season with salt. Sauté for 3 minutes. Place in oven. Roast vegetables for 8 minutes, stirring occasionally, until golden brown. Keep warm until ready to use.

Pasta-Crusted Salmon with Roast Vegetable Sauce and Griddled Shallot Croutons

ROAST VEGETABLE SAUCE

2 tablespoons olive oil
1 medium onion, peeled
    and chopped
2 small carrots, trimmed
    and chopped
1 stalk celery, trimmed and
    chopped
1/2 red bell pepper, seeded
    and chopped
1 small yellow squash,
    trimmed and chopped
2 shallots, peeled and
    minced

2 cloves garlic, peeled and
    minced
1 tomato, cored and
    chopped
5 fresh thyme sprigs
4 cups chicken stock (see
    page 236), plus more if
    needed
5 leaves fresh basil, tied
    together
Fresh lemon juice to taste
Salt to taste

Preheat oven to 375°.

Heat 1 tablespoon oil in a heavy ovenproof saucepan over medium-high heat. When hot, add onion, carrots, and celery and sauté for 5 minutes or until vegetables are golden brown. Place pan in oven and roast for 15 minutes, stirring occasionally. When done, remove pan from oven.

Bring a medium saucepan to medium heat. When hot, add remaining 1 tablespoon oil, then add red pepper, yellow squash, shallots, and garlic. Sauté for 3 minutes and add roasted vegetables. Add tomato, thyme, and chicken stock, bring to a boil, and simmer for 30 minutes. Pour mixture into a blender and purée until very smooth, then check consistency. If sauce is too thick, thin down with additional chicken stock. If sauce is too thin, reduce liquid on stove until it reaches sauce consistency.

Pour sauce mixture into a container and submerge the tied basil in it for at least 10 minutes. Remove basil and season with lemon juice and salt. Keep warm until ready to use.

GRIDDLED SHALLOT CROUTONS

1 small baguette, cut on
    the bias into 1/2-inch
    slices
2 tablespoons olive oil

6 shallots, peeled and
    minced
Salt to taste
2 tablespoons freshly grated
    Romano cheese

Preheat oven to 350°.

Place bread slices in a single layer on a baking sheet. Place in oven and toast slices for 5 minutes or until crisp. Remove from oven, but leave oven on.

Heat a small griddle (or sauté pan) to medium heat. When hot, add oil, then shallots, and sauté, stirring occasionally, for 7 to 8 minutes or until golden brown. Season with salt. Remove from heat.

Spread a thin layer of shallot mixture on top of each crouton and sprinkle with cheese. Place croutons on baking sheet and place in oven for 4 minutes. Remove from heat and serve.

Pan-Seared Swordfish with Toasted Rice Sauce and Broccoli–Pickled Eggplant Stir-Fry

SERVES 4

The Pickled Eggplant in this recipe could stand alone. Stir-fried, the taste is not what you would imagine. In fact, I can't remember eggplant tasting this good.

4 7-ounce swordfish steaks, trimmed of fat, skin, and dark membrane
Salt to taste
1 tablespoon peanut oil

Broccoli–Pickled Eggplant Stir-Fry
Toasted Rice Sauce
¼ cup thinly julienned red bell pepper

Season swordfish with salt.

Heat oil in a large sauté pan over high heat. When hot, add swordfish and sauté for 3 to 4 minutes, or until a crust has formed. Lower heat to medium. Turn swordfish and sauté for 3 minutes or until no longer translucent. Do not overcook.

Place a swordfish steak off center on each of four hot serving plates. Nestle a portion of Broccoli–Pickled Eggplant Stir-Fry up against the fish. Ladle Toasted Rice Sauce on the third of the plate in between the fish and stir-fry. Sprinkle sauce and surrounding plate surface with ground rice and sprinkle stir-fry with julienned red pepper. Serve immediately.

TOASTED RICE SAUCE

*¹/₃ cup plus 2 tablespoons
  uncooked rice*
*1 tablespoon dark
  sesame oil*
*6 large shallots, peeled and
  chopped*
*3 cloves garlic, peeled and
  chopped*
*2 tablespoons grated fresh
  ginger*
2 scallions, chopped
*2 Thai red chilies (or
  serrano chilies),
  chopped*
*¹/₄ cup sweetened rice wine
  vinegar*

*1 tablespoon Thai fish
  sauce*
*1 tablespoon chopped fresh
  cilantro*
*1¹/₂ cups chicken stock (see
  page 236)*
*¹/₂ red bell pepper, seeded
  and membranes
  removed*
*2 teaspoons chopped fresh
  mint leaves*
Salt to taste
Fresh lime juice to taste

Preheat oven to 350°.

Spread uncooked rice on baking sheet and place in preheated oven. Bake for 8 to 10 minutes or until brown. Set aside.

Heat oil in a medium saucepan over medium heat. When hot, add shallots and garlic and sauté for 2 minutes. Add ginger, scallions, chilies, rice vinegar, fish sauce, and cilantro. Bring to a boil. Boil for 3 minutes or until reduced by half. Add ¹/₃ cup browned rice, and chicken stock and bring to a boil. Lower heat and simmer for 30 minutes.

Pulverize red bell pepper in a food processor using a metal blade. Place in a small piece of cheesecloth and squeeze out all juice. Set pulp aside.

Place remaining 2 tablespoons browned rice in a mini–coffee grinder and grind until pulverized. Set aside.

Remove sauce from heat and pour into a blender and purée until smooth. Stir in red bell pepper pulp and mint and season to taste with lime juice and salt. Keep warm until ready to use.

BROCCOLI–PICKLED EGGPLANT STIR-FRY

*1 large eggplant, peeled
and cut into large
julienne*
*1/2 cup plus 2 tablespoons
sweetened rice wine
vinegar*
1/4 cup sugar
*2 tablespoons white wine
vinegar*
*1 shallot, peeled and finely
chopped*

*1 clove garlic, peeled and
finely chopped*
*2 teaspoons finely grated
fresh ginger*
*2 tablespoons chicken stock
(see page 236)*
1/4 cup black soy sauce
1 tablespoon sesame oil
*2 cups uncooked broccoli
florets*
1/2 cup julienned carrots

Place eggplant in a medium bowl. Combine 1/2 cup rice vinegar, sugar, and white wine vinegar and mix thoroughly to dissolve sugar. Pour over eggplant and allow to marinate for at least 1 hour.

Combine shallot, garlic, ginger, remaining 2 tablespoons rice vinegar, chicken stock, and soy sauce in a small bowl and set aside.

Pour eggplant into a strainer and let stand for 10 minutes or until all the liquid has drained off.

Heat sesame oil in a large sauté pan over high heat. When hot, immediately add broccoli and carrots. Stir-fry for 1 minute. Add well-drained eggplant and stir-fry for another 2 minutes, allowing eggplant to brown as much as possible. Add soy mixture, a tablespoon at a time, until vegetables are well seasoned; however, there should be no standing liquid in the pan. Remove and serve immediately.

Grilled Cactus-Pear-Marinated Gulf Grouper with Green Chili Sauce and Fresh Corn Tamales
SERVES 4

"Cactus pear" is the red bloom that pops out on top of a cactus. Though covered with very small stickers, inside is a bright-hued fruit filled with many seeds. Once strained, the vibrant juice has numerous uses, such as in this marinade for fish.

4 7-ounce grouper fillets, trimmed of skin, bones, and dark membrane
8 ripe red cactus pears
1 shallot, peeled and finely chopped
1 clove garlic, peeled and finely chopped
1 serrano chili, finely chopped

2 teaspoons finely chopped fresh cilantro
2 tablespoons corn oil
Salt to taste
Green Chili Sauce
Fresh Corn Tamales
1/2 cup cooked, drained black beans
4 sprigs fresh cilantro

Place grouper in a shallow glass dish. Carefully peel cactus pears and place into a strainer. Place strainer over a bowl and press pulp to extract all the juice. Add shallot, garlic, serrano, and cilantro to juice and stir to combine. Pour over grouper. Cover and marinate, turning fish occasionally, for at least 1 hour.

Prepare grill, making sure grates are clean and lightly brushed or rubbed with oil.

Remove grouper from marinade. Allow excess marinade to drip off, then brush with oil. Season with salt. Place on preheated grill rack, skin side up, and grill about 3 minutes. Turn fillets and cook for another 2 to 3 minutes or until fish is done. Remove from grill.

Place a fillet on each of four hot serving plates. Ladle a small pool of Green Chili Sauce beside each fillet. Place 1 Fresh Corn Tamale on the opposite side of the grouper. Place a spoonful of black beans beside each tamale and garnish with a cilantro sprig. Serve immediately.

GREEN CHILI SAUCE

2 cloves garlic, peeled
3 shallots, peeled
1 serrano chili
1 jalapeño chili
8 tomatillos, husked and
*   cleaned*
3 cups chicken stock (see
*   page 236), plus more if*
*   needed*
4 roasted poblano chilies
*   (see page 232), peeled*
*   and seeded*
1/2 cup diced mango or
*   papaya*
1 small bunch cilantro
*   with roots, washed and*
*   trimmed*
Salt to taste
Fresh lime juice to taste

Place garlic, shallots, serrano, jalapeño, tomatillos, and chicken stock in a medium stockpot over high heat. Bring to a boil. Lower heat and simmer for 20 minutes or until liquid has reduced by one cup. Stir in poblanos and mango, then pour into a blender. Add cilantro. Purée until smooth. If sauce is too thick, add additional chicken stock. If sauce is too thin, return to a boil and cook until reduced to proper consistency. Season with salt and lime juice and keep warm until ready to serve.

FRESH CORN TAMALES

4 large dried corn husks
6 large ears sweet corn,
*   shucked and cleaned*
1/4 cup lard (or olive oil)
1 small onion, peeled and
*   cut into 1/4-inch dice*
1 serrano chili, chopped
3 tablespoons cornmeal
Salt to taste

Place corn husks in warm water to cover for at least 1 hour or until ready to use.

Using a large grater, grate corn kernels from each cob into a large bowl. Using the back side of a knife, scrape pulp from cobs into kernels.

Heat lard in a large saucepan over medium heat. When hot, add onion and serrano and sauté for 3 minutes or until onion is soft. Stir in corn mixture and continue to sauté for 12 to 15 minutes or until liquid has evaporated. When mixture is thick, beat in cornmeal. Stir to combine, then remove from heat. Season with salt and set aside to cool.

Remove corn husks from water. Pat dry. Spread the soft corn husks open on a flat surface. Spoon the cool corn mixture into a small mound in the middle of each husk. Fold two sides of the husk over the corn, making a large cylinder shape. Fold the top of each husk toward the overlapping crease to form a pocket. Crimp the opposite end of each tamale to close. Lay each tamale down in a steamer rack over boiling water and steam for 20 minutes or until firm. Serve hot.

Fried Soft-shell Crabs with Ancho Jam, Served with Spicy Cole Slaw and Smoked Onion Hush Puppies

SERVES 4

I hope my last meal includes soft-shell crabs. I look forward to the start of the summer season to begin eating my way through many upon many fried soft-shell crabs.

2 cups milk
8 small soft-shell crabs, cleaned
2 cups all-purpose flour
1 teaspoon Mansion Pepper Mixture (see page 235)
1 tablespoon Mansion Barbecue Spice Mix (see page 234)

Salt to taste
1/2 cup vegetable oil
Ancho Jam
Spicy Cole Slaw
Smoked Onion Hush Puppies
4 sprigs fresh cilantro

Pour milk over crabs in a large shallow baking dish. Let stand for 20 minutes.

Combine flour, Mansion Pepper Mixture and Barbecue Spice Mix, and salt. Dredge crabs through flour mixture and set aside. Heat oil in a large cast-iron skillet over medium-high heat. When hot, add crabs (in 2 batches, if necessary) and sauté for 3 minutes per side or until golden brown. Drain on paper towel.

Place 2 crabs on each of four hot serving plates. Streak a zigzag pattern of Ancho Jam over each crab. Spoon a portion of Spicy Cole Slaw behind crabs and 2 Smoked Onion Hush Puppies and a cilantro sprig off to the side. Serve immediately.

ANCHO JAM

5 ancho chilies, seeded and washed
1–2 serrano chilies, chopped
1/2 red bell pepper, seeded and membranes removed, chopped
2 shallots, peeled and chopped
2 cloves garlic, peeled and chopped
1 tablespoon finely grated fresh ginger

1 1/2 cups fresh orange juice
1 tablespoon sweetened rice wine vinegar
1 tablespoon chopped fresh cilantro
1 tablespoon honey or to taste
Salt to taste
Fresh lime juice to taste

Combine chilies, red bell pepper, shallots, garlic, ginger, orange juice, and rice vinegar in a medium saucepan over high heat. Bring to a boil. Lower heat and simmer for about 20 minutes or until anchos are very soft. Pour into a blender, add cilantro, and blend until very smooth. Season with honey, salt, and lime juice. Pour jam into a plastic squeeze bottle such as those used for mustard or ketchup.

SPICY COLE SLAW

*2 cups julienned green
cabbage, leafy part
only*

*1 cup julienned red
cabbage, leafy part
only*

*1/2 red bell pepper, seeded
and membranes
removed, cut into
julienne*

*1/2 yellow bell pepper, seeded
and membranes
removed, cut into
julienne*

*1/2 carrot, peeled and cut
into very fine julienne*

1/2 cup mayonnaise

*1 1/2 tablespoons cold-smoked
1/4-inch-dice green bell
pepper (see page 230)*

*2 shallots, peeled and
chopped*

*1 clove garlic, peeled and
chopped*

*1–2 serrano chilies,
chopped*

*1 tablespoon chopped fresh
cilantro*

1 tablespoon maple syrup

1/2 tablespoon malt vinegar

*1/2 tablespoon Dijon
mustard*

*1/2 tablespoon
Worcestershire sauce*

*1/2 teaspoon ground toasted
cumin seeds*

*1/2 teaspoon ground toasted
coriander seeds*

Salt to taste

Fresh lime juice to taste

In a large bowl, combine cabbages, red and yellow peppers, and carrot until well blended.

Process remaining ingredients in a blender until smooth. Adjust seasoning. Pour dressing over vegetables and toss to combine. Recheck seasoning and serve.

SMOKED ONION HUSH PUPPIES

1 cup white cornmeal
1 cup all-purpose flour
1 tablespoon baking powder
1/2 teaspoon salt
2 large eggs, beaten
1 cup buttermilk

*2 tablespoons cold-smoked
finely chopped onion
(see page 230)*
*1 clove garlic, peeled and
minced*
5 cups vegetable oil

In a medium bowl, combine cornmeal, flour, baking powder, and salt. Beat in eggs, buttermilk, onion, and garlic until well combined. Cover and refrigerate.

Heat oil to 375° on a food thermometer in a large stockpot over high heat. When hot, drop batter by the tablespoonful into the oil, a few pieces at a time. Cook for 4 minutes or until golden brown and cooked through. Drain on paper towel and serve hot.

Barbecued Spiced Sea Scallops with Roasted Tomato Butter and Mango

SERVES 4

Chef Robert Del Grande says this recipe should be the mascot dish of the Barbed Wires, our musical group. I told him the only way to have that real Southwest feel for this dish is to use desert scallops found only under rocks.

16 large sea scallops
Mansion Barbecue Spice
    Mix (see page 234)
Roasted Tomato Butter

1½ cups ¼-inch-dice ripe
    mango
Cabbage-Watercress Salad
4 sprigs fresh cilantro

Prepare grill, making sure grates are clean and lightly brushed or rubbed with oil.

Pat scallops dry. Dress with Mansion Barbecue Spice Mix and place on preheated grill rack. Grill over medium heat for 3 minutes or until scallops are warm at the center. Do not overcook. Remove from grill and keep warm.

Ladle Roasted Tomato Butter over surface of each of four warm dinner plates. Sprinkle diced mango over all. Place a portion of Cabbage-Watercress Salad in the center of each plate and place 4 scallops around each salad. Garnish with a sprig of cilantro and serve immediately.

ROASTED TOMATO BUTTER

4 ripe plum tomatoes
2 shallots, peeled
2 cloves garlic, peeled
1 small yellow onion, peeled
    and roughly chopped
2 chipotle chilies, stemmed
1 cup chicken stock (see
    page 236)
4 tablespoons unsalted
    butter, cut into small
    pieces

1 small bunch fresh
    cilantro, finely chopped
1 teaspoon kosher salt or to
    taste
1 teaspoon coarse cracked
    black pepper or to taste
Fresh lime juice to taste

Preheat oven to 350°.

Place tomatoes, shallots, garlic, onion, and chipotles in a small roasting pan and roast in preheated oven for 45 to 60 minutes or until tomatoes blister and are well cooked. Transfer cooked ingredients and any liquid in pan to a food processor fitted with a metal blade. Purée. Transfer purée to a medium saucepan. Add chicken stock and bring to a boil over high heat. Lower heat to a simmer. Cook for 20 minutes, then remove from heat. Whisk in butter and add chopped cilantro. Season with salt, pepper, and lime juice and keep warm until ready to serve.

CABBAGE-WATERCRESS SALAD

¹/₂ head green cabbage
1 red bell pepper, seeded
  and membranes
  removed
1 carrot, peeled
1 bunch watercress, thick
  stems removed

2 serrano chilies, chopped
1 tablespoon walnut oil
Juice of 1 lime
Pinch of sugar
Salt to taste
Ground black pepper to
  taste

Finely julienne cabbage, red pepper, and carrot. Combine with remaining ingredients in a medium bowl and mix well. Adjust seasonings. Cover and keep chilled until ready to use.

CHAPTER FIVE
Poultry and Fowl

Cumin-Coriander Crusted Chicken on Roast Poblano–Corn Sauce and Jalapeño Jack Cheese Spoon Bread

SERVES 4

2 tablespoons toasted cumin
    seeds
2 tablespoons coriander
    seeds
1 tablespoon toasted sesame
    seeds
1/2 tablespoon mustard seeds
1/2 tablespoon white
    peppercorns
1 teaspoon chopped fresh
    thyme
1 teaspoon chopped fresh
    oregano

2 tablespoons vegetable oil
4 large boneless chicken
    breast halves, with skin
    and wing bone
    attached
3 tablespoons honey
Roast Poblano–Corn
    Sauce
Jalapeño Jack Cheese Spoon
    Bread

Combine seeds, peppercorns, and fresh herbs in a coffee grinder. Grind until mixture is well blended and finely ground.

Preheat oven to 350°.

Heat oil in a large ovenproof sauté pan over medium heat. When hot, brown chicken breasts, skin side down, for about 5 minutes or until skin is well browned and crisp. Do not blacken or burn skin. Turn over and brown for an additional 3 minutes. Remove pan from heat. Brush the browned chicken skin with honey. Generously sprinkle the honey-brushed breasts with ground herb-spice mixture, patting down to make it adhere better. Then drizzle remaining honey on top.

Place pan in preheated oven and bake for 8 minutes or until meat is cooked through and firm. Remove pan from oven and place breasts, skin side up, on a warm platter to rest for 4 minutes.

Ladle a small amount of Roast Poblano–Corn Sauce into the center of each of four hot serving plates. Do not allow the sauce to flow to the rim of the plate. Lay a chicken breast on top, crust side up, off center in the plate. Spoon a portion of the Jalapeño Jack Cheese Spoon Bread in back of each breast and serve immediately.

ROAST POBLANO–CORN SAUCE

2 ears sweet corn
1 tablespoon vegetable oil
1 uncooked chicken carcass,
    cut into small pieces
1 large yellow onion, peeled
    and chopped
1 carrot, trimmed and
    chopped
3 cloves garlic, peeled
2 serrano chilies, chopped
2 ancho chilies, seeded
1 small bunch fresh
    cilantro, chopped

4 cups chicken stock (see
    page 236)
1½ tablespoons corn starch
1½ tablespoons cold water
3 roasted poblano chilies
    (see page 232), seeded,
    skinned, and cut into
    ¼-inch dice
1 tablespoon chopped fresh
    cilantro
Salt to taste
Fresh lime juice to taste

Shuck corn and remove silk. Using a large grater, remove kernels and pulp from cobs. Set pulp aside and reserve cobs.

Heat oil in a large sauté pan over medium heat. When hot, add chicken bones and sauté for about 10 minutes or until golden brown. Add onion and carrot and sauté for 5 minutes. Add garlic and serranos and sauté for 1 minute. Add anchos, bunch of cilantro, corn cobs, and chicken stock and bring to a boil.

Dissolve corn starch in water and whisk mixture into boiling stock. Lower heat and simmer for 30 minutes. Remove from heat and strain into a medium saucepan. Place over high heat and bring to a boil. Lower heat and stir in reserved corn pulp, poblanos, and 1 tablespoon chopped cilantro. Remove from heat. Season to taste with salt and lime juice. Keep warm until ready to serve.

JALAPEÑO JACK CHEESE SPOON BREAD

2 jalapeño chilies, seeded
    and finely chopped
2 cloves garlic, peeled and
    finely chopped
2 shallots, peeled and finely
    chopped
2 cups milk
1 cup cornmeal

1 cup grated jalapeño jack
    cheese
1 cup unsalted butter,
    softened
1 tablespoon maple syrup
Salt to taste
4 large eggs, separated
1 tablespoon tequila

Preheat oven to 350°.

Combine jalapeños, garlic, shallots, and milk in a medium saucepan over medium-high heat. Bring just to a boil and immediately stir in cornmeal, beating thoroughly. Lower heat and cook for 5 minutes or until thick. Remove from heat and beat in cheese, butter, syrup, and salt until well combined. Set aside to cool.

Beat egg yolks in a small bowl and stir into cooled cornmeal. Beat egg whites until stiff and fold into cornmeal. Add tequila, stirring to just mix.

Pour into a buttered 2-quart casserole, cover, and bake in preheated oven for about 30 minutes or until the tip of a knife inserted in the center comes out clean. Serve hot.

Roast Chicken with Tortilla Dressing and Fried Corn Sauce

SERVES 4

For years Tortilla Dressing has been the favorite of our patrons at The Mansion on Turtle Creek at Thanksgiving. It brings a new meaning and taste to traditional dressings.

2 3-pound frying chickens, wings and wishbone removed
Salt to taste
Mansion Pepper Mixture to taste (see page 235)

3 tablespoons peanut oil
Tortilla Dressing
Fried Corn Sauce

Preheat oven to 400°.

Generously season each bird, inside and out, with salt and Mansion Pepper Mixture.

Heat oil in a flat roasting pan large enough to hold the 2 chickens. When hot, add chickens and sear for about 5 minutes or until brown on all sides. Place pan in preheated oven and roast chickens for 40 minutes or until done. Baste the birds with pan juices at least twice during roasting. Remove from oven and allow to rest for at least 10 minutes before carving.

When chickens are cool enough to handle, remove leg and thigh quarters from breast, leaving skin to cover breasts. Separate drumsticks and thighs at joint. Opposite the skin side make a slit along the length of the thigh bones and remove bones. Reserve boneless thighs. Use drumsticks and thigh bones for stock if desired. Slice boneless thighs and reconstruct in original shape. Keep warm.

Next remove the breast meat from the carcass to make 2 boneless breast halves from each chicken. Use the sharp point of a knife to cut between the meat and bone starting at the widest part of the breast, separating each half. (Removal of the wishbone and wings before cooking makes this easier.) Slice each breast half against the grain starting with the thicker end. Slice very thin and keep in the shape of the breast half. Arrange slices of chicken from each breast half and a thigh to form a circle around the center of each of four warm serving plates.

Place a portion of Tortilla Dressing in the center of each plate. Ladle Fried Corn Sauce over the dressing, spilling onto the chicken and plate. Serve immediately.

TORTILLA DRESSING

1 cup corn-bread crumbs (see page 233)

8 Flour Tortillas (see page 28), cut into small strips

8 corn tortillas, cut into small strips and crisply fried

1/3 cup cold-smoked 1/4-inch-dice red bell pepper (see page 230)

1 small onion, peeled and cut into 1/4-inch dice

1 stalk celery, trimmed and cut into 1/4-inch dice

2 cloves garlic, peeled and minced

1–2 jalapeño chilies, finely chopped

1 tablespoon finely chopped fresh cilantro

1 tablespoon chili powder

1 teaspoon finely chopped fresh sage

1/2 teaspoon ground cumin seeds

1/2 teaspoon ground coriander seeds

1 cup Tortilla Soup Broth, chilled

1 large egg, beaten

Salt to taste

In a large bowl, combine all ingredients except salt, and allow to sit for 1 hour to absorb all liquid and to blend flavors, tossing occasionally.

Preheat oven to 325°.

Season dressing with salt. Form into small balls and place on a greased baking sheet. Place in preheated oven and bake for 20 minutes or until the inside is cooked and the outside is golden brown. Keep warm until ready to serve.

Tortilla Soup Broth

1 tablespoon corn oil

2 corn tortillas, coarsely chopped

3 cloves garlic, peeled and finely chopped

1/2 tablespoon chopped fresh epazote (or cilantro)

1/2 cup fresh onion purée

1 cup fresh tomato purée

1/2 tablespoon ground cumin

1 tablespoon chili powder

1 bay leaf

2 tablespoons canned tomato purée

4 cups chicken stock (see page 236)

Salt to taste

Cayenne pepper to taste

Heat oil in a large saucepan over medium heat. When hot, add tortillas, garlic, and epazote and sauté for 3 minutes or until tortillas are soft. Add onion and fresh tomato purées and bring to a boil. Add cumin, chili powder, bay leaves, canned tomato purée, and chicken stock. Again bring to a boil. Lower heat, season with salt and cayenne pepper, and simmer, stirring frequently, for 30 minutes. Skim fat from surface if necessary. Strain before using. (Any remaining stock may be frozen for later use.)

FRIED CORN SAUCE

*2 cups Great Grandma
 Wright's Fried Corn
 (see page 60)*

*1 cup veal demi-glace (see
 page 237)*
Fresh lime juice to taste
Salt to taste

Just before fried corn is ready, stir in demi-glace and lime juice. Cook for 2 minutes, season with salt, and keep warm until ready to serve.

Roast Turkey with Corn Bread–Sweet Potato Dressing, Chili-Pecan Sauce, and Cranberry-Jalapeño Relish

SERVES 6

Why are most home cooks terrified of the month of November, knowing they will have to cook a turkey on Thanksgiving Day? Is it the size of the bird that makes people think it must cook all day? I hope this recipe will ease the pain of suffering through the holidays, but maybe it's easier to make reservations at The Mansion on Turtle Creek.

1 12-pound fresh turkey
4 tablespoons olive oil
Salt to taste
Ground black pepper to
    taste
2 cups chicken stock (see
    page 236)
1 onion, peeled and
    chopped

1 stalk celery, trimmed and
    chopped
1 carrot, trimmed and
    chopped
Corn Bread–Sweet Potato
    Dressing
Chili-Pecan Sauce
Cranberry-Jalapeño Relish

Preheat oven to 400°.

Wash turkey well under cold running water. Pat dry. Tuck wings underneath body. Remove excess fat from cavity. Generously coat outside of turkey with 2 tablespoons oil. Season skin and cavity with salt. Season cavity generously with pepper.

Place turkey in roasting pan, uncovered, and place in preheated oven. Roast for 20 minutes or until skin is golden brown. Lower temperature to 325° and roast for 3 hours and 30 minutes (or 18 minutes per pound), basting the breast every 15 minutes with chicken stock and remaining 2 tablespoons oil. (If skin begins to get too brown, cover with aluminum foil.) Put onion, celery, and carrot around turkey in the last hour of cooking. To check for doneness, stick a cooking fork in between the breast and leg at the joint. If juices run clear, turkey is done. Remove pan from oven and carefully place turkey on a warm platter and allow to rest for 15 minutes before slicing.

Bring juices and vegetables to a boil in the roasting pan over medium heat on the stove top. When boiling, cook for 2 minutes, scraping pan, then pour through a fine strainer. With a small ladle, push the solids through. If necessary, remove grease. Reserve 1 cup or more of sauce for Chili-Pecan Sauce. Keep turkey and sauce warm until ready to serve.

When ready to serve, slice four portions

from the turkey breast. Spoon a portion of Corn Bread–Sweet Potato Dressing in the center of each of four hot plates. Fan the sliced turkey over dressing. Ladle Chili-Pecan Sauce over turkey, allowing it to spill out onto the plate. Spoon a small portion of Cranberry-Jalapeño Relish behind dressing. Serve immediately.

CORN BREAD–SWEET POTATO DRESSING

*1 day-old whole Corn
    Bread (see page 233),
    well dried out*
*12 day-old Sweet Potato
    Biscuits (see page 44),
    crumbled and well
    dried out*
*1 tablespoon olive oil or
    bacon fat*
*2 large onions, peeled and
    cut into ¼-inch dice*
*2 stalks celery, trimmed
    and cut into ¼-inch
    dice*

*2 cups chicken stock (see
    page 236) or turkey
    drippings*
*2 teaspoons chopped fresh
    sage*
*1 teaspoon chopped fresh
    thyme*
½ teaspoon celery seeds
*½ teaspoon fresh cracked
    black pepper*
1 large egg, beaten
Salt to taste

Preheat oven to 350°.

In a large bowl, break up the dried corn bread and sweet potato biscuits into small pieces and mix together. Set aside.

Heat oil in a large sauté pan over medium heat. When hot, add onion and celery and sauté for 5 minutes or until onion is transparent. Add chicken stock, sage, thyme, celery seeds, and pepper and bring to a boil. When boiling, pour over the broken-up bread. Stir to combine and let cool slightly. When cool, add egg and mix until thoroughly blended. Season with salt.

Place dressing in a buttered 2-quart casserole. Smooth top. Place in preheated oven and bake for 45 minutes or until firm and light brown. If dressing begins to get too brown, cover top with foil. Serve hot.

CHILI-PECAN SAUCE

1 tablespoon vegetable oil
3 shallots, peeled and cut
 into ¼-inch dice
2 cloves garlic, peeled and
 minced
2 jalapeño chilies, seeded
 and finely chopped
1 tablespoon chili powder
1 teaspoon ground cumin
1 teaspoon ground
 coriander

1 teaspoon finely chopped
 fresh oregano
½ teaspoon cayenne pepper
1 cup or more turkey
 roasting pan sauce
1 cup veal demi-glace (see
 page 237)
½ cup toasted chopped
 pecans
Salt to taste
Fresh lemon juice to taste

Heat oil in a medium saucepan over medium heat. When hot, add shallots, garlic, and jalapeños and sauté for 2 minutes. Add chili powder, cumin, coriander, oregano, and cayenne. Sauté for 2 minutes. Add turkey sauce and demi-glace. Bring to a boil. Lower heat and simmer for 20 minutes. Stir in pecans and season with salt and lemon juice. Serve hot.

CRANBERRY-JALAPEÑO RELISH

1 orange
1 cup whole cranberries
2 teaspoons grated fresh
 ginger
2 teaspoons chopped fresh
 cilantro

2 teaspoons chopped
 jalapeño chili
Maple syrup to taste

Peel zest from orange with a sharp potato peeler. Remove white pith and seeds from orange.

Quickly chop cranberries, orange zest and pulp, ginger, cilantro, and jalapeño in a food grinder using a small die. *Do not purée.* Add maple syrup and mix well. Cover and set aside for at least 30 minutes before using.

Roast Duck with Sweet Potato–Pear Purée and Cranberry–Texas Cabernet Sauvignon Sauce

SERVES 4

At The Mansion on Turtle Creek we use either a Fall Creek Cabernet Sauvignon from our friends Ed and Susan Auler in Tow, Texas, or a Pheasant Ridge Cabernet Sauvignon from our other friends Bobby and Jennifer Cox in Lubbock, Texas. Both are great wines to serve with this dish.

2 5-pound ducks
Salt to taste
Coarsely ground black
pepper to taste
Sweet Potato–Pear Purée
Cranberry–Texas
Cabernet Sauvignon
Sauce

¼ cup Poached
Cranberries
2 teaspoons orange rind cut
into long strings,
blanched
2 teaspoons 1-inch cut
chives
Pecan Garnish

Preheat oven to 375°.

Rinse ducks, inside and out, then pat dry. With a boning knife, remove legs on each duck and reserve them for another use. Remove each duck breast from carcass leaving the skin on the meat. You will have 4 individual duck breasts. Reserve carcasses for Duck Demi-Glace.

Season each breast with salt and pepper. Heat a large sauté pan over medium heat and lay breasts, skin side down, in pan. Cook for 10 minutes, not turning breasts, or until nicely browned. The breasts will render their own fat as the meat cooks, leaving the skin crisp. Do not allow skin to blacken or burn. Turn and cook for 4 minutes. Remove from pan and keep warm.

Spoon a small mound of Sweet Potato–Pear Purée in the center of each of four hot dinner plates. With a sharp slicing knife, very thinly slice each duck breast on the bias. Place a sliced duck breast around the purée, fanning out the breast. Spoon 3 tablespoons of Cranberry–Texas Cabernet Sauvignon Sauce in front of each breast. Garnish top of sauce with Poached Cranberries, blanched orange rind, and chives. Place Pecan Garnish in a small mound beside the purée. Serve immediately.

Roast Duck with Sweet Potato–Pear Purée and Cranberry–Texas Cabernet Sauvignon Sauce

SWEET POTATO–PEAR PURÉE

2 pounds sweet potatoes,
* peeled and cut into*
* large chunks*
1 pound very ripe pears,
* peeled, cored, and cut*
* into large chunks*

2 cinnamon sticks
1 tablespoon finely grated
* fresh ginger*
2 cups apple juice
Salt to taste
Fresh lemon juice to taste

Place potatoes, covered with water, in a medium saucepan over high heat. Bring to a boil. Lower heat and simmer about 30 minutes or until soft. Drain potatoes. In a food processor fitted with a metal blade, purée until smooth.

Combine remaining ingredients in a medium saucepan over high heat. Bring to a boil. Lower heat and simmer for 15 minutes or until pears are soft and all liquid has evaporated. Remove cinnamon sticks and add mixture to sweet potato purée, blending until smooth and well combined. Adjust seasoning, and keep warm until ready to use.

CRANBERRY–TEXAS CABERNET SAUVIGNON SAUCE

¹/₂ bottle Texas Cabernet
* Sauvignon (or other*
* fine cabernet*
* sauvignon)*
2 cups fresh cranberries
1 teaspoon grated fresh
* ginger*
Juice of 1 orange
2 shallots, peeled and
* chopped*

1 serrano chili, finely
* chopped*
1 large dried ancho chili,
* seeded*
1 cup Duck Demi-Glace
Maple syrup to taste
Salt to taste
Fresh lemon juice to taste

Combine wine, cranberries, ginger, juice, shallots, and chilies in a medium saucepan over medium heat. Bring to a boil. Lower heat and simmer for 15 minutes. Add Duck Demi-Glace and cook for an additional 10 minutes or until sauce will coat the back of a spoon. Season with maple syrup (if needed), salt, and lemon juice.

Duck Demi-Glace

MAKES 1–1½ CUPS

1 tablespoon peanut oil
2 uncooked duck carcasses,
excess fat removed with
a knife, chopped into
small pieces
1 onion, peeled and diced
½ carrot, trimmed and
diced
½ stalk celery, trimmed
and diced
2 teaspoons cracked black
pepper

2 shallots, peeled and
chopped
3 large white mushrooms,
cleaned and thinly
sliced
1 small bunch fresh thyme
1 cup veal demi-glace
(see page 237)
2 cups chicken stock
(see page 236)

Heat oil in a large saucepan over medium heat. When hot, add bones and brown evenly for 15 minutes, stirring every 2 minutes to prevent burning. Add onion, carrot, and celery and brown evenly for 10 minutes, stirring constantly to prevent burning. Add pepper, shallots, and mushrooms and sauté for 2 minutes. Add thyme, demi-glace, and chicken stock. Bring to a boil. Lower heat and simmer for 45 minutes to 1 hour, making sure to reduce liquid slowly by half, skimming scum as necessary. Strain through a fine sieve and refrigerate until ready to use.

POACHED CRANBERRIES

½ cup water
½ cup orange juice

2 tablespoons sugar
¼ cup fresh cranberries

Combine water, orange juice, and sugar in a small saucepan over medium heat. Bring to a boil. Add cranberries and return to a boil. Simmer for 3 minutes or until the first cranberry pops and splits open. Remove from heat and let cranberries marinate in the mixture for another 3 minutes. Strain and place on a chilled plate until ready to use.

PECAN GARNISH

½ cup ½-inch-dice lean
salt-cured ham

½ cup pecan halves
2 tablespoons maple syrup

Combine ham and pecans in a medium sauté pan over medium heat. Sauté for 2 minutes. Stir in maple syrup and deglaze pan. Cook for an additional 2 minutes. Remove from heat and keep warm until ready to use.

Grilled Marinated Duck Breasts with Port Wine–Sage Sauce and Eggplant Bread Pudding

SERVES 4

Although this sauce is not a hybrid, it is still one of my favorites from *way* back.

1/3 cup peanut oil
1/3 cup balsamic vinegar
1 tablespoon finely minced shallots
1 teaspoon finely minced garlic
1 teaspoon chopped fresh cilantro
1 teaspoon chopped fresh basil
1 teaspoon chopped fresh thyme

2 dried hot red peppers, chopped fine
1/2 tablespoon cracked black pepper
4 whole boneless, skinless duck breasts, halved and well trimmed of fat and silver skin
Salt to taste
Port Wine–Sage Sauce
Eggplant Bread Pudding

Combine oil, balsamic vinegar, shallots, garlic, herbs, red peppers, and black pepper and pour over duck breasts. Marinate for at least 1 hour.

Preheat grill. Brush clean grates with oil.

Season duck breasts with salt and place on hot grill. Grill for approximately 3 minutes per side for medium-rare. Do not overcook or meat will be tough.

Remove from grill and let rest 2 minutes. Ladle a pool of Port Wine–Sage Sauce in the center of each of four hot serving plates. Lay 2 breast halves on each plate. Spoon a portion of Eggplant Bread Pudding beside the breasts and serve immediately.

PORT WINE–SAGE SAUCE

1 1/2 cups port wine
1/4 teaspoon chopped fresh sage
1/4 teaspoon finely grated ginger
1 tablespoon finely minced shallots
2 white mushrooms, cleaned and finely diced

1/4 cup heavy cream
1 cup unsalted butter, softened and cut into small pieces
Juice of 1/2 lemon or to taste
Salt to taste
Ground black pepper to taste

Combine port wine, sage, ginger, shallots, and mushrooms in a small saucepan over medium heat. Bring to a boil and cook for 5 minutes or until reduced by three-quarters. Stir in heavy cream and again bring to a boil. Reduce until mixture is thick, about 5 minutes. Immediately remove from heat. Whisk in butter, piece by piece. Whisk in lemon juice, salt, and pepper. Strain. Keep warm, but do not bring back to a boil as the butter will separate.

EGGPLANT BREAD PUDDING

4 large eggs
2 cups heavy cream
1 large roasted eggplant, peeled and roughly chopped
1 roasted red bell pepper (see page 232), seeded and diced
1 roasted yellow bell pepper, seeded and diced
1 onion, peeled and diced
2 cloves garlic, peeled and chopped
1 teaspoon crushed black pepper
2 tablespoons chopped fresh chives
1/8 cup basil leaves chiffonade
1 tablespoon roughly chopped fresh parsley
2 teaspoons salt
1 large baguette, sliced and dried (do not toast)

Preheat oven to 350°.

Generously butter an 8-×-8-inch baking dish. Set aside.

Combine eggs and cream and mix thoroughly. Stir in all remaining ingredients, except the baguette.

Place a layer of dried bread in the bottom of the prepared pan. Completely cover it with custard, making sure to evenly distribute vegetables. Add a second layer of bread and again cover it with custard. Add a final layer of bread and custard. Tightly cover top with aluminum foil and place in a larger pan filled with water to a level 1/2 inch up the sides of the pudding pan.

Place in preheated oven and bake for 45 minutes. Uncover and bake for an additional 15 minutes. Let cool before slicing.

Chinese-Style Smoked Pheasant with Shiitake Mushroom–Ginger Gravy and Stir-Fried Wild Rice

SERVES 4

One of the cleverest methods of smoking meats is in this recipe. My sous-chefs came up with this idea, which really gives the pheasant a distinctive Asian smoke flavor by using spices in addition to wood for smoking.

2 3–4-pound pheasants
3 cinnamon sticks
4 star anise
4 cloves
3 tablespoons mustard seeds
*3 tablespoons coriander
    seeds*
2 tablespoons cumin seeds
*3 tablespoons white
    peppercorns*

2 cups brown rice
*2 cups hickory chips, soaked
    in water for 20
    minutes*
Stir-Fried Wild Rice
*Shiitake Mushroom–
    Ginger Gravy*

Remove necks and giblets from pheasants. Clip wings, remove wishbones, and reserve.

Preheat oven to 350°.

Combine spices, brown rice, and chips in a medium bowl. Line a wok with aluminum foil and pour in brown rice mixture. Place a rack over it and place pheasants on rack. Place wok over high heat. Cover and tightly seal top with aluminum foil. Cook for 10 minutes, then lower heat and allow to smoke for 20 minutes. Remove pheasants from smoker and place in preheated oven to finish cooking, about 20 minutes or until done.

Remove meat from pheasant breasts (see page 169) and keep warm. (Reserve carcasses for Shiitake Mushroom–Ginger Gravy and thighs for Stir-Fried Wild Rice.)

When ready to serve, place a portion of Stir-Fried Wild Rice slightly off the center of each of four hot serving plates. Carefully arrange sliced pheasant breast in front of wild rice and ladle Shiitake Mushroom–Ginger Gravy around the pheasant.

Chinese-Style Smoked Pheasant with Shiitake Mushroom–Ginger Gravy and Stir-Fried Wild Rice

Shiitake Mushroom–Ginger Gravy

8 shiitake mushrooms
3 tablespoons peanut oil
1 onion, peeled and
    chopped
1/4 cup chopped scallions
1 stalk celery, trimmed and
    chopped
1 carrot, trimmed and
    chopped
2 cloves garlic, peeled and
    chopped
1 1/2 tablespoons grated
    fresh ginger
1 dried red chili, seeded
2 tablespoons chopped fresh
    cilantro

3/4 cup sweetened rice wine
    vinegar
Chinese-Style Smoked
    Pheasant bones,
    chopped into small
    pieces
6 cups chicken stock (see
    page 236)
1 1/2 tablespoons corn starch
1 1/2 tablespoons water
1 tablespoon soy sauce
1 tablespoon oyster sauce
Salt to taste
Fresh lemon juice to taste

Remove stems from mushrooms and disregard. Slice mushrooms and set aside.

Heat 2 tablespoons oil in a large saucepan over medium heat. When hot, add onion, scallions, celery, and carrot. Sauté for 3 minutes, then add garlic, ginger, chili, and cilantro. Stir to mix. Pour in rice vinegar and cook for 4 minutes or until pan is deglazed. Add smoked pheasant bones and chicken stock. Bring to a boil. Dissolve corn starch in water and pour mixture into stock, stirring until combined. Lower heat and simmer for 1 hour or until sauce has been reduced to 3 cups. Strain through a fine sieve and add soy sauce and oyster sauce. Season with salt and lemon juice. Keep warm.

Heat remaining 1 tablespoon oil in a small sauté pan over medium heat. When hot, add sliced shiitake mushrooms. Sauté for 3 minutes or until just soft. Season with salt and lemon juice, then scrape into warm sauce. Keep warm until ready to use.

Stir-Fried Wild Rice

2 teaspoons sesame oil
4 Chinese-Style Smoked
    Pheasant thighs,
    skinned, boned, and
    julienned
1 cup cooked wild rice or
    Thai black rice

1 cup bean sprouts
1/2 cup julienned red bell
    pepper
1/2 cup sliced scallions,
    white part only
2 teaspoons soy sauce
2 teaspoons honey

Heat sesame oil in a medium sauté pan over medium heat. When hot, stir-fry julienned pheasant meat for 3 minutes. Stir in vegetables, one at a time, and continue to stir-fry until heated through but still crisp. Add soy sauce and honey to mixture, stir to incorporate, and serve immediately.

Oven Roast Pheasant and Pumpkin-Molasses Purée, Served on a Sauce of Apples, Tequila, and Ancho Chilies with Crispy Tortilla Relish

SERVES 4

Keep in mind that roasting a pheasant is almost identical to roasting a chicken. Then you will never be afraid of cooking one. I don't know why, but people tend to think that you have to enroll in cooking school to prepare any game.

*2 2¹/₂-pound pheasants,
    wings and wishbone
    removed
Salt to taste
Mansion Pepper Mixture
    (see page 235)*

*3 tablespoons corn oil
Pumpkin-Molasses Purée
Sauce of Apples, Tequila,
    and Ancho Chilies
Crispy Tortilla Relish
4 sprigs fresh cilantro*

Preheat oven to 400°.

Generously season each bird inside and out with salt and Mansion Pepper Mixture.

Heat oil in a flat roasting pan large enough to hold the birds. Sear birds for 6 minutes or until brown on all sides. Place pan in preheated oven and roast pheasants for 20 to 25 minutes. Baste birds with pan juices at least twice during roasting. Remove pheasants from oven and allow to rest for at least 10 minutes before carving.

When birds are cool enough to handle, remove leg and thigh quarters from breasts. Separate drumsticks and thighs at joint.

Make a slit on the underside of the thigh along the length of the thigh bone and remove bones. Reserve boneless thighs. Use drumsticks and thigh bones for pheasant stock if desired.

Slice the boneless thighs and reconstruct in original shape. Keep warm.

Remove the breast meat from the carcasses to make 2 boneless halves from each breast. Use the sharp point of a knife to cut between the meat and the bones, starting at the widest part of the breast; separate each half. (Prior removal of the wishbone and wings will make this easier.)

Peel off the skin and slice each breast half

against the grain, starting with the thicker end. Slice very thin and keep in the shape of breast halves.

Spoon a portion of Pumpkin-Molasses Purée into the middle of each of four hot dinner plates and arrange slices of breast and thigh meat to form a circle on top of the purée. Surround the pheasant with a ring of Sauce of Apples, Tequila, and Ancho Chilies. Place a small portion of Crispy Tortilla Relish to the side of the pheasant. Garnish with a sprig of cilantro and serve.

PUMPKIN-MOLASSES PURÉE

1 2-pound pumpkin,
    stemmed, seeded, and
    cut in half
¹/₂ cup molasses
¹/₂ cup fresh orange juice
1 tablespoon finely grated
    fresh ginger

1 tablespoon honey
1 cinnamon stick
1 teaspoon ground
    coriander
Pinch of ground cloves
Salt to taste

Preheat oven to 350°.

Place pumpkin halves on a baking sheet and place in preheated oven. Bake for 40 minutes or until pumpkin is very soft. Remove from oven and allow to cool. When cool enough to handle, peel off outer skin of pumpkin and cut pumpkin into small chunks. Set aside.

Heat a medium saucepan over medium-high heat. When hot, carefully add molasses to pan, shaking as you pour. Molasses will bubble and smoke. Continue slowly shaking pan to keep liquid from burning and cook for about 2 to 3 minutes or until molasses is just about to caramelize or burn. (This is called "burning the molasses," a process that burns the heavy sweetness out of the molasses without removing the flavor.) Immediately remove from heat. Slowly and carefully stir orange juice into hot molasses. Add pumpkin and remaining ingredients and return to medium heat. Simmer for 20 minutes, stirring occasionally to prevent sticking. Remove cinnamon stick.

Pour pumpkin mixture into a food processor fitted with a metal blade. Process until thick and smooth. Recheck seasoning. If pumpkin is not thick, return to heat and simmer until reduced, stirring occasionally. Keep warm until ready to serve.

SAUCE OF APPLES, TEQUILA, AND ANCHO CHILIES

5 ancho chilies, seeded
3 tablespoons corn oil
1 large onion, peeled and
*   chopped*
2 Granny Smith apples,
*   cored and chopped*
2 cloves garlic, peeled and
*   finely chopped*
2 serrano chilies, finely
*   chopped*
2 tablespoons chopped
*   almonds*
1 cinnamon stick
1/2 teaspoon ground
*   coriander*

1/4 teaspoon ground anise
1 roasted pheasant or
*   chicken carcass, chopped*
3 cups pheasant stock (see
*   page 236) or chicken*
*   stock*
1 large red Delicious apple,
*   peeled, cored, and*
*   thinly sliced*
1 tablespoon chopped fresh
*   cilantro*
1 tablespoon fine tequila
Salt to taste
Fresh lime juice to taste

Place anchos in warm water to cover and allow to stand for 20 minutes. Drain and reserve.

Heat 2 tablespoons oil in a stockpot over medium heat. When hot, add onion and sauté for 3 minutes. Add Granny Smith apples, 3 anchos, garlic, serranos, almonds, cinnamon stick, coriander, and anise and sauté for 3 more minutes. Add pheasant bones and stock and bring to a boil. Lower heat and simmer for 40 minutes, stirring occasionally. Remove cinnamon stick and all pheasant bones.

Pour mixture into a blender and process until smooth. Strain through a coarse strainer and reserve.

Heat remaining 1 tablespoon corn oil in a medium sauté pan over medium heat. When hot, add Delicious apple slices and sauté for 5 minutes or until golden brown. Cut the 2 remaining anchos into 1/4-inch dice and add to apples along with 2 cups of the reserved spiced apple sauce, cilantro, and tequila. Season with salt and lime juice. Serve immediately.

CRISPY TORTILLA RELISH

1 cup finely julienned
*   tortillas, fried crisp*
*   in oil*
1/2 cup cooked, drained
*   black beans*

1/2 cup finely diced jicama
1/2 cup fresh cooked corn
*   kernels*
3 tablespoons Cilantro-
*   Lime Vinaigrette*

Combine all ingredients and toss well. Serve immediately.

Cilantro-Lime Vinaigrette

1 tablespoon fresh lime
*   juice*
2 tablespoons peanut oil
1 shallot, peeled and
*   minced*

1/2 clove garlic, peeled and
*   minced*
1 tablespoon minced fresh
*   cilantro*
Salt to taste

Whisk all ingredients together until well blended.

Pan-Fried Corn-Bread Quail on Peach–Smoked Poblano Sauce with Green Bean Compote

SERVES 4

Coating the quail with corn-bread crumbs will keep the meat moist and tender when pan-frying. If peaches are not in season, use plums, apples, apricots, or any ripe fruit.

8 whole boneless quail, wings removed
2 large eggs
3 cups corn-bread crumbs (see page 233)
¹/₂ cup vegetable oil

Salt to taste
Ground black pepper to taste
Green Bean Compote
Peach–Smoked Poblano Sauce

Cut each quail in half, lengthwise. Put in a large bowl.

Beat eggs and pour over quail. Toss to coat.

Place corn-bread crumbs in a medium bowl. Press each egg-coated quail half into corn-bread crumbs until fully coated.

Heat oil in a large cast-iron skillet over medium heat. Season quail with salt and pepper and when oil is hot, place in skillet. Cook for 4 minutes or until golden brown, then turn and cook for an additional 4 minutes. (Do not let quail overcook; they should be pink in the breast.) Place quail on paper towel to drain.

Spoon a portion of Green Bean Compote at the "12 o'clock" position on each of four warm serving plates. Ladle Peach–Smoked Poblano Sauce in front of the compote to cover the plate. Lay 4 pieces of quail on the sauce with the legs toward the compote. Serve immediately.

Pan-Fried Corn-Bread Quail on Peach–Smoked Poblano Sauce with Green Bean Compote

PEACH–SMOKED POBLANO SAUCE

5 ripe peaches
3 shallots, peeled and finely
    chopped
1 clove garlic, peeled and
    finely chopped
1–2 serrano chilies, finely
    chopped
1 tablespoon finely grated
    fresh ginger
2 cups chicken stock (see
    page 236)

3 tablespoons cold-smoked
    1/3-inch-dice poblano
    chili (see page 230)
1 tablespoon fresh chopped
    cilantro
Salt to taste
Fresh lime juice to taste
Maple syrup to taste

Peel and pit peaches. Cut 1 into 1/3-inch dice and reserve.

Place remaining 4 peaches, shallots, garlic, serranos, ginger, and chicken stock in a medium saucepan over medium heat. Bring to a boil. Lower heat and simmer for 5 minutes. Remove from heat and pour into a blender. Process until smooth. Strain through a coarse sieve and then stir in diced peach, poblano, and cilantro. Season with salt, lime juice, and maple syrup. Keep warm.

GREEN BEAN COMPOTE

1/4 pound thin green beans,
    trimmed
1 tablespoon vegetable oil
1/2 red bell pepper, seeded
    and membranes
    removed, cut into thin
    julienne
1/2 yellow bell pepper, seeded
    and membranes
    removed, cut into thin
    julienne

2 ounces salt-cured country
    ham, cut into thin
    julienne
1/4 cup pecan halves
1 tablespoon maple syrup
Salt to taste
Ground black pepper to
    taste

Place green beans in boiling salted water for 1 minute. Immediately drain into a sieve and hold under cold running water. When cool, drain well and pat dry.

Heat oil in a large sauté pan over medium-high heat. When hot, add beans, bell peppers, country ham, and pecans. Sauté for 3 minutes or until heated through. Add maple syrup and sauté for 1 minute. Season with salt and pepper. Serve hot.

CHAPTER SIX

Meat and Game

Barbecued Lamb Chops with Baked Black Bean Sauce and Tobacco Onions

SERVES 4

These delicious beans stand alone or will enhance any meat dish.

2 8-rib French-cut racks of
   lamb, trimmed of fat
   and silver skin, cut
   into single chops
1 cup Mansion Barbecue
   Spice Mix (see page
   234)

Salt to taste
Baked Black Bean Sauce
Tobacco Onions

Preheat grill. Make sure grates are clean and heavily brushed with oil.

Dredge each chop through Mansion Barbecue Spice Mix. Season with salt and place on the hot grill. (Wood chips can be added to the grill to give a smoky flavor.) Grill chops for about 3 minutes or just long enough to mark one side. Turn chops and cook about 2 minutes longer or until desired doneness is reached.

Remove chops from grill and place 4 chops on each of four warm serving plates, crisscrossing each pair of rib bones pointing toward the inside of the plate. Ladle Baked Black Bean Sauce in front of chops. Garnish with a mound of Tobacco Onions. Serve immediately.

BAKED BLACK BEAN SAUCE

4 cups cooked, drained
   black beans
1 large onion, peeled and
   finely chopped
1½ cups ketchup
1 tablespoon yellow
   mustard
1¼ cups packed brown
   sugar
¼ cup molasses

1 tablespoon juice from
   sweet gherkin pickles
1 tablespoon cider vinegar
Salt to taste
Ground black pepper to
   taste
¼ pound thickly sliced
   smoked bacon
1 cup veal demi-glace (see
   page 237)

Preheat oven to 350°.

In a 2-quart casserole, combine black beans, onion, ketchup, mustard, brown sugar, molasses, gherkin juice, and vinegar, and season with salt and pepper. Top with strips of bacon placed in a crisscross pattern. Cover with aluminum foil and bake in preheated oven for 1½ hours. Remove foil for last 30 minutes of baking.

Remove from oven and lift bacon from bean mixture. Chop fine. Stir chopped bacon and demi-glace into bean mixture. Keep warm until ready to serve.

175

TOBACCO ONIONS

5 cups peanut oil
3 cups all-purpose flour
1½ teaspoons cayenne
    pepper
1 tablespoon paprika
Salt to taste
Ground black pepper to
    taste

1 Spanish onion, peeled
    and sliced into very
    thin rings
1 red onion, peeled and
    sliced into very thin
    rings

Heat oil in a deep-sided saucepan to 350° on a food thermometer.

Blend flour, cayenne pepper, paprika, salt, and black pepper. Separate onion rings and dredge in flour mixture, shaking off excess flour. Carefully place onion rings in hot oil, a few at a time, making sure rings don't stick together. Fry for 3 to 5 minutes or until golden brown.

Remove with a slotted spoon and drain briefly on paper towel. Place on warm platter and keep warm until all the onions are fried. Serve immediately.

Veal Loins on Basil "Pesto" Sauce with Ratatouille Fettuccine

SERVES 4

I will never forget the day Randall Warder, our night sous-chef, showed me his new creation, this fantastic sauce. I knew then we could do many different styles of hybrid sauces.

2 tablespoons vegetable oil
8 2½–3-ounce "naturally raised" veal loins
Salt to taste

Ratatouille Fettuccine
Basil "Pesto" Sauce
12 long slivers Romano cheese

Heat oil in a large sauté pan over medium heat. Season veal loins with salt and place in hot pan. Sauté for 4 minutes, being careful not to burn meat. Turn each loin and cook for another 3 minutes or until done. Remove from pan.

Place a mound of the Ratatouille Fettuccine at the "12 o'clock" position on each of four hot serving plates. Lay 2 veal loins up against the pasta with the ends overlapping. Ladle a pool of Basil "Pesto" Sauce in front of the veal. Garnish the top of each pasta mound with 3 pieces of slivered cheese. Serve immediately.

BASIL "PESTO" SAUCE

2 tablespoons vegetable oil
1 onion, peeled and chopped
½ stalk celery, trimmed and chopped
½ carrot, trimmed and chopped
5 white mushrooms, cleaned and slivered
1 leek, white part only, cleaned and chopped
1 pound roasted veal shank bones
4 cups chicken stock (see page 236)

2 teaspoons black peppercorns
6 sprigs fresh thyme
1½ tablespoons corn starch
1½ tablespoons cold water
⅓ cup virgin olive oil
1 tablespoon pine nuts
1 tablespoon finely grated Romano cheese
2 cloves garlic, peeled and chopped
Juice of ½ lemon
1 small bunch fresh basil, leaves only
Salt to taste

Heat vegetable oil in a medium stockpot over medium-high heat. When hot, add onion, celery, and carrot. Sauté for 5 to 7 minutes or until browned. Add mushrooms and leek and sauté for 2 minutes. Add bones, chicken stock, peppercorns, and thyme. Bring to a boil. Skim off scum, if necessary. Dissolve corn starch in water and stir into boiling stock. Lower heat and simmer 40 minutes. The sauce should be slightly thick. Strain through a fine sieve and keep warm.

Process olive oil, pine nuts, cheese, garlic, lemon juice, and basil in a blender until smooth.

At service, whisk basil "pesto" into the base sauce, spoonfuls at a time, mixing to incorporate. It may not be necessary to use all the pesto. Season with salt and serve.

RATATOUILLE FETTUCCINE

3 tablespoons olive oil

3 shallots, peeled and chopped

2 cloves garlic, peeled and finely chopped

¹/₄ teaspoon crushed red pepper flakes

4 large ripe red or yellow tomatoes, peeled, cored, seeded, and cut into ¹/₄-inch dice

1¹/₂ cups chicken stock (see page 236)

1 teaspoon chopped fresh thyme

1 teaspoon chopped fresh oregano

1 teaspoon chopped fresh basil

Salt to taste

Ground black pepper to taste

1 onion, peeled and cut into ¹/₄-inch dice

¹/₂ red bell pepper, seeded and membranes removed, cut into ¹/₄-inch dice

¹/₂ green bell pepper, seeded and membranes removed, cut into ¹/₄-inch dice

1 small eggplant, peeled and cut into ¹/₄-inch dice

¹/₂ zucchini, cut into ¹/₄-inch dice

¹/₂ yellow squash, cut into ¹/₄-inch dice

2 cloves garlic, peeled and chopped

¹/₃ pound fettuccine, cooked al dente

Heat 1 tablespoon oil in a medium saucepan over medium heat. When hot, add shallots, 2 cloves garlic finely chopped, and pepper flakes and sauté for 1 minute. Add tomatoes and sauté for 5 minutes, stirring constantly. Add chicken stock and bring to a boil. When boiling, lower heat and simmer for 30 minutes, stirring occasionally.

Pour tomato sauce into a blender and process until smooth. Pour back into saucepan. Add herbs and season with salt and black pepper. Keep warm.

Heat remaining 2 tablespoons oil in a wide-mouth stockpot over medium-high heat. When oil starts to smoke, add onion and sauté for 3 minutes or until brown. Lower heat, add bell peppers, and sauté for 1 minute. Add eggplant, zucchini, and yellow squash and sauté for 2 minutes, stirring occasionally. Stir in 2 cloves chopped garlic and sauté for 1 minute. Add reserved tomato sauce and bring to a boil. Stir to combine and immediately remove from heat. Check seasonings.

Toss the *al dente* pasta with the sauce. Stir to combine and serve immediately.

Veal Loins on Basil "Pesto" Sauce with Ratatouille Fettuccine

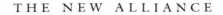
Tenderloin of Beef on White Beans and Jalapeño Jack Cheese with a Barbecued Corn Sauce

SERVES 4

2 tablespoons corn oil
1 onion, peeled and
    chopped
4 ancho chilies, seeded
½ cup chicken stock (see
    page 236)
¾ cup grated jalapeño jack
    cheese
2 shallots, peeled and
    chopped
2 cloves garlic, peeled and
    minced
1 jalapeño chili, seeded and
    chopped

2 cups cooked white navy
    beans
¼ cup chopped fresh
    cilantro leaves
Salt to taste
Fresh lime juice to taste
2 tablespoons peanut oil
4 8-ounce tenderloin fillets,
    trimmed of fat and
    silver skin
Mansion Pepper Mixture
    to taste (see page 235)
Barbecued Corn Sauce
4 sprigs fresh cilantro

Heat 1 tablespoon corn oil in a small saucepan over medium heat. When hot, add onion and sauté for 3 minutes or until transparent. Add anchos and chicken stock and bring to a boil. Lower heat and simmer for about 10 minutes or until anchos are soft. Pour mixture into a blender. Add jalapeño jack cheese and blend until smooth. Reserve.

Heat remaining 1 tablespoon corn oil in a medium sauté pan over medium heat. When hot, add shallots, garlic, and jalapeño. Sauté for 1 minute. Add beans and sauté for 1 minute. Add reserved ancho mixture and stir to combine. Add chopped cilantro. Season with salt and lime juice to taste. Remove from heat and keep warm.

Heat a large cast-iron skillet to medium-high heat. When hot, add peanut oil. Season tenderloins with salt and Mansion Pepper Mixture. Add to pan and sauté for 5 to 7 minutes. Turn and sauté for an additional 5 minutes. Remove from pan.

Spoon a portion of white bean mixture into the center of each of four hot serving plates. Place a fillet on top of the beans. Surround the fillet with Barbecued Corn Sauce, garnish with a cilantro sprig, and serve immediately.

BARBECUED CORN SAUCE

2 tablespoons corn oil

2 onions, peeled and cut
into ¹/₂-inch dice

2 shallots, peeled and
chopped

2 cloves garlic, peeled and
chopped

1 jalapeño chili, seeded and
chopped

¹/₂ pound roasted veal bones

2 tablespoons chili powder

1 tablespoon molasses

1 tablespoon ketchup

2 tablespoons cider vinegar

1 teaspoon ground cumin

1 teaspoon ground
coriander

1 teaspoon ground
cinnamon

1 teaspoon dry mustard

2 tomatoes, cored and diced

4 ancho chilies, seeded

1 cup chicken stock (see
page 236)

1¹/₂ cups veal demi-glace
(see page 237)

1 tablespoon corn starch

1 tablespoon water

1¹/₂ cups cooked sweet corn

¹/₂ red bell pepper, seeded
and membranes
removed, cut into
¹/₂-inch dice, and cold
smoked (see page 230)

¹/₂ yellow bell pepper, seeded
and membranes
removed, cut into
¹/₂-inch dice, and cold
smoked

1 poblano chili, seeded and
membranes removed,
cut into ¹/₂-inch dice,
and cold smoked

¹/₄ cup chopped fresh
cilantro

Salt to taste

Juice of 1 lime or to taste

Heat oil in a medium saucepan over medium-high heat. When hot, add onions and sauté for 8 minutes or until brown. Do not burn. Add shallots, garlic, and jalapeño and sauté for 2 minutes. Add veal bones, chili powder, molasses, ketchup, cider vinegar, cumin, coriander, cinnamon, mustard, tomatoes, and anchos. Bring to a boil and cook for 4 minutes or until all liquid has evaporated. Add chicken stock and demi-glace. Return to a boil. Dissolve corn starch in water and whisk into boiling stock. Lower heat and simmer for 30 minutes. Strain into a small saucepan. Add corn, smoked bell peppers, poblano, and cilantro and season with salt and lime juice. Keep warm until ready to serve.

Wood-Grilled Veal Chops on Tortilla–Jalapeño Jack Cheese Sauce with Barbecued Fire-Roasted Onions

SERVES 4

This Southwestern-style sauce has been a favorite for us throughout the years. The combination of flavors, the earthy taste of the tortillas against the spicy, creamy taste of the cheese, makes a perfect match.

4 9–10-ounce "naturally raised" veal chops, bone in, trimmed of fat
Salt to taste
Tortilla–Jalapeño Jack Cheese Sauce

Barbecued Fire-Roasted Onions (see page 52)
8 sprigs fresh cilantro

Prepare grill for grilling over a wood fire. Make sure grates are clean and lightly brushed or rubbed with oil.

Place chops on hot grill and cook for 4 minutes. Turn each chop and cook for about 4 minutes more, depending on the thickness of the chops. When cooked to desired doneness, remove from grill and let meat rest for a few minutes before serving.

Ladle Tortilla–Jalapeño Jack Cheese Sauce over half of the bottom of each of four warm dinner plates. Place a chop in the middle of each plate. Spoon 3 onions behind the bone of each chop. Nestle cilantro sprigs by the onions and serve immediately.

TORTILLA–JALAPEÑO JACK CHEESE SAUCE

1 tablespoon corn oil
1 large yellow onion, peeled and chopped
1/2 carrot, peeled and chopped
3 cloves garlic, peeled and finely chopped
2 serrano chilies, finely chopped
3 whole corn tortillas, cut into large strips
2 dried ancho chilies, seeded

1 large tomato, quartered
1/2 pound roasted veal bones
1 small bunch fresh cilantro with roots, washed
3 cups chicken stock (see page 236)
1 cup heavy cream
1 cup grated jalapeño jack cheese
Salt to taste
Fresh lime juice to taste

Heat oil in a medium saucepan over medium heat. Add onion and carrot and sauté for 5 minutes or until lightly browned. Add garlic, serranos, tortillas, and anchos and sauté for 2 minutes. Add tomato, veal bones, cilantro, and chicken stock and bring to a boil. Lower heat and simmer for 20 minutes, stirring occasionally to prevent sticking. Add cream and return to a boil. Lower heat and simmer for 10 minutes.

Remove bones and pour mixture into a blender. Add cheese and process until smooth. Season with salt and lime juice. Strain and keep warm.

Wood-Grilled Veal Chops on Tortilla–Jalapeño Jack Cheese Sauce with Barbecued Fire-Roasted Onions

Rack of Lamb with Mustard Crust, Served with Roast Garlic–Horseradish Sauce and Cheddar Cheese Scalloped Potatoes

SERVES 4

I am always amazed at how many racks of lamb we prepare each night. It's great to see the wonderful change in attitude toward lamb. I must admit that the recipe for Cheddar Cheese Scalloped Potatoes by itself is worth buying this book for.

2 8-rib French-cut racks of lamb, trimmed of fat and silver skin, rib bones cut off 3 inches from meat
Salt to taste
Mansion Pepper Mixture (see page 235)
1 tablespoon olive oil
1 tablespoon mustard seeds
2 teaspoons coriander seeds
2 teaspoons white peppercorns
2 tablespoons Dijon mustard

1 tablespoon whole-grain or Cajun Creole mustard
1 teaspoon minced fresh thyme
1 teaspoon minced fresh basil
1 teaspoon minced fresh rosemary
1 cup dry bread crumbs
Cheddar Cheese Scalloped Potatoes
Roast Garlic–Horseradish Sauce
4 sprigs fresh Italian parsley

Preheat oven to 450°.

Make sure rib bones and meat are well trimmed, free of fat and silver skin. Season each rack with salt and Mansion Pepper Mixture.

Preheat a large ovenproof sauté pan to medium-high heat. Add oil. When hot, lay racks down in pan, on opposite side of the rib bones. Brown for 3 minutes. Turn racks over so they are lying on the rib bone side and place pan in preheated oven. Roast racks for 12 to 15 minutes for medium-rare or to desired doneness. Remove pan from oven and place lamb on a warm platter and let rest for 4 minutes.

Preheat oven broiler.

Grind mustard and coriander seeds and white peppercorns in a mini–coffee grinder. In a small bowl, mix ground seeds together with mustards and fresh herbs. When well combined, smear a heavy coat of mustard mixture on top of each rack. Sprinkle bread crumbs over mustard, coating evenly. Place racks in a small roasting pan, crumb side up, and place under preheated broiler. Broil for 2 minutes or until bread crumbs are evenly golden. Remove

Rack of Lamb with Mustard Crust,
Served with Roast Garlic–Horseradish Sauce and Cheddar Cheese Scalloped Potatoes

from broiler and place racks on a cutting board.

Using a large, sharp French knife, carefully cut between each rib bone.

Spoon a portion of Cheddar Cheese Scalloped Potatoes at the "12 o'clock" position on each of four hot serving plates. Place 4 chops circling the potatoes, 2 chops on each side, crisscrossing their bones toward the edge of the plate. Ladle Roast Garlic–Horseradish Sauce around the rim and garnish with Italian parsley tucked between the chops and scalloped potatoes. Serve immediately.

ROAST GARLIC–HORSERADISH SAUCE

2 tablespoons olive oil
10 cloves garlic, peeled
4 large white mushrooms, cleaned and sliced
4 large shallots, peeled and chopped
1/2 pound roasted lamb bones
2 teaspoons cracked black pepper

1 small bunch fresh thyme
2 cups chicken stock (see page 236)
1 cup veal demi-glace (see page 237)
1/4 cup grated fresh horseradish
Salt to taste
Fresh lemon juice to taste

Preheat oven to 350°.

Heat 1 tablespoon oil in a small ovenproof sauté pan over medium heat. When hot, add garlic cloves and sauté for 4 minutes or until golden brown. Place in preheated oven and roast for 10 minutes, stirring occasionally to prevent burning. Remove from oven. Remove garlic from pan and allow to cool. Set aside until ready to use.

Place remaining 1 tablespoon oil in a large saucepan over medium heat. When hot, add mushrooms and sauté for 1 minute. Add shallots, lamb bones, and pepper and sauté for 1 minute. Add thyme, chicken stock, and demi-glace and bring to a boil. Skim off scum. Lower heat and simmer for 20 to 30 minutes or until sauce is reduced by one-third. Remove lamb bones and strain into a small saucepan. Add roasted garlic and grated horseradish. Bring to a boil. Remove from heat. Let sauce sit for 5 minutes to capture as much flavor from the garlic and horseradish as possible. Season with salt and lemon juice. Keep warm until ready to serve.

CHEDDAR CHEESE SCALLOPED POTATOES

*3 large baking potatoes,
peeled and thinly sliced*
*1/4 cup cooked 1/4-inch-dice
country ham*
*3 shallots, peeled and finely
chopped*
*2 cloves garlic, peeled and
finely chopped*

1 1/2 cups heavy cream
*3/4 cup grated white
cheddar cheese*
Salt to taste
Cayenne pepper to taste

Preheat oven to 350°.

Combine all ingredients. Adjust seasonings. Spread mixture evenly across the bottom of a medium glass baking dish. Tightly cover dish with foil. Place dish in a larger ovenproof pan filled with water to 1/2 inch up the sides. Bake in preheated oven for 1 1/2 hours or until potatoes are soft. Remove foil 15 to 20 minutes before taking potatoes out of oven to brown the top. Remove from oven and keep warm.

Beef Tenderloin Marinated in Molasses and Black Pepper, Served with Compote of Smoked Bacon, Wild Mushrooms, Glazed Sweet Potatoes, and Pecans

SERVES 4

Truly an interesting way to prepare beef. The flavor of this meat marinated in a molasses mixture gives a totally different taste.

2 pounds center-cut beef
    tenderloin (or venison),
    trimmed of all fat and
    silver skin
1 cup molasses
2 tablespoons balsamic
    vinegar
2 tablespoons fresh cracked
    black pepper
2 cloves garlic, peeled and
    finely chopped
1 large shallot, peeled and
    finely chopped

2 teaspoons finely grated
    fresh ginger
1 teaspoon finely chopped
    fresh thyme
Crushed red pepper flakes
    to taste
Salt to taste
2 tablespoons vegetable oil
Compote of Smoked Bacon,
    Wild Mushrooms,
    Glazed Sweet Potatoes,
    and Pecans
4 sprigs fresh watercress

Place beef tenderloin in a glass dish.

In a small bowl, combine molasses, balsamic vinegar, black pepper, garlic, shallot, ginger, thyme, and pepper flakes. When well blended, pour over beef. Cover. Refrigerate, allowing meat to marinate, for 24 hours, turning occasionally. Remove meat from marinade, reserving 1/2 cup for Smoked Bacon Compote and 4 tablespoons to deglaze pan. Place on cutting board, and using a sharp knife, cut into 8 portions. Season with salt.

Heat oil in a large cast-iron skillet over medium-high heat. When hot, lay beef medallions in skillet and brown for 3 minutes. Turn and brown for 2 minutes or until desired degree of doneness is reached.

Just before removing meat, add 4 tablespoons reserved molasses marinade to skillet to deglaze the pan as well as to glaze the medallions. Quickly turn meat over to glaze other side. Remove from skillet immediately.

Place 2 medallions near the center of each of four hot serving plates, overlapping each other. Spoon the Smoked Bacon Compote next to the medallions, letting the sauce flow out onto the plate. Place a sprig of watercress in between the meat and the compote. Serve immediately.

Beef Tenderloin Marinated in Molasses and Black Pepper, Served with Compote of Smoked Bacon, Wild Mushrooms, Glazed Sweet Potatoes, and Pecans

COMPOTE OF SMOKED BACON, WILD MUSHROOMS, GLAZED SWEET POTATOES, AND PECANS

¹/₂ cup reserved molasses marinade
1 cup veal demi-glace (see page 237)
1 cup ¹/₂-inch-dice smoked slab bacon
1 tablespoon vegetable oil
2 cups wild mushrooms (any type)
2 tablespoons unsalted butter
1 cup sweet potato balls
¹/₂–³/₄ cup pearl onions, peeled
1 tablespoon brown sugar
2 teaspoons cider vinegar
¹/₂ cup Glazed Pecans
Salt to taste
Fresh lemon juice to taste

Reduce reserved marinade in a small saucepan over medium-high heat for 5 minutes or until reduced by half. Add demi-glace and bring to a boil. Lower heat and simmer for 5 minutes or until sauce coats the back of a spoon. Remove from heat and keep warm.

Render bacon in a small sauté pan over medium-high heat for 5 to 7 minutes or until golden brown. Drain and reserve.

Heat oil in a medium sauté pan over medium-high heat. When hot, add mushrooms and sauté for 3 minutes or until cooked. Remove from pan and reserve.

Preheat oven to 350°.

Melt butter in an ovenproof medium sauté pan over medium heat. When hot, add sweet potato balls and pearl onions. Sauté for 3 minutes. Add brown sugar and cider vinegar and stir to combine. Sauté for 2 minutes. Place pan in oven and cook for 7 minutes, stirring occasionally to glaze evenly. Remove from oven. Add bacon, mushrooms, reduced marinade, and Glazed Pecans. Stir to combine. Season with salt and lemon juice and serve.

Glazed Pecans

¹/₂ cup water
¹/₂ cup sugar
2 dried red chilies

1 cup whole fresh pecans
¹/₄ cup molasses

Preheat oven to 250°.

Combine water, sugar, and chilies in a small saucepan over high heat. Bring to a boil. Add pecans and return to a boil. Lower heat and simmer for 10 minutes.

Drain and place pecans on a baking sheet. Place in preheated oven and bake for 45 minutes, stirring occasionally. Remove pecans from oven and pour into a small bowl. Add molasses and toss to coat. Return nuts to baking sheet and place in oven. Bake for an additional 45 minutes or until pecans are very crisp and crunchy but not burned.

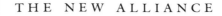

Barbecued Texas Venison on Smoked Corn "Chili" Sauce Streaked with Cilantro Cream

SERVES 4

If venison can't be obtained, try other meats such as beef, lamb, or chicken. The Mansion Barbecue Spice Mix makes the difference here.

2 tablespoons corn oil
4 7-ounce venison fillets, trimmed of all fat and sinew
Mansion Barbecue Spice Mix (see page 234)

Salt to taste
Smoked Corn "Chili" Sauce
Cilantro Cream
Tobacco Onions (see pages 55, 176)

Heat oil in a large cast-iron skillet over medium heat. Press both sides of the fillets in Mansion Barbecue Spice Mix. Remove and season with salt. Place fillets in hot skillet and sear for about 5 minutes or until crusty golden brown. Turn fillets and sear other side for 2 minutes or until desired degree of doneness is reached. Remove from pan.

Ladle the Smoked Corn "Chili" Sauce to cover the bottom of each of four hot serving plates. Place a fillet in the center. Squirt a zig-zag pattern of Cilantro Cream on top of the fillets. Place a mound of Tobacco Onions beside each fillet. Serve immediately.

Barbecued Texas Venison on Smoked Corn "Chili" Sauce Streaked with Cilantro Cream

SMOKED CORN "CHILI" SAUCE

3 ancho chilies, seeded
2 pasilla chilies, seeded
3 large ears sweet corn, shucked and cleaned
2 tablespoons corn oil
1 large yellow onion, peeled and chopped
3 cloves garlic, peeled and chopped
2 serrano chilies, chopped
1 jalapeño chili, chopped
1 small bunch fresh cilantro
6 sprigs fresh thyme
6 sprigs fresh oregano
2 teaspoons toasted cumin seeds
5 tomatillos, husked and chopped

3 cups chicken stock (see page 236)
1 cup veal demi-glace (see page 237)
Salt to taste
Fresh lime juice to taste
1 small sweet potato, peeled and cut into 1/4-inch dice
1 medium red bell pepper, seeded and membranes removed, cut into 1/2-inch dice
1 medium yellow bell pepper, seeded and membranes removed, cut into 1/2-inch dice
1 cup cooked, drained black beans

Preheat oven to 400°.

Put ancho and pasilla chilies on a baking sheet, place in preheated oven, and roast for 3 minutes. Remove from heat and set aside.

Prepare smoker for cold smoke (see page 230).

Remove kernels from corn cobs and place in a small pan. Place both kernels and cobs in a prepared smoker. Smoke kernels for 5 minutes and cobs for 15 minutes. Remove and reserve.

Heat oil in a large sauté pan over medium heat. When hot, add onion and sauté for 5 minutes or until lightly golden brown. Add garlic, roasted anchos and pasillas, serranos, jalapeño, cilantro, thyme, oregano, cumin, tomatillos, reserved smoked corn cobs, and chicken stock. Bring to a boil. Lower heat and simmer for 30 minutes, stirring occasionally to prevent sticking. Remove cobs from stock and pour mixture into a food processor fitted with a metal blade. Process until smooth.

Place mixture in a saucepan over high heat. Bring to a boil. Lower heat and add demi-glace. Simmer for 20 minutes or until the sauce coats the back of a spoon. Strain through a medium-gauge sieve. Season with salt and lime juice. Keep warm.

Place sweet potato in a small saucepan of boiling salted water. Cook for 2 minutes or until just blanched. Drain under cold running water. Pat dry.

Place bell peppers into a saucepan of boiling water and cook for 30 seconds or until just blanched. Drain under cold running water. Pat dry.

Add sweet potato, bell peppers, black beans, and reserved smoked corn kernels to the sauce. Serve warm.

CILANTRO CREAM

*1 small bunch fresh
    cilantro, chopped*
*1 clove garlic, peeled and
    chopped*

1 serrano chili, chopped
1 cup sour cream
Salt to taste
Fresh lime juice to taste

Blend cilantro, garlic, and serrano in a blender until smooth. Do not use a food processor.

Remove from blender and whisk into sour cream. When well blended, season with salt and lime juice. Pour into a plastic squeeze bottle such as those used for ketchup or mustard. Keep cold until needed.

Grilled Texas Antelope with Bourbon Cream Corn and Apple-Pecan Fritters

SERVES 4

The garnish of Bourbon Cream Corn with the Apple Pecan Fritters will enhance the accomplishment of any dish. It is a true favorite of our Dallas patrons.

8 3-ounce antelope tenderloin medallions, trimmed of all fat and silver skin
3 tablespoons oil

Mansion Pepper Mixture to taste (see page 235)
Salt to taste
Bourbon Cream Corn
Apple-Pecan Fritters

Prepare grill. Level coals or wood, making sure grates are clean and lightly rubbed with oil.

Brush antelope with oil and season with Mansion Pepper Mixture and salt. Grill meat 2 minutes per side for medium-rare, or until desired degree of doneness is reached.

Place 2 antelope medallions overlapping each other in the center of each of four hot serving plates. Spoon a portion of Bourbon Cream Corn behind the meat and place 2 hot Apple-Pecan Fritters beside the corn to the right side of the plate. Serve immediately.

BOURBON CREAM CORN

6 ears sweet corn, shucked, cleaned, and kernels removed
1/2 red bell pepper, seeded and membranes removed, cut into 1/4-inch dice, and cold smoked for 3 minutes (see page 230)

1/2 green bell pepper, seeded and membranes removed, cut into 1/4-inch dice, and cold smoked for 3 minutes
1 ounce Jim Beam bourbon
1/2 cup heavy cream
Salt to taste

Place corn, smoked bell peppers, and bourbon in a small sauté pan over high heat. Flame the bourbon. Lower heat and cook for 3 minutes or until liquid is reduced to one tablespoon. Add cream and cook for 5 minutes or until quite thick. Season with salt. Keep warm until ready to use.

APPLE-PECAN FRITTERS

1/2 cup bread flour
1 3/4 cups all-purpose flour
1 teaspoon salt
3 teaspoons baking powder
3 teaspoons ground ginger
2 large eggs, well beaten
3 tablespoons maple syrup
2 cups milk

1/2 Granny Smith apple, cored and cut into 1/4-inch dice
1/2 red Delicious apple, cored and cut into 1/4-inch dice
3/4 cup chopped pecans
3 cups vegetable oil

Combine dry ingredients in a mixing bowl. Blend eggs, maple syrup, milk, apples, and pecans in a separate bowl and stir into flour. Mix until just incorporated.

Heat oil to 350° on a food thermometer in a deep-sided saucepan over high heat. Spoon batter into hot oil. Fry for 3 minutes or until golden brown. Remove from oil and drain on paper towel. Serve warm.

Scallopine of Venison with Persimmon-Cinnamon Sauce and Sweet Potato Hash Browns

SERVES 4

Mike Hughes of the Texas Wild Game Co-op in Ingram, Texas, is the man responsible for all venison served at The Mansion on Turtle Creek. With the newly found health values of venison, I'm sure we will be seeing more of it in the 1990s.

8 2¹/₂-ounce pieces venison tenderloin scallopine, trimmed of all fat and silver skin
Salt to taste
Ground black pepper to taste

1 cup cornmeal
3 tablespoons vegetable oil
Persimmon-Cinnamon Sauce
Sweet Potato Hash Browns

Lightly season venison with salt and pepper.

Dredge venison through cornmeal until fully coated.

Heat 1¹/₂ tablespoons oil in a large sauté pan over medium heat. Add half the venison, making sure not to overlap. Sauté for 1 to 2 minutes or until brown. Turn and sauté for an additional 1 to 2 minutes. Remove from pan and drain on paper towel. Using remaining 1¹/₂ tablespoons oil, repeat process for remaining scallopine.

Ladle Persimmon-Cinnamon Sauce around the rim of each of four hot serving plates. Then alternate 2 scallopines with 2 Sweet Potato Hash Browns, having them overlap each other in the center of each plate. Serve immediately.

PERSIMMON-CINNAMON SAUCE

3 tablespoons vegetable oil
1 pound venison (or beef)
    marrow bones, cut into
    small pieces
2 onions, peeled and cut
    into 1-inch dice
1/2 stalk celery, trimmed
    and cut into 1-inch
    dice
1/2 carrot, trimmed and cut
    into 1-inch dice
5 cups chicken stock (see
    page 236)

1 teaspoon cracked black
    pepper
1 small bunch fresh thyme
2 shallots, peeled and
    chopped
6 very large persimmons,
    stemmed and
    quartered
2 cinnamon sticks
1/4 cup brandy
1 tablespoon corn starch
1 tablespoon water
Salt to taste

Heat 2 tablespoons oil in a stockpot over medium heat. When hot, add bones and sauté for 6 minutes or until evenly brown, stirring occasionally. Add onions, celery, and carrot and sauté for 5 to 7 minutes or until vegetables are brown. Add stock and bring to a boil. Lower heat and simmer for 20 minutes. Skim off any scum that surfaces. Add cracked pepper and thyme and simmer for an additional 20 minutes. Strain through a fine sieve and reserve.

Heat remaining 1 tablespoon oil in a medium saucepan over medium heat. When hot, add shallots and sauté for 1 minute. Add persimmons and cinnamon sticks and cook for 5 minutes or until juices have condensed. Add brandy and cook for 5 minutes or until juices have again condensed. Add reserved stock and bring to a boil.

Dissolve corn starch in water and whisk into boiling stock. Lower heat and simmer for 20 minutes or until a saucelike consistency is reached. Remove cinnamon sticks and strain through a coarse strainer, extracting as much pulp as possible. Season with salt and keep warm.

SWEET POTATO HASH BROWNS

2 medium sweet potatoes,
    peeled
1 bunch scallions, trimmed
    and chopped
3 large eggs

1/2 cup all-purpose flour
Salt to taste
Ground black pepper to
    taste
2 tablespoons vegetable oil

Coarsely grate sweet potatoes. Combine in a medium bowl with all remaining ingredients except oil and stir to blend. Form into 8 patties the size of the venison scallopine.

Heat oil on a griddle over medium-high heat. When hot, add patties and fry for 3 minutes per side or until lightly browned. Serve hot.

CHAPTER SEVEN

Desserts and Breads

To MOST PEOPLE the desserts could be the best part of the book, and they are always the most lasting impression of any meal. Robert W. Zielinski, our executive pastry chef, and I have worked together for a long time at The Mansion on Turtle Creek. These are his recipes, outstanding favorites highly rated by our patrons. I dedicate this chapter of the book to him.

Phoenix Texas Star

SERVES 4

A salute to our new home state.
—RWZ

2 oranges, peeled and
   sectioned
4 to 5 strawberries, washed
   and hulled
1/2 pint raspberries, washed

1/4 pint blackberries,
   washed
1 banana, peeled and sliced
Grand Marnier Glaze
Gingerbread

Preheat broiler.

Divide fruit into four equal portions. Arrange a complete portion of fruit in a circular pattern on each of four ovenproof serving plates. Pour Grand Marnier Glaze over fruit to cover. Place plates under preheated broiler for 2 minutes or until fruit is lightly browned. Serve with 2 pieces of warm Gingerbread cut into a Texas star shape.

GRAND MARNIER GLAZE

5 large egg yolks
1/4 cup sugar

3 tablespoons Grand
   Marnier

Beat egg yolks and sugar in the top half of a double boiler over simmering water for 10 minutes or until ribbon consistency is reached. Remove from heat and cool slightly. Whisk in Grand Marnier.

GINGERBREAD

1/2 cup unsalted butter,
   softened
1/2 cup sugar
1 large egg, beaten
1 cup molasses
1 cup boiling water
2 1/2 cups all-purpose flour

1 1/2 teaspoons baking soda
1 teaspoon ground
   cinnamon
1 teaspoon ground ginger
1/2 teaspoon ground cloves
1/2 teaspoon salt

Preheat oven to 350°.

Grease and flour a 10-×-15-inch cake pan.

Cream butter and sugar in a mixing bowl until light and fluffy. Beat in egg, then molasses and boiling water. In a separate bowl, sift together remaining ingredients and add to creamed mixture. Pour batter into prepared pan and bake in preheated oven for approximately 35 minutes or until cake tester inserted in center comes out clean. Use a five-pointed-star cake cutter to cut out 8 stars. Serve warm.

Banana-Peanut Cheesecake with Oreo Cookie Crust and Peanut Butter Sauce

MAKES ONE 10-INCH CAKE

3 cups ground Oreo cookie crumbs, minus filling
2 cups sugar
4 tablespoons unsalted butter, melted
2¼ pounds cream cheese, softened
5 large eggs, at room temperature

1 teaspoon pure vanilla extract
1 cup very ripe banana purée
1 cup chopped unsalted peanuts
Peanut Butter Sauce

Preheat oven to 325°.

In a medium bowl, combine ground cookie crumbs, ¼ cup sugar, and melted butter until thoroughly blended. Cover the bottom and approximately 1 inch of the sides of a greased 10-inch springform pan. Set aside.

Beat cream cheese until smooth. Add remaining 1¾ cups sugar and continue mixing, scraping bowl often. Add eggs, one at a time, beating until well incorporated. Beat in vanilla. Fold in banana purée and chopped peanuts. Pour into prepared crust and bake in preheated oven for approximately 1 hour and 15 minutes or until center is set. Cool on wire rack; then refrigerate 24 hours before serving.

When ready to serve, place a small slice on each chilled serving plate and drizzle with Peanut Butter Sauce.

PEANUT BUTTER SAUCE

1 cup smooth peanut butter
2 cups milk

½ cup ground unsalted peanuts

Combine all ingredients in a saucepan and cook, stirring constantly, over low heat for about 10 minutes or until slightly thickened. Cool to room temperature before using.

Bourbon-Pecan Crème Brûlée with Milk Chocolate Sauce

SERVES 6

6 large eggs, separated
1¼ cups sugar
3 cups heavy cream
1 vanilla bean, split
   lengthwise

¼ cup good-quality
   Kentucky bourbon
1 cup chopped pecans
6 baked Puff Pastry shells
Milk Chocolate Sauce

Combine egg yolks and ½ cup sugar in the top half of a double boiler over simmering water. Whisk for 10 minutes or until lemon-colored and the consistency of mousse. Remove from heat, pour into a bowl, and set aside.

Place cream and vanilla bean in a heavy saucepan over medium heat. Bring to a strong boil and remove from heat. Strain and slowly pour into egg mixture, whipping rapidly as you pour.

Return mixture to top half of double boiler, and double boiler to heat, and cook mixture over simmering water for about 10 minutes or until very thick. Remove from heat. Stir occasionally while mixture cools until it reaches the consistency of a very thick custard. Stir in bourbon.

Preheat broiler.

Spread a single layer of pecans over the bottom of each of 6 Puff Pastry shells. Pour cooled cream over the pecans to top of shell. Refrigerate for at least 1 hour. When well chilled, sprinkle top with sugar and place under broiler for 2 minutes or until golden brown. Coat each of six serving plates with Milk Chocolate Sauce and set a Crème Brûlée in the center of each. Serve immediately.

Bourbon-Pecan Crème Brûlée with Milk Chocolate Sauce

PUFF PASTRY

2 cups all-purpose flour
Pinch of salt
1 cup unsalted butter

¹/₂ cup ice water,
   approximately
1 teaspoon fresh lemon juice

Combine flour, salt, and 3 tablespoons butter. Cut butter into flour using a pastry cutter or food processor.

Combine water and lemon juice. Add to flour, mixing to form a pliable dough. Knead by hand for 2 to 3 minutes or process in a food processor until dough forms a ball.

Roll dough on a lightly floured, chilled surface, preferably a marble slab. Surface *must* be

chilled. Roll dough to an 8-×-12-inch rectangle. Place pastry with short side facing you. Remaining butter should be cool but malleable. Place butter in center of rectangle and fold the near third of pastry toward the center. Repeat with the far third of pastry to form three layers. Press edges of pastry lightly with a rolling pin to seal. Give pastry a quarter turn and roll again into a rectangle; fold and seal as before. Be careful that butter does not break through during rolling. If it does, immediately dust lightly with flour and roll again. Wrap and chill at least 15 minutes.

Repeat rolling, folding, and chilling five more times, chilling 30 minutes each time. Chill 1 hour after final rolling.

Preheat oven to 350°.

When pastry is well chilled, roll out as thin as possible on a lightly floured, *chilled* surface. To make shells, cut out six 6-inch rounds. Line the ungreased cups of a Texas-size (3½-×-1½-inch) muffin pan with the rounds, pressing pastry evenly into cups and trimming edges. Line each cup with a small coffee filter or parchment paper and fill to the top with dried beans (or commercial pastry weights).

Place in preheated oven and bake for 20 to 30 minutes or until pastry is crisp and golden. Remove beans (or weights) and filters (or paper) and allow shells to cool to room temperature.

MILK CHOCOLATE SAUCE

1 cup milk
5 teaspoons heavy cream
¼ cup sugar

2½ tablespoons unsalted
   butter, softened
9 ounces milk chocolate,
   chopped

Combine milk, cream, sugar, and butter in a heavy saucepan over medium heat, stirring occasionally. Bring to a boil. When boiling, pour over chopped chocolate and stir until chocolate is melted and a smooth sauce is formed. Cool.

Bailey's Irish Cream Cheesecake

MAKES ONE 10-INCH CAKE

My wife, Debbie, was sitting having a cup of coffee one cold winter night with Bailey's Irish Cream liqueur in it and thought this would be a great flavor for a cake of some kind. I started experimenting with it, and this recipe is the result. It is one greatly enjoyed even by non-lovers of cheesecake.

—RWZ

1 tablespoon unsalted butter, softened
2 cups graham cracker crumbs
2 cups sugar
1/2 cup unsalted butter, melted
2 1/4 pounds cream cheese, softened
5 large eggs, at room temperature

1 teaspoon pure vanilla extract
1 cup Bailey's Irish Cream
1 cup heavy cream
1 tablespoon confectioners' sugar
1–2 ounces semisweet chocolate

Preheat oven to 325°.

Coat bottom and sides of a 10-inch spring-form pan with softened butter.

Using a fork, combine graham cracker crumbs, 1/2 cup sugar, and melted butter in a medium bowl until well blended. Then evenly press crumb mixture onto the bottom and 1 inch up the sides of buttered pan.

Beat cream cheese in a mixing bowl until smooth. Add remaining 1 1/2 cups sugar and beat until smooth, scraping down sides of bowl as needed.

Add eggs, one at a time, making sure to scrape sides after each addition. Beat until well incorporated and very smooth. Beat in vanilla and Bailey's Irish Cream until well mixed.

Pour into prepared pan and bake in pre-heated oven for approximately 1 hour and 15 minutes or until center is the consistency of set Jell-O.

Remove from oven and let cool on a wire rack away from drafts. When cool, remove spring form and refrigerate until ready to serve.

When ready to serve, whip heavy cream with confectioners' sugar and garnish top of cake with whipped cream rosettes. Shave chocolate over top.

Banana Soft Tacos with Grand Marnier Glaze and Papaya and Strawberry Salsas
SERVES 4

A classic with a Southwest flair.
            —RWZ

1 cup cake flour
1 cup bread flour
2 tablespoons sugar
Pinch of salt
2 cups milk
4 large eggs, beaten
4 large egg yolks, beaten
¹/₂ cup unsalted butter,
     melted and still hot

¹/₄ cup cognac
Glazed Bananas
Grand Marnier Glaze (see
     page 200)
Papaya Salsa
Strawberry Salsa

In a mixing bowl, combine both flours, sugar, and salt. Slowly beat in milk, eggs, and egg yolks. Whisk in butter, then cognac. Stir well to combine. Allow to sit for 15 to 20 minutes.

Lightly butter an 8-inch sauté or crêpe pan and place over medium heat. Pour in approximately 1 tablespoon batter and swirl in a circular motion to cover bottom of pan. Cook for 2 to 3 minutes or until lightly browned. Turn crêpe over and cook for an additional 2 to 3 minutes. Continue until all batter is used. Do not stack crêpes one on top of the other or they will stick together.

Preheat broiler.

Spoon 6 or 8 slices of Glazed Banana in the center of each crêpe and roll up like a soft taco. Place 2 on each of four ovenproof serving plates. Pour Grand Marnier Glaze across the top of the tacos and place under preheated broiler for 2 minutes or until lightly browned. Spoon 4 or 5 more banana slices on top and serve with Papaya and Strawberry Salsas on the side.

GLAZED BANANAS

¹/₂ cup unsalted butter
1 cup packed light brown
     sugar
2 tablespoons fresh orange
     juice

2 tablespoons Grand
     Marnier
6 bananas, peeled and
     sliced

Combine butter and brown sugar in a small saucepan over medium heat. Cook for 3 minutes or until liquefied. Stir in orange juice and Grand Marnier and cook for 5 minutes. Remove from heat and stir in sliced bananas. Serve warm.

Banana Soft Tacos with Grand Marnier Glaze and Papaya and Strawberry Salsas

PAPAYA SALSA

1 papaya, peeled, halved, and seeded
3 tablespoons sugar

1 teaspoon ground cinnamon

Cut one papaya half into ¼-inch dice and set aside.

In a blender, purée remaining half with sugar and cinnamon. Pour purée over diced papaya and stir to combine. Set aside.

STRAWBERRY SALSA

1 pint strawberries, washed and hulled

3 tablespoons light brown sugar

Cut one half of the strawberries into ¼-inch dice. Set aside.

In a blender, purée remaining strawberries with brown sugar. Pour purée over diced strawberries. Stir to combine. Set aside.

Double Chocolate Mousse Cake

MAKES ONE 9-INCH CAKE

1¹/₂ cups sifted cake flour
³/₄ teaspoon baking soda
³/₄ teaspoon salt
1 cup sugar
6 tablespoons cocoa powder
¹/₂ cup buttermilk
2 extra-large eggs,
    separated

¹/₃ cup vegetable oil
Rum Syrup
Chocolate Mousse
Chocolate Ganache
Chocolate Glaze
1 cup semisweet chocolate
    shavings

Preheat oven to 350°.

Grease and flour a 9-inch springform pan and line with parchment paper or wax paper. Butter and flour paper. Set aside.

Sift together cake flour, baking soda, salt, ³/₄ cup sugar, and cocoa in a mixing bowl. Combine buttermilk and egg yolks in a separate bowl. Alternately combine dry and liquid ingredients, small amounts at a time, to form a batter, beating with an electric mixer at high speed until smooth. Add oil and blend until shiny.

In a mixing bowl, beat egg whites until they form soft peaks, gradually adding ¹/₄ cup sugar. Fold beaten egg whites into batter. Pour batter into prepared pan and bake in preheated oven for 20 to 30 minutes or until cake tester inserted in center comes out clean. Remove from oven and let cake cool on wire rack. When cool, remove spring form. Carefully remove bottom and peel off paper. Slice horizontally into 3 layers.

Fit a piece of parchment paper on a baking sheet and place the ring from a 9-inch springform pan on paper. Place 1 layer of cake into the ring. Brush and soak cake with Rum Syrup. Spread on about 1¹/₂ inches of Chocolate Mousse, then cover with a second cake layer. Repeat procedure. Place final cake layer on top and soak with Rum Syrup. Tightly cover and place cake in freezer for at least 8 hours.

Run a knife around the edges between the cake and the ring and put a hot towel around the outside of the ring to loosen the cake onto a serving platter. Totally cover the sides and

Double Chocolate Mousse Cake

top of the cake with Chocolate Ganache. Refrigerate for 20 minutes. Remove from refrigerator and completely cover ganache with Chocolate Glaze. Refrigerate again for 15 minutes or until glaze is set. When set, cover top of cake with chocolate shavings. Keep cold until ready to serve.

RUM SYRUP

1 cup sugar
1 cup water

¼ cup rum (or brandy,
Grand Marnier, etc.)

Combine all ingredients in a small heavy saucepan over high heat. Bring to a boil. Boil, stirring constantly, for about 2 minutes or until sugar is dissolved. Remove from heat and cool. May be stored, tightly covered and refrigerated, for up to 3 months.

CHOCOLATE MOUSSE

8 ounces bitter chocolate
8 ounces milk chocolate
7 large eggs, separated
¾ cup sugar

4 cups unsweetened
whipped cream
¼ cup Myers's rum

Melt both chocolates together in the top half of a double boiler over water that has just boiled. Remove from heat and set aside.

Whip egg whites and half of the sugar to soft peaks. Set aside.

Beat egg yolks and remaining sugar in a mixing bowl for 10 minutes or until pale yellow and of a ribbon consistency. Slowly pour in melted chocolate. Carefully fold in whipped egg whites. When well combined, gently fold in whipped cream. While mixing, add rum. Store in refrigerator until ready to use.

CHOCOLATE GANACHE

20 ounces semisweet
   chocolate
1 cup heavy cream

¼ cup unsalted butter,
   softened
2 tablespoons sugar

Chop chocolate into bite-size pieces. Reserve.

Bring cream to a boil in a stainless steel or non-stick 1-quart saucepan. Do not use aluminum! When cream comes to a boil, remove from heat and immediately beat in chocolate, butter, and sugar. Stir until smooth. Set aside to cool completely.

Ganache can be made in advance and kept in the refrigerator until ready to use. Bring to room temperature before using.

CHOCOLATE GLAZE

1 cup unsalted butter
2 tablespoons light corn
   syrup
¼ cup dark rum

12 ounces bittersweet
   chocolate, finely
   chopped

Place all ingredients in a heatproof bowl over a double boiler bottom filled with simmering water. Allow to melt completely, stirring occasionally. Keep warm. If mixture will not be used immediately, cover and store at room temperature until needed.

(The glaze can also be made in advance as this recipe makes a generous amount, which can be stored, covered and refrigerated, for a long period.)

Heath Bar Cake

MAKES ONE 13-×-9-×-2-INCH CAKE

Cara LeFebvre, my assistant pastry chef, and I worked this recipe out for her father, who loves Heath Bars.

—RWZ

1 cup packed light brown sugar
½ cup sugar
½ cup unsalted butter, softened
1 large egg, beaten
1 cup buttermilk
1 teaspoon pure vanilla extract

2 cups sifted all-purpose flour
1 teaspoon baking soda
8 Heath Bars, frozen and chopped
½ cup chopped pecans

Preheat oven to 350°.

Grease and flour a 13-×-9-×-2-inch cake pan.

In a mixing bowl, cream sugars and butter. When well mixed, beat in egg and slowly add buttermilk. Beat in vanilla, flour, and baking soda. Pour into prepared pan. Sprinkle candy and nuts over top. Bake in preheated oven for 45 minutes or until a cake tester inserted in the center comes out clean. Cool on wire rack.

Blueberry Sour Cream Cake

MAKES ONE 9-INCH CAKE

This recipe is a perfect marriage of two items, blueberries and sour cream. It looks very dense, but is very light.

—RWZ

1 cup all-purpose flour
1 cup sugar
1½ teaspoons baking
powder
½ cup unsalted butter, at
room temperature, cut
into small pieces

1 large egg
2 cups sour cream
2 large egg yolks
2 pints blueberries, washed
and dried

Preheat oven to 350°.

In a mixing bowl, combine flour, ½ cup sugar, and baking powder. Add butter and mix until smooth. Add egg and blend until combined. Dough will be very soft and some extra flour for handling will be needed. Refrigerate until ready to use.

Beat sour cream and remaining ½ cup sugar until sugar is almost dissolved. Add yolks, one at a time, until well blended.

Remove dough from refrigerator and line bottom and 1 inch up the sides of a 9-inch springform pan that has been sprayed with non-stick pan release. Add half of the blueberries and cover with sour cream mixture. Bake in a 350° oven for approximately 35 to 40 minutes or until center is set.

When done, cool at room temperature for 45 minutes and then refrigerate 3 to 4 hours.

Remove spring form and place remaining blueberries neatly on top.

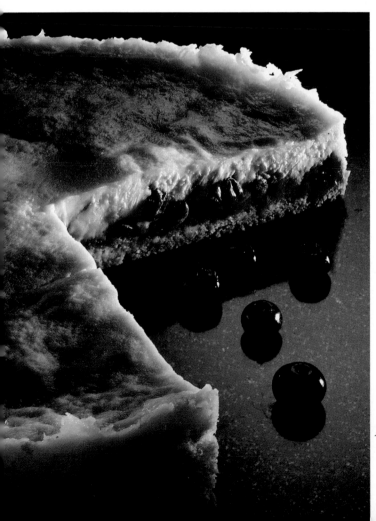

Blueberry Sour Cream Cake

Mississippi Mud Pie

MAKES ONE 13-INCH CAKE

This mud could be addictive—watch out.
—RWZ

1/2 cup unsalted butter,
  softened
1 cup sugar
3 large eggs
3/4 cup all-purpose flour
1/2 teaspoon baking powder
Dash of salt
1/4 cup plus 1 1/2 teaspoons
  cocoa powder, sifted

1 teaspoon pure vanilla
  extract
1 cup chopped pecans
1 10-ounce package
  marshmallows
Chocolate Frosting

Preheat oven to 325°.

Grease and flour a 13-×-9-×-2-inch glass baking dish.

In a mixing bowl, cream butter until light and fluffy. Gradually add sugar and beat until well incorporated. Add eggs, one at a time, beating well after each addition. Combine flour, baking powder, salt, and cocoa and add to creamed mixture. Stir in vanilla and pecans.

Spoon batter into prepared dish and bake in preheated oven for 15 to 18 minutes or until top is barely soft to the touch. Remove from oven and cover the top with marshmallows. Return to oven and bake for about 3 minutes or until marshmallows are soft. Remove from oven and spread marshmallows over the top. Immediately cover with Chocolate Frosting. Let frosting set before cutting pie into serving squares.

CHOCOLATE FROSTING

1/4 cup unsalted butter,
  softened
1/4 cup plus 2 tablespoons
  cocoa powder, sifted
3 cups confectioners' sugar,
  sifted

1/4 cup plus 3 tablespoons
  warm milk
1 teaspoon pure vanilla
  extract

In a mixing bowl, cream butter. Add cocoa, mixing well. Gradually beat in confectioners' sugar, adding warm milk as necessary, until spreading consistency is reached. Stir in vanilla. Immediately spread over warm marshmallows.

Buttermilk Pie

MAKES ONE 9-INCH PIE

Dean and I were visiting Kentucky one summer, and Dean's mother
made this for us. I told her I had to have the recipe.

—RWZ

1 9-inch pie tin, lined with
All-Purpose Pastry,
unbaked (see page
233)
3 large eggs
³/₄ cup sugar
3 tablespoons all-purpose
flour
1¹/₂ cups buttermilk
³/₄ teaspoon pure vanilla
extract

3 tablespoons fresh lemon
juice
1 teaspoon grated lemon
rind
1 tablespoon unsalted
butter, melted
¹/₂ teaspoon ground
nutmeg

Preheat oven to 350°.

Cover unbaked pie shell with parchment paper or a coffee filter. Press down to fit and fill with commercial pastry weights or dried beans. Place weighted shell in preheated oven and bake for 10 minutes. Remove from oven and empty out weights. Discard parchment and set pastry shell aside.

Raise oven to 375°.

Beat eggs and sugar until light and lemon-colored. Add flour and beat until well mixed. Add buttermilk, vanilla, lemon juice, lemon rind, and butter. Pour into baked crust and dust with nutmeg. Bake in preheated 375° oven for 25 to 30 minutes. Cool slightly on wire rack before serving.

Jack Daniels Chocolate Chip–Pecan Pie

MAKES ONE 10-INCH PIE

I spent five years in Kentucky and loved it. This recipe really reminds
me of some wild times.

—RWZ

3 extra-large eggs, lightly
beaten
1 cup sugar
2 tablespoons unsalted
butter, melted
1 cup dark corn syrup
1 teaspoon pure vanilla
extract
¹/₄ cup Jack Daniels
whiskey

¹/₂ cup semisweet chocolate
bits
1 cup whole pecans
1 10-inch pie tin, lined
with All-Purpose
Pastry, unbaked (see
page 233)

Preheat oven to 375°.

In a mixing bowl, beat eggs, sugar, butter, corn syrup, vanilla, and Jack Daniels until well combined. Strain. Sprinkle chocolate chips over bottom of unbaked pie shell, cover with pecans, and pour filling over all.

Place in preheated oven and bake for 35 to 40 minutes or until a knife inserted halfway between the center and the edge comes out clean. Let set at least 30 minutes before serving.

Cherry Almond Cream Pie

MAKES ONE 9-INCH PIE

¹/₂ *cup slivered almonds,*
  finely chopped
1 *recipe All-Purpose Pastry*
  (see page 233)
1 *15-ounce can sweetened*
  condensed milk
¹/₃ *cup fresh lemon juice*

1 *teaspoon pure vanilla*
  extract
¹/₂ *teaspoon almond extract*
1 *cup heavy cream,*
  whipped
Cherry Glaze

Preheat oven to 350°.

Add almonds to pastry dough when adding water. Roll out as directed and fit into a 9-inch pie tin. Prick only sides of pie crust. Cover unbaked pie shell with parchment paper or a coffee filter. Press down to fit and fill with commercial pastry weights or dried beans. Place weighted shell in preheated oven and bake for 15 minutes or until lightly browned. Remove from oven and empty out weights. Discard parchment and set pastry shell aside to cool on a wire rack.

In a mixing bowl, combine condensed milk, lemon juice, vanilla, and almond extract, beating until thick. Fold in whipped cream and spoon into cooled shell. Cover with Cherry Glaze and refrigerate for at least 3 hours before serving.

CHERRY GLAZE

²/₃ *cup cherry juice*
¹/₄ *cup sugar*
1 *tablespoon corn starch*

2 *cups pitted sour cherries,*
  well drained

Combine cherry juice, sugar, and corn starch in a small saucepan over medium heat. Cook, stirring constantly, for 10 minutes or until thickened and clear. Stir in cherries. Set aside until ready to use.

Peach Pie

MAKES ONE 10-INCH DEEP-DISH PIE

Jeff Smith, the pastry chef at our sister hotel, the Crescent Court in
Dallas, gave me this truly wonderful summer recipe.

—RWZ

³/₄ cup all-purpose flour
1 cup sugar
¹/₂ cup packed brown sugar
¹/₂ teaspoon ground
  cinnamon
Juice of 1 lemon

10 cups sliced fresh peaches
1 10-inch deep-dish pie tin,
  lined with All-Purpose
  Pastry, unbaked (see
  page 233)
Cinnamon Topping

Preheat oven to 375°.

Mix dry ingredients together in a large
bowl. Squeeze lemon juice over sliced peaches.
Toss peaches with dry ingredients and mix
well. Place peaches into unbaked deep-dish pie
shell. Cover with Cinnamon Topping and
bake in preheated oven for 30 minutes or until
top is light brown. Serve warm.

CINNAMON TOPPING

2 cups all-purpose flour
2 cups sugar
2 teaspoons ground
  cinnamon

1 cup cold unsalted butter

Combine flour, sugar, and cinnamon. Cut in
cold butter until mixture crumbles. Keep cool
until ready to use.

Apple-Cranberry Pie with Cheddar Cheese Crust

MAKES ONE 9-INCH PIE

*1 recipe Cheddar Cheese
    Pie Dough*
³/₄ cup brown sugar
¹/₃ cup sugar
¹/₃ cup all-purpose flour
*2 teaspoons ground
    cinnamon*

*4 cups peeled, cored, and
    sliced tart apples*
*2 cups cranberries, washed
    and dried*
*2 tablespoons unsalted
    butter*

Preheat oven to 425°.

Roll out 2 crusts of Cheddar Cheese Pie Dough for a 9-inch pie. Line a 9-inch pie tin with 1 crust, and set both crusts aside.

In a large bowl, combine brown sugar, sugar, flour, and cinnamon. Add apples and cranberries and toss until well coated. Pour into unbaked pie shell. Dot with butter. Place top crust on and seal and flute edges. Slit top to allow steam to escape.

Bake in preheated oven for 40 to 50 minutes or until golden brown and bubbly. Cool on wire rack before serving.

CHEDDAR CHEESE PIE DOUGH

MAKES ENOUGH FOR 1 DOUBLE-CRUST PIE

3¹/₂ cups all-purpose flour
*1 cup shredded cheddar
    cheese*
*¹/₂ cup unsalted butter,
    softened*

*1¹/₂ cups solid vegetable
    shortening*
¹/₂ teaspoon salt
2 tablespoons sugar
¹/₂ cup ice water

Sift flour and set aside.

In a mixing bowl, cream cheddar cheese and butter until smooth. Gently mix shortening into cheese mixture until slightly combined. Cut flour into cheese mixture by hand until mixture resembles coarse meal. Dissolve salt and sugar into ice water, and gradually add water to cheese mixture. Mix by hand until firm ball is formed. Do not overmix. Divide dough into 2 balls, seal in plastic wrap, and chill for at least 30 minutes before rolling out. When chilled, roll each ball out to about ¹/₈-inch thickness on a lightly floured surface, to a size 2 inches larger than the pan into which it will be fitted (or cut dough into whatever size or shape desired). After bottom crust is fitted into pan, trim edges and finish as directed.

Butterfinger Candy Tart

MAKES ONE 9-INCH TART

I love this candy bar.
—RWZ

2 large eggs
1/2 cup water
1 1/2 cups sugar
1/4 cup all-purpose flour
1/4 teaspoon salt
1/2 cup unsalted butter
8 Butterfinger candy bars,
roughly chopped

1 9-inch pie tin, lined with
All-Purpose Pastry,
unbaked (see page
233)
Whipped cream

In a mixing bowl, beat eggs lightly. Stir in water, sugar, flour, and salt until well combined.

Melt butter in a small saucepan over low heat. While still hot, stir butter into batter until well combined. Stir in 6 chopped Butterfingers. Refrigerate for 8 hours (this will help bring out the candy taste).

Preheat oven to 325°.

Pour chilled mixture into unbaked pie shell and bake in preheated oven for 45 minutes. Tart will be quite loose. Refrigerate for at least 12 hours. Serve garnished with whipped cream and 2 remaining chopped Butterfingers, if desired.

Butterfinger Candy Tart

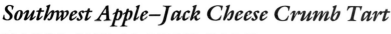

Southwest Apple–Jack Cheese Crumb Tart

MAKES ONE 10-INCH TART

1 recipe Puff Pastry dough
   (see page 203)
³/₄ cup Pastry Cream
1 cup grated jalapeño jack
   cheese
5 Granny Smith apples,
   peeled, cored, and
   thinly sliced

¹/₄ cup Cinnamon Sugar
Crumb Topping
2 tablespoons confectioners'
   sugar

Preheat oven to 400°.

Roll pastry dough into a 10-inch circle ¹/₈ inch thick. Place circle of dough on a cookie sheet. Spread Pastry Cream on dough, leaving 1 inch clear all around the edge. Cover Pastry Cream with grated jack cheese. Leaving the edge clear, overlap apple slices to form an outer circle. Sprinkle with Cinnamon Sugar. Then form an inner circle of slices which partially covers the outer circle. Cover with Crumb Topping, still leaving 1 inch around the outside clear (the puff dough will form its own edge this way).

Bake in preheated oven for approximately 30 minutes or until puff pastry is flaky and golden brown. When tart is done, dust top with confectioners' sugar. Serve warm with ice cream, if desired.

PASTRY CREAM

1 cup milk
¹/₄ teaspoon pure vanilla
   extract
¹/₃ cup sugar
2 tablespoons corn starch
   dissolved in 2
   tablespoons milk

3 extra-large eggs, lightly
   beaten

Combine milk, vanilla, and half of the sugar in a small saucepan over medium heat. Bring to a boil, stirring frequently. Remove from heat. Combine dissolved corn starch, eggs, and remaining sugar in a mixing bowl. Add a bit of hot liquid to eggs, stirring vigorously. Slowly whisk egg mixture into hot milk.

Return pan to medium heat and cook, stirring constantly, until mixture just comes to a boil. Remove from heat immediately, still stirring. Stir for a few minutes off heat, then let cool. Refrigerate for at least 2 hours or until completely chilled.

CINNAMON SUGAR

¹/₄ cup sugar

*¹/₂ teaspoon ground
    cinnamon or to taste*

Thoroughly combine sugar and cinnamon.

CRUMB TOPPING

*¹/₂ cup unsalted butter,
    softened*
¹/₄ cup sugar
¹/₄ cup brown sugar

1³/₄ cups all-purpose flour
*¹/₂ teaspoon ground
    cinnamon*
2 tablespoons almond paste

Using your hands, mix all ingredients together
until small crumb is formed.

*Grapefruit Tequila Sorbet
with Flour Tortilla
Cinnamon Crisps*

Grapefruit Tequila Sorbet with Flour Tortilla Cinnamon Crisps

MAKES APPROXIMATELY 1 QUART

2 cups sugar
1¹/₃ cups water
*2 cups cold fresh grapefruit
    juice*

¹/₂ cup tequila
Cinnamon Crisps

Combine sugar and water in a small saucepan over medium heat and bring to a boil. Boil, stirring constantly, for 3 minutes or until sugar is dissolved. Remove from heat. Cool, then refrigerate until well chilled.

Combine cold grapefruit juice, tequila, and 2 cups chilled sugar syrup. Pour into an ice cream maker and freeze according to manufacturer's directions. Serve with Cinnamon Crisps on the side.

CINNAMON CRISPS

*8 Flour Tortillas (see page
    28)*
1 cup vegetable oil

1 cup sugar
¹/₄ cup ground cinnamon
1 tablespoon ground cloves

Cut tortillas into eighths. Heat oil to 350° on a food thermometer in a deep-sided pan over high heat. Deep-fry tortillas for 1 minute or until crisp. Drain on paper towel.

In a mixing bowl, combine sugar, cinnamon, and cloves. Gently toss tortilla pieces in mixture to coat well.

Peanut Butter–Chocolate Chip Ice Cream

MAKES APPROXIMATELY 1½ QUARTS

6 extra-large egg yolks
1 cup sugar
1 cup heavy cream
2 cups cold milk
1 vanilla bean, split
　　lengthwise

¾ cup peanut butter
1 cup mini–semisweet
　　chocolate chips

Combine egg yolks and sugar in a small bowl, beating until smooth and lemon-colored. Set aside.

Place cream, milk, and vanilla bean in a small saucepan over medium heat and bring to a boil. Immediately remove from heat and cool slightly. Remove vanilla bean and add a small amount of cream to yolks, stirring briskly. Slowly add yolks to remaining cream, stirring constantly. Strain through cheesecloth or a fine sieve.

Slowly stir cream mixture into peanut butter. Beat until well mixed. Chill. When well chilled, pour into an ice cream maker. Freeze according to manufacturer's directions. When slightly frozen, fold in chocolate chips and continue to freeze.

Honey Pecan Ice Cream

MAKES APPROXIMATELY 1½ QUARTS

6 extra-large egg yolks
1 cup sugar
1 cup heavy cream
2 cups cold milk

1 vanilla bean, split
　　lengthwise
6 ounces pecan pieces
¼ cup honey

Combine egg yolks and sugar in a small bowl, beating until smooth and lemon-colored. Set aside.

Place cream, milk, and vanilla bean in a small saucepan over medium heat and bring to a boil. Immediately remove from heat and cool slightly. Remove vanilla bean and add a small amount of cream to yolks, stirring briskly. Slowly add yolks to remaining cream, stirring constantly. Strain through cheesecloth or a fine sieve.

Stir honey into cream mixture and chill. When well chilled, pour into an ice cream maker. Freeze according to manufacturer's directions. When slightly frozen, fold in pecans and continue to freeze.

Marvel Cream Cheese–Chocolate Brownies

MAKES 24

Dean's neighbor Gloria Shaw won many contests at the state fair with
this recipe, which brings a new meaning to brownies for the nineties.

—RWZ

*4 ounces unsweetened
    chocolate*
1 cup unsalted butter
½ cup unsalted margarine
2¼ cups flour
1 teaspoon baking soda
½ teaspoon salt
3 large eggs

*1 teaspoon pure vanilla
    extract*
2 cups sugar
1 cup chopped walnuts
*1 cup cream cheese,
    softened*
2 cups confectioners' sugar

Preheat oven to 325°.

Grease and flour a 14-×-12-inch sheet cake pan.

Melt chocolate, ½ cup butter, and margarine in top half of a double boiler over boiling water, stirring to blend. When melted, remove from heat and allow to cool.

Sift together flour, baking soda, and salt and set aside. In a mixing bowl, beat 2 eggs and vanilla until frothy. Add sugar and continue beating until thick and lemon-colored. Gradually beat in flour mixture until well combined. Stir in chocolate mixture, scraping down sides of bowl as necessary. When well blended, pour into prepared pan. Smooth top and sprinkle with ½ cup walnuts. Set aside.

Beat cream cheese and remaining ½ cup butter until light and fluffy. Add remaining egg and beat to combine. Add confectioners' sugar and beat until well blended.

Spread cream cheese mixture over top of brownies, leaving ½-inch border all around, using a rubber spatula to smooth the surface. Sprinkle with remaining ½ cup walnuts.

Place in preheated oven and bake for 30 to 40 minutes or until set.

Remove from oven and cool on a wire rack for 2 hours before cutting into squares.

Date and Nut Chews

MAKES 36 COOKIES

A great holiday treat after eating that big turkey.

—RWZ

³/₄ cup all-purpose flour
¹/₄ teaspoon salt
2 large eggs
¹/₂ cup sugar
¹/₂ cup corn syrup
¹/₂ teaspoon pure almond
*   extract*

1 cup finely chopped dates
1 cup chopped pecans
¹/₃ cup sifted confectioners'
*   sugar*

Preheat oven to 375°.

Grease bottom of two 8-inch square baking pans.

Sift flour with salt and set aside. In a mixing bowl, beat eggs with sugar, corn syrup, and almond extract until light and fluffy. Stir in flour, dates, and pecans and mix until well blended.

Pour batter into prepared pans and bake in preheated oven for 20 minutes or until done. Immediately cut into 1¹/₂-inch squares. When squares have cooled slightly, roll into balls or fingers and coat with confectioners' sugar. Let cool before serving.

Pumpkin Spice Bread

MAKES TWO 9-INCH LOAVES

If you want your house to smell like your mom's did at the holidays, this recipe will do the trick. It not only tastes great, but the smell while it's baking really reminds me of home.

—RWZ

2¹/₄ cups sugar
⁵/₈ cup vegetable oil
1 14-ounce can pumpkin
*   purée*
3 large eggs
3 cups all-purpose flour
1¹/₂ teaspoons baking soda
1³/₄ teaspoons salt

³/₄ teaspoon baking powder
³/₄ teaspoon ground
*   nutmeg*
³/₄ teaspoon ground allspice
³/₄ teaspoon ground
*   cinnamon*
¹/₄ teaspoon ground cloves
¹/₂ cup milk

Preheat oven to 350°.

Grease and flour two 9-×-5-×-3-inch loaf pans.

In a mixing bowl, combine sugar, oil, pumpkin, and eggs and beat until smooth. Sift together flour, baking soda, salt, baking powder, and spices. Add to pumpkin mixture until well combined. Slowly beat in milk. Pour into prepared pans and bake in preheated oven for about 1 hour or until a cake tester inserted in the center comes out clean. Serve warm or at room temperature.

Southwest Corn Muffins

MAKES APPROXIMATELY 2 DOZEN

¹/₂ cup unsalted butter, softened
¹/₂ cup confectioners' sugar
2 large eggs
¹/₂ teaspoon salt
3¹/₂ cups cake flour
2 tablespoons baking powder
2¹/₂ cups coarsely ground cornmeal
2 cups milk, approximately
¹/₂ green bell pepper, seeded and membranes removed, finely chopped

¹/₂ red bell pepper, seeded and membranes removed, finely chopped
¹/₂ yellow bell pepper, seeded and membranes removed, finely chopped
1 carrot, trimmed and finely grated
2 ears corn, kernels only
¹/₄ cup grated sharp yellow cheese
¹/₄ cup grated jalapeño jack cheese

Preheat oven to 400°.

In a mixing bowl, cream together butter and confectioners' sugar. Slowly add eggs. Combine dry ingredients and add alternately with milk to make a stiff batter.

Toss together vegetables and cheese and fold in by hand until well combined. Fill 2 ungreased muffin tins three-quarters full and bake in preheated oven for approximately 30 to 35 minutes or until firm and lightly browned. Serve warm.

Apple Carrot Muffins

MAKES 1 TO 1¹/₂ DOZEN

We were in the process of looking for new muffin recipes when one of our pastry cooks, Katy Reddick, came to us with this one, which has become a big breakfast hit.

—RWZ

2 cups all-purpose flour
1¹/₄ cups sugar
2 teaspoons baking soda
2 teaspoons ground cinnamon
¹/₂ teaspoon salt
2 cups grated carrots
¹/₄ cup dark raisins
¹/₄ cup light raisins

¹/₂ cup chopped pecans
¹/₂ cup shredded coconut
1 cup finely chopped Granny Smith apple
1 cup vegetable oil
3 eggs, lightly beaten
2 teaspoons pure vanilla extract

Preheat oven to 350°.

In a mixing bowl, combine flour, sugar, baking soda, cinnamon, and salt. Toss carrots, raisins, pecans, coconut, and apples together and add to dry ingredients.

Beat oil into eggs, add vanilla, and combine with carrot mixture. Mixture will be very thick. Pour into greased muffin tins and bake in preheated oven for approximately 25 minutes or until firm and lightly browned. Serve warm.

PART THREE

New Alliance Basics

Smoking

The flavor of smoked foods is integral to Southwest cuisine; many indigenous foods are enhanced by the subtle effects of cooking or flavoring with smoke. This ancient method of cooking and preserving food has been elevated to an art form in the Southwest!

Meats and fish have long been cooked by the smoking process, exposure to low heat and smoke over a long period of time (several hours, even days) to "cook" the meat. But Southwest cuisine has added a new dimension to smoking. Good smoked meats are increasingly available at quality food stores, and may be used in our recipes, but I recommend that you try smoking your own—the results will be worth the effort. Vegetables are very lightly smoked to give them a flavor that is often too subtle for even the most experienced palate to identify but will add an unforgettable accent to food.

Preparation, time, and temperature of the "smoke-cooking" process differ from those of the "smoke-flavoring" process. The former requires soaking the meat in a brine (see recipe below) to achieve a full flavor when smoking for a period of time over very low but measurable heat. The latter involves a matter of minutes over "cold smoke."

SMOKE COOKING

The easiest, most reliable smokers to use at home are outdoor cookers sold as "smokers" or "water smokers." The pan that holds the coals is in the bottom of the 2- to 3-foot-tall cooker, about 1½ feet in diameter. A pan—to hold water (or stock for additional flavor) and lower the inside temperature—rests between the coals and the cooking rack. A dome lid traps the smoke.

The smokers, some with two racks for cooking, can easily accommodate whole turkeys, several chickens, ducks, fish, or pheasants, large briskets, or roasts. The food is more flavorful and tender if it has a natural layer of fat to baste the meat as it slowly cooks. Leaving the skin on fish or fowl serves this purpose as does larding lean meats. Most smokers come with explicit instructions for their use, but the rule of thumb to follow when smoking is to allow ½ hour smoking time per pound of meat, fish, or game to be smoked.

Wood (such as hickory) or wood charcoal is the preferred fuel. It is more natural and more flavor-intensive than other fuels. Mesquite

wood charcoal is my choice at The Mansion on Turtle Creek because it gives the food a true Southwestern character.

Charcoal briquettes, especially those infused with liquid starter, can give off fumes that mar the flavors of fresh, delicate foods, and I do not recommend their use. I prefer using a large amount of charcoal so that the coals will burn slowly. I recommend using an electric starter because it imparts no fumes to the charcoal. A chimney starter, fueled by newspaper, is also an acceptable method for firing coals.

Wood chips or pieces (such as hickory, pecan, apple, or cherry) are soaked in water and placed on top of the wood (or wood charcoal) once it has burned down to a gray ash. If the wood is green, it does not need to be soaked before being placed on the gray coals. Dry pieces must be soaked well, however, so they give off smoke instead of burning. This gives the food a wonderful smoky flavor. Any aromatic wood can be used to smoke foods; even fresh herbs, especially woody ones such as rosemary, can be fired. If wood chips burn down, add fresh chips to keep smoke constant.

SMOKE FLAVORING (COLD SMOKING)

This process does not cook the vegetables; it flavors them! The vegetables should still be crisp when taken from the smoke. This process can also be used to impart a smoke flavor to meat or seafood, such as sweetbreads or shrimp, which will be cooked through using a different process, often stir-frying.

Several types of outdoor grilling equipment can be used. Before the kitchen at The Mansion on Turtle Creek was equipped with a commercial smoker, I relied on a Weber Kettle Grill. These small, dome-covered cookers are designed primarily for grilling steaks and chickens on decks or patios, but their convenient size and design make them ideal for imparting a smoke flavor to vegetables usually smoked in small quantities.

Light 4 to 5 pieces of charcoal (a chimney-type starter that uses newspaper to ignite the coals is very handy for this). Mound the hot coals in the bottom of the cooker and let them burn down to gray ash. Spread them into a single layer and lay soaked or green wood chips or pieces (such as hickory, pecan, apple, or cherry) over the ash. You may also use pieces of fresh or dried fruit and/or fresh or soaked, dried herbs. This process lowers the heat of the coals to "cold smoke."

Usually, the bottom damper should be closed. The top vent, in the lid, should be open just a crack to draw the smoke. Place the vegetables to be smoked on the grate above the coals, to the side, not directly over the coals. (When smoking vegetables that have been diced, place them on a layer of foil so they do not fall through.) The grate should be very clean so it does not leave black marks on the vegetables. Smoke for the amount of time specified in each recipe. If none is specified, smoke for about 20 minutes. If wood chips burn down, add fresh chips to keep smoke constant.

Gas grills can also be used for this process. Preheat one side of the grill for about 10 minutes or until thermostat registers "low." Turn off heat. Place soaked or green wood chips or pieces on the preheated grill rocks. Place the vegetables to be smoked on the cool side of the grill or on the small warming rack that sits above the cooking grate on some models. (When smoking vegetables that have been diced, place them on a layer of foil so they do not fall through.) The grate should be very clean so it does not leave black marks on the vegetables. Smoke for the amount of time specified in each recipe, usually about 20 minutes.

BRINE FOR SMOKING GAME, FOWL, OR MEAT

1 gallon water
1 cup salt
1 large onion, peeled and chopped
1 stalk celery, chopped
1 small carrot, peeled and chopped
1/4 cup white wine

1/4 cup white wine vinegar
2 cloves garlic, chopped
2 serrano chilies, chopped
1 sprig fresh thyme
1 sprig fresh basil
1 sprig fresh cilantro
1 sprig fresh parsley
1 bay leaf

Combine all ingredients in a large stockpot over high heat and bring to a boil. Reduce heat and simmer for 20 minutes. Remove from heat and cool completely. Strain brine through a fine sieve.

Submerge meat in brine and soak for at least 1 hour. (The soaking time required for all game, fowl, and meat is 1/2 hour per pound.) Remove meat from brine and shake off excess moisture. Brine may be refrigerated or frozen and used 2 to 3 times for soaking game, fowl, or meat for smoking. You may want to boil brine before reusing.

Place meat in prepared smoker and smoke according to manufacturer's directions.

Roasted Peppers

Bell pepper (or any other pepper as called for in type and quantity)

Using a fork with a heatproof handle or with the handle wrapped with a towel or hot pad to protect your hand, hold pepper over open flame, such as the burner of a gas stove.

Hold as close as possible without allowing the flames to touch the pepper, until the skin puffs and is charred black. Turn as necessary to char the entire pepper.

Immediately place the charred pepper in a plastic bag and seal. Allow pepper to steam for about 10 minutes.

After pepper has steamed, remove from bag and pull off charred skin. Remove stem and seeds. Chop or purée as required in the specific recipe.

If using an electric stove, place whole pepper in a large, dry, cast-iron skillet over medium-high heat. Slowly cook pepper, turning frequently, until charred on all sides. Continue as above.

To roast several peppers at a time, place on a sheet pan under preheated broiler, as close to heat as possible without touching the flames. Roast until skin puffs and is charred black, turning as necessary to char entire pepper. Proceed as above to remove skin and prepare peppers.

All-Purpose Pastry

MAKES ENOUGH FOR 1 DOUBLE-CRUST PIE

3 cups all-purpose flour
1 teaspoon salt
3 tablespoons sugar
*1 cup very cold unsalted
    butter, cut into pieces*

*2 extra-large egg yolks,
    lightly beaten*
¹/₄ cup ice water

Combine flour, salt, and sugar in a mixing bowl. Cut in butter with a knife or pastry blender until mixture resembles coarse meal. Gradually add egg yolks and ice water until a firm ball is formed. Do not overwork dough.

Seal the dough in plastic wrap and chill for at least 30 minutes before rolling out.

When chilled, roll out to about ¹/₈-inch thickness on a lightly floured surface 2 inches larger than pan into which it will be fitted or cut into desired size or shape. When fitted into pan, trim edges and finish as directed.

Corn Bread

1 cup yellow cornmeal
1 cup all-purpose flour
¹/₄ cup sugar
4 teaspoons baking powder
¹/₂ teaspoon salt

1 cup milk
2 large eggs, lightly beaten
*¹/₄ cup melted unsalted
    butter, olive oil, or
    bacon grease*

Preheat oven to 400°.

Grease a 10-inch cast-iron skillet and place in oven.

In a mixing bowl, combine cornmeal, flour, sugar, baking powder, and salt. Add milk, eggs, and butter. Stir with a few rapid strokes until dry ingredients are just moistened.

Pour batter into hot pan. Place in preheated oven and bake for 20 to 25 minutes or until edges are light brown and bread is firm. Serve hot.

To make corn-bread crumbs: Allow corn bread to dry at least 24 hours. Break into pieces and chop in a food processor fitted with a metal blade.

Mansion Vinaigrette

MAKES ABOUT ⅔ CUP

2 large shallots, minced
2 large cloves garlic,
  minced
1 teaspoon minced fresh
  basil
1 teaspoon minced fresh
  thyme
1 teaspoon minced fresh
  parsley
1 teaspoon minced fresh
  tarragon

1 teaspoon minced fresh
  chives
1½ tablespoons white wine
  vinegar
1 tablespoon balsamic
  vinegar
4 tablespoons canola oil
2 tablespoons virgin olive
  oil
Juice of ½ lemon or to taste
Salt to taste

Combine shallots, garlic, herbs, and vinegars in a small bowl. Whisk in oils. Season with lemon juice and salt. Mix well to blend.

Mansion Barbecue Spice Mix

MAKES ABOUT ⅓ CUP

2 tablespoons paprika
1 tablespoon chili powder
1 teaspoon ground cumin
1 teaspoon ground
  coriander
1 teaspoon sugar
1 teaspoon salt

½ teaspoon dry mustard
½ teaspoon black pepper
½ teaspoon dried thyme
  leaves
½ teaspoon curry powder
½ teaspoon cayenne pepper

Mix all ingredients together and store in a cool, dry place.

Mansion Pepper Mixture
MAKES ABOUT 1½ CUPS

1 cup ground black pepper
⅓ cup ground white pepper

1½ tablespoons ground
  cayenne pepper

Combine all ingredients. Cover tightly and store in a cool place. Use to season red meats and game before cooking.

Fish Stock
MAKES ABOUT 3 CUPS

1 pound fish skeletons (saltwater fish such as sole, John Dory, turbot, halibut, or other very fresh non-oily fish), cut into pieces
2 tablespoons vegetable or other flavorless oil
½ onion, peeled and sliced

1 small stalk celery, sliced
1 cup dry white wine
4 cups water, approximately
1 bouquet garni (2 sprigs each of fresh parsley and thyme plus 1 small bay leaf tied together)

Clean the fish bones under cold running water, removing the gills from the head and any traces of blood on the frames.

Heat oil in a large saucepan over medium heat. Add fish bones and vegetables and lower heat. Place a layer of wax paper directly on bones and vegetables in pan and cook over low heat for 10 minutes, stirring once or twice to prevent them from browning.

Remove paper. Add wine, then enough water to cover the bones and vegetables by 2 inches. Add bouquet garni. Raise heat to high and bring to a boil. Skim the surface, reduce heat, and simmer for 20 to 25 minutes.

Strain the stock through an extra-fine sieve (preferably a chinois). Refrigerate, tightly sealed, for 2 to 3 days or freeze in small quantities, for ease of use, for 2 to 3 weeks. (After 3 weeks the flavor begins to fade.)

Chicken Stock (or Pheasant or Quail) and Demi-Glace

MAKES ABOUT 4 CUPS STOCK
OR 2 CUPS DEMI-GLACE

*1 chicken carcass (or 2
    pheasant or 8 quail
    carcasses)*
*2 tablespoons corn, peanut,
    or vegetable oil*
*2 cups coarsely chopped
    onion*
*³/₄ cup coarsely chopped
    carrots*
*³/₄ cup coarsely chopped
    celery*

3 sprigs fresh thyme
3 sprigs fresh parsley
1 small bay leaf
*1 tablespoon white
    peppercorns*
5 cups water to cover
*For demi-glace: 1¹/₂
    tablespoons corn starch
    mixed with 1¹/₂
    tablespoons cold water*

Have butcher cut carcass into small pieces or use a cleaver to do so at home. Heat 1 tablespoon oil in a large saucepan over medium heat. Add carcass. Cook, stirring often, until well browned.

Add remaining oil with onion, carrots, and celery. Cook, stirring frequently, until vegetables are golden brown. Pour off oil. Add thyme, parsley, bay leaf, and peppercorns. Stir to blend and add water to cover.

Bring to a boil, reduce heat, and simmer about 1¹/₂ to 2 hours, skimming surface as necessary, until reduced to 4 cups.

Line a bowl with an extra-fine sieve (preferably a chinois). Pour mixture into the sieve and strain, pushing solids with a wooden spoon to extract as much liquid as possible. Discard solids. Skim off any surface fat. Refrigerate, tightly sealed, for no more than 2 days, or freeze in small quantities (for ease of use) up to 3 months.

To make demi-glace: Bring finished stock to a boil over high heat. Stir in corn starch and water mixture, whisking constantly. Lower heat and simmer until reduced to 2 cups or thick enough to coat the back of a spoon. Stir occasionally as demi-glace cools to keep it from separating.

Demi-glace will keep up to 1 week in the refrigerator or for 2 to 3 months in the freezer, tightly sealed. For ease of use, store demi-glace in small quantities.

Brown Veal Stock and Demi-Glace

MAKES ABOUT 12 CUPS STOCK
OR 4 CUPS DEMI-GLACE

3/4 cup vegetable or olive oil
3–4 pounds veal (or beef,
venison, or lamb)
marrow bones, cut into
2-inch pieces
3 onions, peeled and
quartered
1 carrot, peeled and
coarsely chopped
1 stalk celery, coarsely
chopped

1 tomato, quartered
1 bay leaf
1 tablespoon black
peppercorns
2 sprigs fresh thyme
3 cloves garlic, crushed
1 gallon water
For demi-glace: 4
tablespoons corn starch
mixed with 4
tablespoons cold water

Preheat oven to 450°.

Using ¼ cup oil, lightly oil bones. Spread bones in a single layer in a large roasting pan. Place pan in preheated oven and roast, turning occasionally, for about 20 minutes or until bones are dark golden brown on all sides.

When nicely browned, transfer to a large stockpot. Add remaining oil and stir in onions, carrot, celery, and tomato. Cook, stirring frequently, until brown. Add bay leaf, peppercorns, thyme, and garlic.

Pour off fat from the roasting pan. Deglaze pan with 2 cups water, scraping up any particles sticking to the bottom of the pan. Add this liquid to the stockpot and pour in remaining water. It should cover bones by 2 inches. Bring to a boil, reduce heat, and let mixture simmer, uncovered, at least 6 to 8 hours, skimming foam and fat as necessary. Chill 12 hours or overnight.

Strain liquid through a sieve into a clean stockpot. Remove any traces of foam or fat. Bring stock to a rolling boil. Lower heat and cook until flavor is full-bodied and liquid slightly reduced. There should be about 3 quarts.

Refrigerate, tightly sealed, for 2 to 3 days or freeze in small quantities (for ease of use) for 2 to 3 months.

To make demi-glace: Bring finished stock to a boil over high heat. Stir in corn starch and water mixture, whisking constantly. Lower heat and simmer until reduced to 1 quart or until liquid is thick enough to coat the back of

a spoon. Stir occasionally as demi-glace cools to keep it from separating.

Demi-glace will keep up to 1 week in the refrigerator and for 2 to 3 months in the freezer, tightly sealed. For ease of use, store demi-glace in small quantities.

NOTE: If veal bones are used, stock has a neutral flavor and can be used in almost any recipe calling for a mild homemade stock.

Vegetable Stock

SERVES MAKES ABOUT 4 CUPS

1 tablespoon olive oil
4 onions, peeled and
    chopped
2 stalks celery, chopped
2 carrots, chopped
1 zucchini, chopped
1 yellow squash, chopped
4 bell peppers (any color),
    seeded and chopped
2 tomatoes, chopped
1 ear of corn, shucked and
    broken into small pieces
5 cloves garlic, peeled and
    smashed

1 jalapeño chili, chopped
1 tablespoon black
    peppercorns
1 tablespoon chopped fresh
    thyme
1 tablespoon chopped fresh
    parsley
1 tablespoon chopped fresh
    cilantro
1 tablespoon chopped fresh
    basil
8 cups water

Heat a stockpot over medium-high heat. When hot, add oil, onions, celery, and carrots, then brown slowly for 8 minutes. Add zucchini, yellow squash, and bell peppers and sauté for 5 minutes. Add all other ingredients, bring to a boil, and simmer for 2 hours or until reduced to 4 cups. Strain. Refrigerate, tightly sealed, for 2 to 3 days or freeze in small quantities, for ease of use, for 2 to 3 months.

Index